Connecting with the Arcturians 4

THE PSYCHOLOGY OF PLANETARY DEVELOPMENT

channeled through DAVID K. MILLER

Other Publications by

David K. Miller

Connecting with the Arcturians

Connecting with the Arcturians 2

Connecting with the Arcturians 3

Teachings from the Sacred Triangle, Volume 1

Teachings from the Sacred Triangle, Volume 2

Teachings from the Sacred Triangle, Volume 3

New Spiritual Technology for the Fifth-Dimensional Earth

Kaballah and the Ascension

Raising the Spiritual Light Quotient

Biorelativity

Arcturians: How to Heal, Ascend, and Help Planet Earth

A New Tree of Life for Planetary Ascension

Enseñanzas Del Sagrado Triángulo Arcturiano

Fifth-Dimensional Soul Psychology

Expand Your Consciousness

Connecting with the Arcturians 4

THE PSYCHOLOGY OF PLANETARY DEVELOPMENT

channeled through

David K. Miller

Light Technology PUBLISHING

For more information about special discounts for bulk purchases, please contact Light Technology Publishing Special Sales at 1-800-450-0985 or publishing@LightTechnology.com.

ISBN-13: 978-1-62233-078-2
ebook ISBN: 978-1-62233-817-7

Published and printed in the United States of America by

Light Technology PUBLISHING

PO Box 3540
Flagstaff, AZ 86003
1-800-450-0985 • 928-526-1345
LightTechnology.com

Table of Contents

Introduction

David K. Miller

This book is based on lectures and teachings I received from the Arcturians that focused primarily on the Arcturian perspective of our current planetary condition and development. I am fascinated by their observation that other planets in our galaxy go through similar developmental stages.

Earth's current stage of development threatens the entire biosphere, and if the conflicts in this stage are not resolved, the destruction of our planet could occur. In these lectures, the Arcturians often refer to the conflicts in this current stage of development as either leading to our self-destruction or, if they are resolved, to a new spiritual awakening and era of unity consciousness.

This volume begins with a look at life on Arcturus, a fifth-dimensional planet. It also explores some of the advanced healing techniques that Arcturians use on their planet. We learn, for example, that Arcturians experienced similar third-dimensional conflicts as Earth's, including a mass-destruction event. Earth's current event is manifesting through the sixth mass extinction, which can be compared to the mass extinction that occurred 55 million years ago when an asteroid hit Earth near the current Yucatan Peninsula. That event led to the eradication of almost 90 percent of all life forms. What is different about Earth's current event is that humanity (rather than an asteroid) is the main cause.

Other chapters cover the important subject of Earth's feedback loop system. This is a self-adjusting system in which Earth regulates or modifies data or planetary input conditions around the globe. Earth's feedback loop system uses this data to maintain proper temperatures and oxygen levels so homeostasis on the planet can be maintained. This allows the biosphere to support all life forms. Because of humans' abuse of the Earth, it's uncertain if Earth's feedback loop system can maintain the balance necessary for humans and other life forms to survive. Earth could be so overburdened that proper homeostasis cannot be maintained, which could lead to mass extinctions.

This book explores the important subject of ascension and the work leading to ascension. The Arcturians present a model based on their observations that precipitating events of ascension occur when the third dimension and fifth dimension intersect. At the time of that intersection, a powerful spiritual energy will download into Earth's energy field. It can uplift those who are at the highest vibrations and prepared for ascension.

The Arcturians introduce us to galactic anthropology. Most of us are familiar with modern anthropological research, especially as it relates to modern anthropologists visiting primitive cultures across the globe. Some anthropologists live in primitive cultures to study how they deal with rites of passage, marital relations, medical and healing issues, and social customs. Galactic anthropology is the study of planetary civilizations and cultures throughout our galaxy. The Arcturians study galactic civilizations in a way similar to how we on Earth study primitive cultures. It is interesting to consider what a powerful and interesting opportunity it would be to study different cultural developments in the galaxy. It should be noted that the study of galactic anthropology includes scientific anthropology and advances in technology.

More New Concepts

Another concept introduced in this volume is the idea of holographic healing. In holography, a piece of an object can represent the whole. In this Arcturian theory, a person on Earth is only a part of his or her whole self. Other parts can include the past self, which is the self in other lifetimes, and the future self, which is the self that will live and evolve in future times. There is also a multidimensional self that exists on this and other dimensions. The Arcturians look to Australian Aboriginal dreamtime as an example of what it is like to be a multidimensional being, since we exist as multidimensional beings in our dream worlds.

During this time of planetary crisis, the Arcturians explore how we starseeds can cope with dramatic changes, such as updating our immune systems and dealing with electromagnetic energies and energy fields. They offer recommendations for helping us cope with these overwhelming planetary changes.

While discussing life on Arcturus, the Arcturians introduce the concept of the philosopher king, a concept introduced in ancient Greece to represent an enlightened ruler who can judiciously direct a country. Arcturian leaders are trained from young ages to make decisions. The Arcturians explore why the concept of the philosopher king was a good option for their leadership and how it might be a way for us to rule our lands.

Other themes introduced in this volume include the concept of messianic energy as a healing force, in which a number of righteous people are necessary for a messianic intervention to occur. Righteous people can and should include a number of starseeds, which ties into the concept of a core number of starseeds who reach a certain level of consciousness and help prepare for messianic energy. Messianic energy transcends logic and can help overcome many of the obstacles that seem insurmountable in our current situation. The Arcturians also explore the concepts of time travel and new physics and how these relate to our spiritual development.

Finally, the Arcturians introduce the concept of the next evolutionary stage of humankind, called the omega man/woman. This represents a higher being, a higher consciousness, that can be described as the best level of humanity. This best level of humanity includes fifth-dimensional consciousness, which is an essential and necessary ingredient for higher evolution. They explain that beings are only able to reach evolutionary heights during a crisis, and I think most of us would agree that Earth's current situation represents a planetary crisis.

This is volume 4 of *Connecting with the Arcturians*, but the book stands on its own; you do not need to read earlier volumes to grasp and benefit from the ideas presented here. I provide certain aids, such as an expanded glossary that defines many terminologies and spiritual-technology terms used by the Arcturians. I also provide an appendix with questions and answers, as I believe many readers will benefit from reviewing common questions people ask the Arcturians.

The Group of Forty

I would like to spend a little time talking about the Group of Forty. The Group of Forty is an Arcturian meditation spiritual group focused on planetary healing, personal healing, and ascension. I originally began channeling the Arcturians in 1996. At that time, they asked me to establish this group to promote higher consciousness, planetary healing, and a method for distributing and teaching new spiritual technologies.

The Arcturians continue to emphasize new spiritual technologies. This book takes into consideration many scientific discoveries about the universe, holographic events, and unity consciousness. I briefly touch on some concepts I introduced in earlier volumes, such as Sacred Triangle energy, which is the energy of unifying different spiritual traditions. The concept of galactic spirituality — the ability to understand higher dimensions, beings from other levels, and ascension, as well as the galactic civilizations besides Earth — represents an important contribution to Sacred Triangle energy. The Group of Forty continues to be a strong group. As of this writing, over 900 members from around the world participate in our meditations and planetary healing exercises.

Another important planetary healing technique is biorelativity. I have added several biorelativity exercises and meditations in the appendix. Essentially, biorelativity is the use of meditations that seek to telepathically communicate with Earth and Earth's feedback loop system. The goal is to modify the interaction of the Earth so it positively protects and helps maintain a balance of the biosphere. Group consciousness and meditations are powerful methods that can also affect the noosphere, which is the collective-thought-field energy around the planet. The Arcturians maintain that we now operate from a lower model of subconscious energies, affirmations, and visual inputs. They recommend that we upgrade the noosphere by using more positive affirmations and visualizations that can help our planet and civilization manifest higher light and consciousness.

The image of the higher evolutionary stage of development known as the omega man/woman represents the most positive and optimistic outcome from this current planetary crisis. The Arcturians' unique perspective is very helpful. I see more and more people and starseeds around the planet eager for and open to the fifth-dimensional ideas offered in *Connecting with the Arcturians*.

Channeling Explained

All of the lectures in this book were channeled. A channeling is an experience that has been described as automatic speaking. I go into a light trance to attain a higher state of consciousness. In that state, I connect telepathically with higher beings. I have studied psychology, psychotherapy, hypnosis, and altered states of consciousness for many years. I am particularly interested in the study of Kabbalah and the relationship of higher consciousness to sacred energies, chanting, shamanism, and different methods of experiencing the altered state of consciousness known as the fifth-dimensional state of consciousness.

These lectures were recorded live as I channeled them, but they have been edited and corrected for grammar and clarity so readers can more easily read and understand the concepts. While the core energy and concepts have been preserved, normal channeling can be described as stream-of-consciousness communication that does not conform to normal spelling, sentence structure, or grammar.

It is my hope that this new volume assists readers in understanding the current spiritual condition and crisis we live in. I also hope this volume stimulates and activates many starseeds around this planet to come together and participate in ascension and planetary healing.

Chapter 1

Life on Arcturus, Part One

Juliano and the Arcturians

We were living on a third-dimensional planet but transitioned our planet into the fifth dimension through our spiritual development and advancements. Like Earth, we went through early stages of planetary development, which I refer to as stage one. Our system had several third-dimensional planets with stage-one civilizations. At that time, we experienced conflicts and wars. In fact, Earth is not unique in its conflicts, dualities, and polarizations; many planets in the galaxy have had major conflicts and wars.

One of our polarized conflicts ended with the total destruction of a planet. I am not referring to a localized nuclear conflict where cities were destroyed, but a conflict that ended in the planet's total annihilation. This was extremely traumatic, and the energy, memories, and trauma from that event have stayed in our archetypical memory.

The nearby star system called Lyra also had military conflicts. The Lyran constellation and planetary systems are believed to be the origin of humans, or *Homo sapiens*. Historical accounts of wars within the Lyran system existed even before the Arcturian wars. In these conflicts and the conflicts on Arcturus, refugees, including scientists and spiritual masters, left their planets and colonized other planetary systems. Part of the purpose of their escape was to ensure the survival of their species. They were concerned that a military event might occur that would lead to the total destruction of one of the Lyran planets. In fact, a military campaign did lead to its destruction.

On Earth, scientists discuss colonizing Mars, which would be a similar attempt to ensure the survival of Earth's human species. I like to use the term "Earth's human species" to distinguish Earth beings from other human species that live and thrive throughout the galaxy.

Arcturian Life

Let us turn to Arcturian life. After the trauma that occurred eons before our ascension, a major spiritual infusion of light came to those who were still in the Arcturian star system. After the war that led to the destruction of our planet, our forefathers gathered in spiritual unity. They promised that polarization and duality would never again be allowed to result in the destruction of a civilization or an entire planet. This commitment to harmony led to an acceleration of our spiritual advancement. It also helped push us into ascending our planet into the fifth dimension.

Regarding our current planetary fifth-dimensional civilization, all our activities would look spiritual from your perspective. We live in an extremely spiritual manner. We have no disease, polarization, or war. We live in harmony with our planet through the practice of biorelativity, in which we telepathically communicate with the planet's spirit. This advanced telepathic communication helps stabilize and modify disruptions from weather, earthquakes, and other natural events.

We teach the practice of biorelativity to you on Earth, because we know it is a key activity of advanced planetary civilizations. You might have studied the galaxy from the viewpoint of astrophysics and understand that the galaxy is a dangerous place. Asteroids and comets strike planets, and exploding stars emit dangerous radiation. Aberrant stars and planets veer off course. One of these planets has been described as the twelfth planet that came close to your Earth at the time of the Sumerian civilization, approximately 4,000 Earth years ago.

Circumstances also occur in which planets from one dimension go into another dimension. This can happen because special portals and corridors exist around solar systems. Your scientists refer to these as wormholes, which are circular-shaped energy vortexes. If a planet passes near such a vortex, it can be thrown into other parts of the galaxy or even into others dimensions.

We assign a large part of our population to the following activities: meditation, biorelativity, spiritual healing, temple work, and planetary cities of light projects.[1] Planetary cities of light projects are the basis of unity on Arcturus.

We are a small planet compared to Earth. Our planet would be considered one-third the size of Earth and more in alignment with Mars. We have four to five million inhabitants. Two moons in our star system are also in the fifth dimension. Because our planetary systems are in the fifth dimension, you cannot observe them with Earth-based, third-dimensional telescopes. When we ascended, we moved our planet into the fifth-dimensional realm.

Arcturian Consciousness

Let us look at what our lives are like. You might wonder if Arcturians die. The answer is yes, our lives do end, but not in the same way as yours. In your Earth lives, death gives the illusion that you have ended. Our deaths are actually transitions; we have total awareness of going from one lifetime to another. We do not even call it death; we call it a transitional time.

In order to explain some other aspects of Arcturian life, I need to explain Arcturian consciousness. Consciousness is the final frontier. Your space program *Star Trek* calls space the final frontier, but in our perception, it is consciousness. Arcturians have three states of consciousness you are aware of: the normal waking state, the dream state, and the sleep state. These are so well separated in your life that most of the time you do not remember your dream state. You forget what you dreamed even thirty seconds after you wake up. Some practices can help you remember your dream states. Certain "primitive" civilizations or societies work on the dream state and encourage people to write down their dreams or tell them as stories in group meetings.

The third state of consciousness is the sleep state where no dreaming occurs. This state is so far removed from your consciousness that you have no memory of what happens. In fact, you are in what could be called a mini-state of death.

1. A project on Earth directed by the author's meditation group, known as the Group of Forty, recognizes sacred areas and energies around cities on Earth.

Each of these states of consciousness has its own benefits and purposes. Earth humans have sharp divisions between these three states. Your psychologists and neuropsychologists can describe them in terms of brain waves, and in the dream state you also experience rapid eye movement. If you do not dream, such a deficit can lead to insanity. You need to have periods of dream-state consciousness, and you get there by transitioning from the sleep state to the dream state. This can sometimes require several hours of deep relaxation.

We Arcturians also have these three states, but we experience all three at once with total consciousness and awareness. In our daily lives, we can interact with total awareness in all three states, including the conscious state — what you would call the normal, perceptual state — the dream state, and the deep-sleep state. One of the many benefits of experiencing the dream state is "active dreaming," in which we can control and change the outcomes of events in dreams. You have a term for this active dreaming, lucid dreaming, where you are aware of being in the dream state. This ability is rare; only a few highly evolved people have this advanced active-dreaming ability.

You are evolving, and many of you already experience active daydreaming, which is a predecessor of active dreaming in rapid-eye-movement consciousness. Daydreaming is active dreaming while in the awake state of consciousness. In this state, you retreat from the conscious state and go to the edge of the dream state without deep sleep.

Active daydreaming gives you an introduction to Arcturian consciousness and how we use these different states in our waking lives. The deep-sleep state is difficult to describe, because it contains no memories, verbalizations, or images. In the deep-sleep state, you are in a state of oneness and cosmic unity. This cosmic unity is so deep that you have no anchor, but it provides important rejuvenation for the body.

The mind, not the brain, is multidimensional. Your mind exists in the third dimension as well as in the fifth dimension, the dream state, the deep-sleep state, and in expanded consciousness where you experience all states simultaneously.

Galactic Anthropology

On Arcturus, we consider ourselves galactic anthropologists. Our missions and studies are enhanced by the planetary cities of light and what are known as the sister planetary cities of light in the galaxy. We continually work to create energy fields of higher frequency within our cities, primarily through our temple work. One temple master you might be familiar with is Tomar; he offers instruction in Arcturian temple methods. Together, we create the thought-energy field for our fifth-dimensional planet using thought constructs and thought constellations.

Energy fields can be seen from several different perspectives. The basic energy field on Earth sets the manifestations or materializations of events. The concept for an object or an event first resides in the noosphere, which is a combination of the planetary subconscious, unconscious, and auric energy fields. After an object or event has been in the noosphere, it can manifest.

We have learned the importance of working with the noosphere. In advanced civilizations, inhabitants can systematically download higher thinking, images, visualizations, and thought projections into the noosphere. This is how a proper energy field for a higher planet is created. A higher planet means that all energy input is based on unity thinking, downloaded into the noosphere. Unity thinking is based on fifth-dimensional principles, including love, equality, brotherhood and sisterhood, and the unity of All There Is.

To that end, we have a sophisticated system that inputs into the noosphere. Full-time employees (not an actual Arcturian term, but one you can understand) meditate and work on downloading information and energy into the noosphere. In order to be a full-time employee in one of these temples, an individual must have advanced training. This advanced training is so specialized that people are chosen and introduced to these techniques when they are very young. In Earth terms, they would be children.

Arcturian Society

Our life spans are longer than yours. We live 600 to 700 years in Earth time. Therefore, age 60 is not old from our standpoint; that is about the age when we have children. Children that come to us are fully consciousness of their past lives. They know their goals and missions. As parents, we have the child's full background in our consciousnesses when he or she is born, and we know what soul lessons or missions each child is here to learn. We provide children with the maximum support, education, and direction they need to accomplish these goals. We provide excellent guidance and support for our children, especially when you consider how old and mature we are when we have children. When children come into a family, they are closely connected to their dream time and past lives.

We often talk about our past lives and continually seek methods of healing from past events. I mentioned earlier that we still carry the trauma in our collective unconscious from the annihilation of one of our planets eons ago. Those memories are strong. People who lived on that planet reincarnate now to our planet. They have gone through soul training and learned soul lessons. They are ready to enter our realm and heal those traumas.

Some starseeds are from Arcturus and have reincarnated on Earth. Some of you were on Arcturus when it was in its third-dimensional system. You might have had the experience of living on that planet during the planetary wars. You might have experienced death at the time of the annihilation. There is something to say about repetition in reincarnation and repetition compulsion in incarnational learning. You have reincarnated now on a planet that is also on the brink of destroying itself.

This learning process might be a repetition for you, but you do not have to die this time. You can use this opportunity for spiritual advancement. It is a strange paradox that when planets are close to destroying themselves, an extraordinary amount of spiritual light and energy surrounds them. We always hope that spiritual light will dominate and bring harmony and balance. This is a galaxy that is at times filled with violence, which means planetary duality has not been successfully resolved.

On another note, we have no diseases in our Arcturian system. I also want to talk about our food and how we eat. You might have seen pictures of us. We have been described very kindly by some people as similar to ballet dancers. That is because we have thin bodies, and we do not look muscularly endowed or strong. We use an advanced form of mental power called telekinesis, which is the ability to move objects using our minds. While muscular energy and power are helpful and desirable on third-dimensional planets, we do all things with the mind on our fifth-dimensional planet. We have no need for muscle strength.

Our food system is based on what you would call liquid light. I also use the term manna, a food described in the book of Exodus in the Hebrew Bible that was used when the Israelites were in the desert for forty years. Being in the desert at that time, they were not able to grow crops or raise animals. Higher beings dropped food down to them in the form of manna. This story offers a useful description of manna. It is a perfect food. It produces no biological waste. After eating it, you never have to go to the bathroom, because everything is totally used. Manna can be vibrationally attuned to your physical structure. Because there is no waste, you do not gain weight. Every molecule in the food is vibrationally attuned to you. Manna also comes in the form of liquid light or drinks.

We do not eat meat or devote large periods of time to raising food or eating meals. On Earth, you have three meals per day, which consumes large amounts of your energy and time. I realize there are social consequences and social events during your meal time. We do not have such ceremonies or events during our meals.

We Arcturians have digestive systems without your complex intestinal tracts, because everything we eat is used, resulting in no residual toxins. This means our other organs are smaller and more streamlined. For example, your kidneys and livers process toxins. Since our food contains no toxins, we do not need complex kidneys, livers, or large intestinal systems. This is one reason we have overcome disease.

Regarding marriage and social customs, we mate and marry, but we do not have divorce. I have been with my partner Helio-ah now for several lifetimes. Arcturians have what I call "expanded relationships." These are powerful and spiritual relationships that can go beyond marriage relationships. Our relationships are harmonious. Our sexual encounters are pure vibrational energy unity. A sexual encounter reaches the state that you might call ecstasy or higher pleasure, but it involves a unity of vibrational energy fields without a physical component. This level of vibrational unity brings true pleasure.

Arcturian Temples

Some of you are already students of Tomar, an Arcturian temple master and teacher. Our temple meditators have been trained since childhood and go into temples as "employees." They are trained to download thoughts into our noosphere. Accelerating and downloading thoughts requires a certain power we call "arcan" power.

We use crystals in Arcturian temples to increase our thought power. These crystals are specially programmed and much more powerful than crystals on Earth. Powerful crystals also exist on Earth, which brings me to the subject of crystal mining. Some have talked about how extraterrestrial civilizations came to ancient Earth to mine and take Earth's resources. There is truth to this. They also mined special crystals. Higher civilizations, and even some lower extraterrestrial civilizations, know very well the power of Earth's crystals. These high-powered crystals are located throughout the Earth, and some of the most powerful were removed by extraterrestrial beings over the eons. Even though many were removed, many still remain. We Arcturians do not mine Earth for these crystals.

In our Arcturian temples, we use high-powered crystals to help us amplify our thoughts during meditations. The crystal temple has special portals in which thoughts can download into the noosphere of our planet. An aura surrounds the planet, in which thought forms exist and are continually updated from our crystal-temple work. Some lower thought forms are purified or upgraded. We always look for ways to upgrade all thought forms in our noosphere.

Arcturian temples allow us to go into the past, present, and future. More advanced past, present, and future work is done in the holographic chambers that cover these time periods. We travel through the galaxy and time travel. Time travel is based on the concept of folding space and time. When you look at the night sky, the star systems you see are many light-years away. In the case of Arcturus, our star system is thirty-six light-years from Earth. So when you look into the night sky and see Arcturus, you see our star as it was thirty-six years ago, not as it is today.

In order to see Arcturus as it is now, you would have to use the positive-energy process of folding space. Everything in the universe has a positive and a negative charge. In time travel, a reverse process allows you — through acceleration — to use special corridors and thought forms and go forward in time. You can use a similar space-and-time folding process to go backward in time.

Robots and Holographic Healing

We are sometimes asked if we use robots. We do, but we call them computer-bots, in your language. We especially use these highly advanced computers in our spaceships. A special advanced program implanted in all computer bots prevents them from taking over our planet or society in any way. This special download prevents using computers and robots for war. You do not often see us with robots, because we do many tasks with telekinesis. We use highly advanced computers in our spaceships and healing chambers.

I want to give you an idea of the power of these computers. The highly specialized computer on my spaceship could read your energy field. Your energy field — your aura — contains everything that has happened in your life, including all diseases, imbalances, and events. Your energy field also contains all the information about what will happen in your future, based on your current energy reading. Another level of the computer can tie into your past lives. This means that your aura system is more complex and filled with much more information than you can imagine.

Let me speak now about Helio-ah and holographic work, because holographic work is based on time differentials and unity consciousness. Unity consciousness occurs when you integrate your waking consciousness with your dream time and sleep time. In Helio-ah's healing chambers, you can visually record and portray any event in your past, present, or future life. This is particularly important, because visualizations and pictures are one of the most important aspects of dream time. When you are in the dream state, you usually dream in images. When you try to remember a dream, you must visualize images. In certain dream experiences, there are no words.

When masters like Tomar work in their temples, they often meditate in images. They also use affirmations. Powerful affirmations are considered an advanced form of working with the noosphere. In our temple work, we use imagination, visualizations, and affirmations. All three are keys to personal and planetary healing. Our holographic chambers are based on holographic healing computers and are called Helio-ah's healing chambers.

People who were in Arcturus when some planets were destroyed had severe trauma from those past lives. One benefit of the holographic healing chamber is that it can reprogram and heal past-life traumas. One way we do this is by recreating the visual traumatic event on the computer screen. For example, say you were on the planet when it was destroyed. How can that possibly be healed? We take you back to the minutes before the actual destruction and help you create a visual image of you ascending or being rescued.

We then download the image of the ascension or upliftment into the image of the past trauma, which then shifts the event in your memory. The memory shifts in the collective unconscious, and you now have a beautiful and new image in your mind. This is one of the secrets of Helio-ah's holographic healing. This holographic method is also used in planetary work.

On our planet, we teach and work with planetary healing using gigantic computers that are large in scope but not in size. We can holographically heal a planet by working with our holographic planetary computers. We can holographically work with the future time of a planet and download images from our advanced and perfected future into our present. Our planetary healing work is advanced.

Arcturian Aid to Earth

I have called us galactic anthropologists, because we are interested in studying and working spiritually with other planetary systems. We know that all living beings in this galaxy have a collective unconscious and a collective energy field. So if you experienced trauma on Earth, you can reincarnate on another planet and have the opportunity to heal. We strongly believe in cosmic karma, and that incarnational systems work cosmically throughout the galaxy.

We come to Earth and work with you as galactic anthropologists. We come to study, help, provide guidance, and teach. One reason we downloaded the twelve etheric crystals on Earth is that these are energy points you can use to shift the noosphere of the planet. The etheric crystals can raise the arcan power of any thought of high nature, which can then be downloaded into the noosphere of Earth.

Earth's noosphere is still in its early form of development. This is good, because it means the noosphere is open to new input. On the negative side, the noosphere still needs to be developed with higher thought forms. We need to raise the vibration and skill level of noorelativity practitioners. Noorelativity is the ability to send thoughts and energy into the noosphere for the purpose of manifesting higher healing light throughout a planet.

People have asked us how we travel and why we need spaceships if we can transport ourselves with the power of thought. The answer is that many of our excursions go from our fifth-dimensional planet into interdimensional space, and in some cases we travel to third-dimensional planets. This requires physical ships. Temple masters on our ships create the ship's energy field and connect our core vibrational thoughts with the Arcturian planetary home base.

Chapter 2

Life on Arcturus, Part Two

Juliano and the Arcturians

I will begin by comparing the fifth dimension to the third dimension. In your ascending numerical description of each dimension, the third is lower than the fifth, and the fifth is lower than the seventh. From this numerical perspective, you might conclude that the fifth dimension is better than the third dimension. I do not necessarily look at dimensions in terms of better or worse. Each has unique qualities, merits, and values for your soul's development. I see the third dimension as having certain characteristics and limitations, rather than being lower or inferior.

You are on a soul journey, and your soul incarnates on different planets and in different dimensions. Different aspects of your soul can only manifest in the third dimension, which is a very important concept. The fifth dimension is focused on unity and higher consciousness. Weaknesses or blemishes on the soul cannot manifest on the fifth dimension. The third dimension allows a unique opportunity for certain "weaknesses" in the soul to manifest and heal. Therefore, the third dimension is a school; it is a necessary part in your soul development.

You are eager to leave the third dimension, and ascension and entry into the fifth dimension will offer you great happiness; it will feel as if you are returning home. But please remember that you had a specific reason for coming to the third dimension. It was not an accident; you wanted and needed this third-dimensional energy and perspective.

Arcturian Schools and Training

Schools for young students in Arcturus offer a variety of different themes and subjects, one of which is galactic anthropology. In this course, I teach students about the different planetary systems in the Milky Way galaxy. I explain that each third-dimensional planet has a unique perspective based on many different factors, including the planet's position in relation to the structure of the galaxy: Planets closer to the center of the galaxy are generally older and more advanced, while planets in the outer galaxy tend to be newer and contain younger, more introductory life forms.

The Earth is two-thirds of the way from the center of the Milky Way galaxy. In astronomical terms (there are several different estimates, but one of the more recent ones is presented here), Earth is 26,000 light-years from the center of the galaxy. To give you an idea of its full size, the diameter of the galaxy could be as long and as wide as 100,000 light-years. Each planetary position has a unique perspective. When I teach our students on Arcturus about perspective, I use the same example I often give you, my students on Earth.

Every year or two, there is a solar eclipse. Sometimes it is observable in North America; sometimes it is only observable in South America, Africa, or Asia. Astronomers spend great effort, time, and money traveling to different parts of the world to observe the eclipse. You might think if they've observed one eclipse, that is enough. But they see each eclipse from a different perspective on the planet.

I tell my students on Arcturus that Earth has a unique perspective. In fact, each third-dimensional planet has a unique perspective. The Creator manifests life forms throughout the galaxy, and certain opportunities and insights can only be experienced from Earth. Likewise, some opportunities for experiencing the Creator on Arcturus are unique. For example, because we are on the fifth dimension, we experience more closeness with the Creator. But this does not diminish the spiritual power and energy you can experience from Earth. Remember, it is not that the fifth dimension is better; it is just a different perspective. You need this duality available on the third dimension for your training.

We have spiritual schools on Arcturus. We do not call our spiritual schools religious; we call them Arcturian temples. We offer special trainings and meditations for experiencing higher light and higher energy. In a religious teaching on Earth, the Creator told Moses that anyone who saw the Creator's face would die, and therefore he could only be shown the shadow. Moses could not see the Creator directly, because the nature of higher light and frequencies is too strong for an Earth body to tolerate. It is like looking directly at the sun; you must have protection.

On the fifth dimension, we experience the face of the Creator. We are in contact with the higher frequency of light you cannot directly experience on the third dimension. This is a great gift and a great advancement for those of you leaving the third dimension and entering the fifth dimension. You have a greater sustainability, and a greater ability to tolerate increased light frequencies.

Even on Arcturus, we have to train our students and build their spiritual strength. I have compared spiritual strength to running a race. You have to practice every day; you must train. You must build up your lung capacity, heart rate, and muscle strength. In the same way, you must train your body system and spiritual vibratory system to tolerate and hold higher light. That higher light can be damaging if you do not have the right training, and on the third dimension it could actually destroy you.

Our energy fields are stronger than your energy fields on the third dimension. We have stronger chakra systems. Our auras vibrate at much higher vibrational speeds. Our chakras are open to the different dimensions. On Arcturus, we are in direct contact with our multidimensional selves. We live in total expanded consciousnesses, so it is normal for us to experience our multidimensional selves. In the Arcturian schools, we train our students in multidimensional cohabitation or multidimensional habitation on the third dimension so they can be on the fifth dimension and have an existence on the third dimension; they can be aware of both.

The movie *Avatar* portrays multidimensional presence. In this movie, a scientific experiment projects people into incarnations on another planet. It introduces the idea of multidimensional presence. We have a method to experience our multidimensional selves. Crystal rooms allow us to go into the third dimension in our multidimensional selves and, when necessary, even occupy a karmic incarnation.

Arcturian Spirituality versus Earth Religions

I also want to talk about spirituality on Arcturus compared to Earth religions. On Earth, you have beliefs called atheism and agnosticism. These philosophical thought systems are based on the doubt or disbelief in the existence of the Creator. We Arcturians believe in the Creator. We do not doubt this, especially since we have more direct experience with the Creator than you have on the third dimension. Direct contact with the Creator is rare, but it does happen on the third dimension. Even then, these contacts are often short-lived, and those people who claim to have them can be subjected to criticism. In some cases, prophets have been put to death for having direct contact with the Creator.

In the third dimension, rational mind and rational thought have been the basis and tradition of your civilization for the past 2,500 to 3,500 years. Some even say the time span is longer. We have studied and visited your planet at least since the time of Atlantis and Lemuria. We visited during the time of Egypt. The point is that the rational mind, the logical mind, is a recent development in the evolution of humanity. It has brought many technological benefits, but it can lead to distortions. The rational mind is still what I consider a part of the "small mind." For example, Albert Einstein had one of the greatest rational minds on the planet, and he made many advanced discoveries. But his rational mind could not accept the existence of the quantum world. He even made a rather humorous statement saying that God did not play with dice. The quantum world is not logical, and Einstein could not accept that.

When we on Arcturus study the different religious systems on Earth, we have to view them from the perspective of the rational mind. In many cases, over-emphasis on the rational mind leads to atheism (disbelief in the Creator), which leads into the small mind versus the large mind. The large mind can transcend logic and still incorporate and use logic, without being totally dependent on it.

We are aware of the many varieties of religious experiences on Earth. *The Variety of Religious Experiences*, a famous book written by William James, details some of the religious perspectives that have developed on Earth. Having access to the many religious experiences on Earth is one key advantage of being in a freewill zone. It is one reason we visit Earth: We are fascinated by the different varieties of religious experiences. It is similar to the variety of languages on this planet. Most planets we visit and study do not have as many different languages or religious expressions. A downside is that adherence to different religious expressions has led to wars and terrible conflicts. That is a downside of third-dimensional duality. But the freewill zone is one of the main attractions of Earth, why we study it, and why you came here.

Parts of your soul can only be explored and manifested on the third dimension, and it is only through that manifestation that you can correct or heal those parts of the soul. So you have good reasons for coming to the third dimension. Some Eastern religions are more focused on an indefinable God that sometimes can be called the force or energy of the universe. There is even a beautiful term called the Tao, which is an impersonal expression of the universal force.

The varieties of religious experiences on Earth can be explained in two types of systems: One uses a personal Creator and the other uses an impersonal Creator. The systems in most Eastern cultures focus on the impersonal, which is beautifully described by the Tao. It is said that the Tao is not the Tao.[1]

One of the beautiful contributions of Eastern religions is the duality of yin and yang — male and female, good and bad, beautiful and ugly. Divisions came from the unity. First there was One and then there was separation; that was the beginning of duality in the third dimension. The symbolic representation of the Tao is two half circles, united. Each half circle has within it a dot of the opposite color. This signifies that even in the dark there is some light, and even in the light there is some dark. Even in the bad, there is some good, and in the good there is some bad.

How does this lesson transfer into the lives of prophets and spiritual teachers? All the great prophets and teachers on this Earth had human weaknesses. The ascended masters do not expect you to be

1. Tao is the name for the unnamable energy of the Creator in the Chinese philosophy and religion known as Taoism. The name Tao implies that nothing can be said to describe the Creator. Actually, the Tao is sometimes referred to as the life force or the first energy of unity. The Tao manifested a duality called yin and yang.

perfect; you are human. But what is it like to be human on the third dimension? Being human means you have some weaknesses and frailties. Having weaknesses does not prevent you from ascending.

Advantages of the Fifth-Dimension

What are the advantages of being on Arcturus? What are the benefits of being on the fifth dimension? I mentioned that our aura systems are stronger than yours on the third dimension. Our auras vibrate at higher speeds, which means we have higher protective shielding, and we can travel interdimensionally without problems. We do not, for example, have attachments on our auras or holes in them.

We also have advanced telepathic powers, and this has a great effect on our relationships. On Arcturus, we can read each other's thoughts. We have a telepathic method in which we can block anyone from coming into our thought fields, but most of the time this is not necessary. We use telepathic communication and do not hide our thoughts or feelings in relationships. Can you imagine what it would be like on Earth if you had relationships based on telepathic thought communication?

We can speak, and we share a single language. There were ancient languages on Arcturus, and our schools teach linguistic studies that explore many different languages. Our schools teach many different subjects. One is telepathic communication and another is telekinesis: how to move objects. On Arcturus, our sensory perceptions, such as the colors we see and the music we hear, are much stronger than yours on Earth.

We have a perception called synesthesia, which is defined as the ability to have two modalities of perception at the same time. For example, when you hear music you also see the notes float in front of your eyes. This is a highly advanced form of perception. Some people on Earth with expanded consciousness occasionally experience synesthesia. On Earth, if you see notes floating in the air, other people might worry and think you are hallucinating instead of realizing that you are in an advanced state of perception.

Our training in the Arcturian schools enhances all these perceptual abilities. Our telepathic abilities are effective in close proximity to the subject and remotely; we train ourselves to have remote telepathic communications with people who are far away.

Arcturian Healing Methods

Another subject or theme in the Arcturian school system is healing. We teach all our students a healing method based on what you would call vibrational healing medicine. Every cell in the body vibrates at a certain frequency, and the body's overall frequency can be measured in hertz or kilohertz. If a disease or something else attacks the energy system, the energy system changes frequency. We do all our healing with this vibrational method. We teach this to some of our students on Earth. This is a fifth-dimensional technique useable on the third dimension.

Many different intrusions can affect the aura on the third dimension, including electromagnetic interference from different technologies and lower fourth-dimensional beings causing disruptive energy vibrations. All these discordant energies have the potential to create disease. The good news is that they can all be removed and the individual brought back into a healthy vibrational energy field.

Arcturian healing techniques are based on several main methods. The first is a holographic healing method taught by my colleague Helio-ah. In brief, it is based on the idea that one part of the body is in resonance with the main or most healthy part. You then use that part to restructure the whole energy system to come into balance.

The second method we use is the crystal healing technique, in which we subject a person to high, intense crystal light. We calibrate the light frequency so the person can integrate it. One main issue with this healing technique is that the proper calibration must be done. If not, the person cannot absorb or integrate the light. I talked about Creator light and how you must have a certain developed frequency to tolerate and integrate it. In this crystal healing method, we first have to calibrate how much crystal-light frequency a person can receive and tolerate, and then we slowly and carefully upgrade it.

In working with humans, we also do what some have called psychic surgery. We identify a specific organ dysfunction in the human body. For example, there might be a cyst on the ovary or the pituitary gland. I can calibrate and send direct frequencies and direct rays of light into that diseased part of the organ to break up and remove the discordant parts. This is an advanced healing method based in vibrational medicine.

Other methods we use and teach in our vibrational energy school are based on what I call the pulsing technique and the contracting and expanding technique, using the aura. We stabilize the aura energetically and encourage the person to contract their aura to the point of a singularity. The word "singularity" has special meanings. In the world of astrophysics, it is defined as one infinitely dense point that is the origin of all. In talking about the universe, the singularity would be the point of density that contained All That Is right before the explosion of the Big Bang. Modern physics defines a singularity as infinitely dense and infinitely small — smaller than the head of a pin.

A singularity is also you. Imagine all that you are, all that you have been, and all that you will be, contracted to a point of singularity. In one of our healing methods, we help people contract to a point of singularity, located at the center of the stomach. It is almost like starting over again. By doing this method, we contract the energy into a single point that helps flush everything out. After holding that singularity point for twenty or thirty seconds, the person expands the singularity into the shape of a small ball. As the energy goes out from the stomach, it pushes out all discordant or lower-vibrational energies in the body.

I am now going to use a vibrational frequency that will be very healing for you. In vibrational medicine, the frequency is the healer. [Chants]: "Oooohhhh, yeeeaaahhhh." Contracting to the singularity can be compared to a birth, or a "resetting of your aura." When I guide people into this reset, I bring them first into a higher vibration using this method of sound. It is like clearing or setting the vibrational energy field into a new, receptive vibrational field. So much of vibrational healing is based on receptivity.

Living on a Fifth-Dimensional Planet

What does it mean to be on a fifth-dimensional planet? The Earth is a third-dimensional planet, which means it is still based on duality. One of the effects of planetary duality is geological and weather changes that can result in earthquakes and storms. You are seeing tremendous polarizations and dualities now on Earth. Because Arcturus is a fifth-dimensional planet, we do not have dualities and polarizations. Arcturus is an evolved planet with special spiritual abilities; it can telepathically communicate with us. In order for a planet to become fifth-dimensional, people on the planet must be evolved and moving toward the fifth-dimensional evolutionary cycle. No planet can become fifth dimensional without higher spiritual beings on it.

On Arcturus, we meet in person with the great ascended masters, which include Jesus/Sananda, Buddha, Lao-Tse, Moses, the archangels (including Archangel Michael), Chief White Eagle, and Quan Yin. We meet with them regularly, and they offer classes and instruction to us on Arcturus. One of the benefits of being on Arcturus is that fifth-dimensional masters, the great prophets, can directly communicate with us in our schools.

It is wonderful to be on a fifth-dimensional planet, and I know you have a great desire to bring Earth into a fifth-dimensional state. To do this, you need to telepathically communicate with her. Opening up telepathic communications with the spirit of Earth helps her evolve.

Singularity Meditation Exercise

Visualize your aura. I, Juliano, am here with my students from Arcturus, sending high-frequency blue light into your aura. After reading this chapter, you should be very receptive. Your receptivity and vibrational speed increase. Your aura might extend eight to ten inches from your physical body. Contract it to six inches. Contract it to four inches. Contract it to the surface of your body. Now contract it inward. As we go inward, we will go to the point that I call the singularity of you — all that you are, all your powers. Bring your aura into a ball of light in the center of your stomach.

Rotate the ball; it is at your command. It has great power and is filled with Arcturian blue light. Hold all that energy in the singularity point in the center of your stomach.

At the count of three, gently but firmly expand that singularity point. One, two, three. The ball gets larger and fills your stomach and your other organs, expelling all lower vibrations. These energies might include inflammation, disease, or any other dense energy.

The ball is now on the surface of your body. It grows two inches, six inches, eight inches. All lower densities are now discharged. Your aura expands to ten inches and to twelve inches. It vibrates at a higher speed as all lower densities continue to discharge.

Go into a short meditation as you experience this discharge. You are vibrating nicely and rhythmically, and your energy aligns at a healthy and balanced rhythm.

This is one of the methods we teach our students in the Arcturian school for healing and light work. Our students are happy to work with you.

Chapter 3

Earth's Feedback Loop System

Juliano and the Arcturians, Chief White Eagle, Chief Buffalo Heart, and Helio-ah

Juliano and the Arcturians: In this chapter, we will look at Earth's feedback loop system and work with representatives of Native American energies, including Chief White Eagle. The concepts of planetary healing and Earth's feedback loop system are tied together with Sacred Triangle energy. Major conflicts and polarizations exist on planet Earth between technology and wisdom as well as technology and heart energy.

In this chapter, you will come to understand the importance of using heart energy to connect with planet Earth. It is apparent to the Arcturians that advanced technology on Earth has greatly contributed to closing humanity's heart to the planet. This could be one of the greatest tragedies of the twentieth and twenty-first centuries. It is our opinion that hearts closed to the Earth is the primary cause of the current mass-extinction crisis.

We offer a new model for bringing Earth back into balance. We refer to this model as a groundwork or basis for planetary healing. Planetary healing is an Arcturian concept we describe as a group of open-hearted, sensitive starseeds working together to send healing energy and balance to the spirit of Earth for the purpose of healing the planet and helping return it to its natural strength and beauty. This is a big job on a large planet like Earth with well over 8 billion people. You might think that millions of planetary healers work around the clock to bring about a beautiful outcome, but starseeds are not that plentiful. They work diligently and with great dedication, but they must work hard to overcome this planetary crisis.

The Sacred Triangle System

We Arcturians have developed an elaborate system called the Sacred Triangle system and Sacred Triangle energy. This is one of the key concepts we teach humanity. It is part of our mission to encourage people to study, discuss, and implement the Sacred Triangle. We will work primarily with one side of the Sacred Triangle in this chapter — the Native American aspect.

The Sacred Triangle has three sides. One is the mystical White Brotherhood/White Sisterhood, which includes great ascended masters like Sananda/Jesus, Moses, Quan Yin, Archangel Michael, and many others who have contributed to the spiritual development and mystical experiences on Earth. The second part of the Sacred Triangle is what I call galactic spirituality, consisting of the Arcturians and many other, higher fifth-dimensional galactic beings from the Pleiades, Antares, and special planets near the Central Sun. It also includes masters and teachers from other galaxies, including the Andromeda galaxy, which is the sister galaxy of the Milky Way. (It is rather surprising that the Andromeda galaxy is the closest galaxy to Earth, yet it is still very far away, perhaps 5 million light-years. This gives you an idea of the vastness of our universe.)

The final side of the Sacred Triangle is native peoples, including those of North and South America, Central America, Africa, and elsewhere around the planet. Native peoples have a special ability to relate to the heart of Mother Earth, and this ability is necessary for returning Earth to balance. Native peoples have the knowledge and teachings to guide planetary healers to this new balance, but they have many problems bringing and implementing their teachings into a powerful system all starseeds can learn from. Part of the problem comes from historical conflicts and domination that have occurred over the past three centuries and even longer. This has led to intense distrust and alienation toward Europeans and the dominant North American and South American cultures on this planet

Some might say it is ironic that at a time of crisis we return to working with native peoples, because historically the exact opposite occurred. The dominant society sought to control, dominate, and eradicate native peoples. Fortunately, this did not succeed, even with genocide. In our work as planetary healers, we call on native peoples to join in the Sacred Triangle work.

In the next section, Chief White Eagle, an ascended master and teacher, will offer his spiritual guidance and wisdom on planetary healing. He is highly esteemed on both the fifth and third dimensions, and he has many followers on Earth.

A Native American Perspective

Chief White Eagle: Heya-ho. Greetings. We are all brothers and sisters. I am honored to be working with Juliano and you, the starseeds and planetary healers, and you who are the followers of the Arcturian teachings. We all agree that this is a dangerous time for the planet, with a need for great spiritual wisdom and teachings that will move people. We believe that this movement must come through open hearts and heart energy.

I will talk about Earth's feedback loop system from the Native American teachings that are generally used across the planet by shamans and other native cultures in many different countries. First, I must tell you a little about Earth's feedback loop system — what it is and how we view it. The Earth's feedback loop system is a self-regulating planetary system that keeps Earth in balance on hundreds of different levels. The most obvious level is temperature. Humanity and most animal and plant life need a special, moderate temperature to survive.

Modern man is looking at Mars with great interest as a possible planet for life. Mars has some temperatures above freezing — 40 to 50 degrees Fahrenheit on certain summer days — but nighttime temperatures can fall between 200 to 300 degrees below zero. That is extremely difficult to live with. If humans were to colonize Mars, you would probably have to live underground, which might not be the most exciting place to live. In this case, Mar's feedback loop system cannot keep a temperature range comfortable for humans.

Besides maintaining a moderate temperature, the feedback loop system moderates the chemical composition of the atmosphere. Plants, animals, and humans need a certain percentage of oxygen and nitrogen in the air. Other areas regulated by Earth's feedback loop system include ocean currents, jet streams, and the production of oxygen in general. Much of the production of oxygen on this planet comes from rain forests. It has been said that rain forests are the lungs of planet Earth. How has humanity been treating its lungs lately? Are we honoring them or destroying them?

Earth's Aura and Mind

Where is the feedback loop system of Earth located? In order to answer this question, I must give you a brief description of Earth. Earth is a living being; it is a living spirit. We call it a living spirit, because it has the characteristics of a living spirit or a living being. The most prominent feature is self-regulation — the ability to maintain certain temperatures and chemical compositions, for example. The Industrial Age has been going on for three to four hundred years, and much of the contamination it has produced could have tipped the balance earlier. But Earth's self-regulating system adapted and has kept the parameters of temperatures and chemicals to match the needs of humanity and other life forms.

The Earth has an aura, like humans have auras. The feedback loop system is in the mind of Earth, which is multidimensional. The human mind cannot directly be observed. It is true that you can do physiological experiments and study the electro-currents in the brain, and you can stimulate certain parts of the brain and see reactions. But even though you can study the brain and its chemical transitions and reactions, that is only the effect you are seeing on the third dimension.

Your mind is divided into the greater mind and the lesser mind. The greater mind is an over-viewer. It has the ability and need to exist in multidimensional realms. In fact, when you die, your mind still exists and will continue to exist. The Earth's mind is similar to the human mind in that it transcends physical reality. You can stimulate certain parts of Earth's mind by working with Earth's meridians. Many of you do not experience the mind energy of Earth unless you do certain techniques or ceremonies.

The Earth feedback loop system is a program that has been placed and activated within the mind of Earth for the purpose of maintaining a biosphere in which life can exist. This program is difficult to access; it is closely guarded. Even today, some native people, such as the Hopi, work throughout the year to guard the Spirit of Earth and Earth's feedback loop system. The Hopi are devoted to protecting and interacting with that system. Many people from the outside world consider what the Hopi do as rather primitive, but the exact opposite is true. They use highly advanced ceremonial techniques to interact with and talk to the Spirit of Earth.

Requirements to Access the Feedback Loop System

Anyone who wants to access the feedback loop system in the mind of Earth must have a certain level of spiritual advancement. Not just anyone is allowed to interact with or try to change the feedback loop-system program. A person must have dedication, have a heart open to Earth, and be willing and ready to follow ceremonies. For example, starseeds talk about codes of ascension and being able to follow a certain spiritual path; you must follow certain steps to open the codes of ascension in your mind. Accessing Earth's feedback loop system also requires certain steps, and this is a sacred path. It is not something done lightly.

The person or people accessing Earth's feedback loop system must also have expanded consciousness and perspective. Expanded consciousness includes the ability to accept Earth as a living spirit, named Gaia. An expanded consciousness means you can telepathically communicate with the Spirit of Earth. Perspective refers to the whole global view of the planet. If someone in a ceremony tries to communicate with Earth's feedback loop system, they must have a global perspective. For example, a planetary healer might want to push out a storm that is causing havoc in a certain area, but once pushed out, that dangerous storm could go to somewhere else and cause more damage.

To work with Earth's feedback loop system, you must have a global perspective and take into consideration the entire system. This is a big problem, because most planetary activities do not take into consideration global consequences. One example is building a nuclear-power plant on or near an earthquake fault. In the case of Fukushima, Japan, it proved to be a disastrous idea. Perhaps the people who designed and built the plant only considered the local consequences of a meltdown and not the global consequences. The same can be said of the Chernobyl nuclear accident in Russia. Did anyone consider that a meltdown would affect Europe? It did, of course. Many examples exist of the importance of a global perspective.

A Call for Ceremony

Heya ho! Oh Father/Mother, Creator of all, we call on you now to bring divine wisdom and teachings to our brothers and sisters. Help us teach them correctly. Help them learn this knowledge so they can use it wisely. Help them open their hearts to the planet. Heya ho, heya ho, heya ho.

I know you feel a great love for Mother Earth. You respect her, because in your language you call her your mother. The basis of your ascension comes from your connection to Mother Earth. This might be a new and controversial teaching, but Earth is a multidimensional planet with a multidimensional mind, and special energies within the Earth help you in your ascension. [Chants]: "Heya-ho, heya-ho, heya-ho."

Some of these energetic places are of great beauty, such as Lago Puelo in Argentina. Lightworkers there experienced a great heart opening to Mother Earth. She responded by showing those lightworkers beautiful sunsets, great weather, and powerful vibrational energy waves from her highest mind. We teach our people to communicate with the feedback loop system and the Spirit of Earth through ceremonies. We native peoples perform many rituals and ceremonies.

I earlier said that the opening to the feedback loop system is not for everyone; not everyone can access the mind of Earth. I want to return again to the Hopi who do long and elaborate ceremonies to talk to the feedback loop system in order to access the mind of Earth. Most people without training would find these ceremonies too long and maybe even boring. The most sacred parts of the ceremonies are not even shown or taught to outsiders.

There must be a major change in how humanity relates to Earth, because the planet needs more people to do these ceremonies. The planet needs more planetary healers. Planetary healers cannot remain isolated, and this is why we call for all native peoples to come together and work in union with all brothers and sisters and lightworkers. The calling goes out to share this knowledge of how to communicate with the feedback loop system.

Humans are the first species on this planet with the ability to interact and change a program — Earth's feedback loop system. Earth's feedback loop system is complicated, so it requires knowledgeable intervention. We cannot just allow anyone without the proper training, supervision, and perspective to access and try to change Earth's feedback loop system.

Cause-and-Effect Program

This leads me to another important aspect of Earth's feedback loop system. It is currently programmed and based on the laws of cause and effect. These are basic core realities of physics and the basis for the operational program for Earth's feedback loop system. Cause and effect is a fundamental concept in physics and karma. You do activity A, and B is the result. In Earth's feedback loop system, sometimes completing activity A delays activity B. There comes a point where the pressure of activity A becomes so strong that the result — activity B — must occur.

This simple idea can be applied to the environment, for example in contamination and nuclear radiation. Much contamination and pollution are in the atmosphere and oceans now. This affects the biosphere. After a certain point, blockages will result in the meridians that affect the feedback loop system. If the meridians cannot stay open, then Earth will look for alternative meridian systems. If none can be found, the blockages will continue, and Earth's feedback loop system will look for other ways to keep the balance.

Sometimes it reaches a point where there are no new pathways. One of the roles of planetary healers is to develop and encourage the opening of existing meridians, and, if necessary, develop new meridian systems. This is one role of the Arcturian-etheric-crystals system downloaded around the globe. I have jokingly called these twelve etheric crystals "bypass surgery." Many of the meridian systems are so blocked that they do not function well. But the twelve-etheric-crystals system can be viewed as bypass surgery, because we are placing new pathways, new meridians, into the planet.

Contamination is a major reason for blockages. One way to change the outcome is to clean contamination, which removes the blockages. So the laws of cause and effect can also work in your favor. Unfortunately, it is our opinion that the planet is at a tipping point, which means the amount of damage, contamination, and blockage is so overwhelming that it is unlikely the effect can be reversed without rapid intervention. Very simply, global warming and contamination of the environment are real, and will become worse by 2050. Major interventions need to take place now, which seems highly unlikely in the present political climate on the planet.

The Earth's feedback loop system operates in the mind of the planet. The system is within Earth's aura, just like your mind is energetically in an energy field around you and within your aura. The mind is not just physical neurons, synapses, and axons. The real mind is located in the electromagnetic energy field in the multidimensional space around your human body.

The second alternative program for the operation of the feedback loop system of Earth is a fifth-dimensional program that transcends cause and effect. This program receives quantum energy and light and omega energy and light. This program contains the codes and energy for Earth's ascension into the fifth dimension. This is a newer program for Earth's feedback loop system. As a planetary healer, you can begin to call on this higher program, interact with it, and use newer fifth-dimensional techniques, energies, and activations for fifth-dimensional Earth. You have a great desire to nurture Earth into her fifth-dimensional, planetary beauty, and this will happen.

The direct way to communicate with Earth's mind and Earth's feedback loop system is through heart energy. We must work together to open the hearts of as many humans as possible to the pain and suffering of the planet. We must make people aware of the blockages in the meridians causing disruptions to the center of Earth, because Earth needs to be healed. Our mother is sick and she needs our help. I am now going to turn you over to Chief Buffalo Heart. This is Chief White Eagle. We are all brothers and sisters. Ho!

Heart Energy

Chief Buffalo Heart: Heya-ho, heya-ho, heya-ho! I am Chief

Buffalo Heart. My specialty is heart energy, and I help people open their hearts. The planet has experienced much pain lately. It is a real spiritual accomplishment to have an open heart, and it is a special developmental advancement to have an open heart to Earth. I speak about the buffalo, because that is my power animal. Maybe some of you have power animals. Power animals are signs that the natural world can provide assistance in your mission as a planetary healer. Some of you have the bear. Some of you have the leopard. Some of the power animals are now extinct, but they still exist in the spirit world.

In buffalo heart energy, we seek to gather personal power so we can teach people about how powerful their heart energy is in communicating with Earth's mind. This communication with Earth is expressed in the buffalo ceremony, fire ceremony, and pipe ceremony. We give honor and respect to Mother Earth. We feel gifted that we can walk on her ground and see her beauty. You all know of the great beauty of Earth. Think about how Earth's beauty can expand your consciousness.

You might have had a peak experience in your lifetime that expanded your consciousness. You can thank these powerful, higher states of consciousness experienced through a sunset on an ocean, a majestic mountain, a morning sun, or beautiful clouds. You have felt the beauty of Mother Earth, and you have opened your heart to her. You have opened your mind to her mind and telepathically communicated by admiring her beauty. Think of Earth as your beloved pet. Your pet loves to be admired by you and wants your love and acknowledgement of their beauty. It is the same with Earth. Earth is moved when you acknowledge her beauty, thank her, and give her gratitude.

I come from the Buffalo Clan. The buffalo has given so much to the native peoples in North America. Native peoples were grateful for the buffalo. Buffalo provided meat for food and skins for tipis and clothes. No part of the animal was wasted. Native hunters honored the buffalo and only took the animals they needed. They asked permission from the herd, and they prayed for the buffalo they were going to take. They thanked the spirit of that buffalo for providing sustenance.

People from Europe came and hunted the buffalo for sport. Their hearts were not open to the buffalo, and they hunted them as a game. The buffalo did not protest; the buffalo was an accepting, compassionate animal. Likewise, Earth is a loving and compassionate planet and understands what modern humans are doing. For all the damage and destruction that modern technology has caused, Mother Earth is still loving, compassionate, and understanding. Is that not moving? Mother Earth accepts your prayers, ceremonies, medicine wheel, and love. We honor you, Mother Earth, with our hearts. I am Chief Buffalo Heart. Ho!

Holographic Healing

Helio-ah: Greetings, I am Helio-ah, an Arcturian guide and teacher. I work with Juliano. In this closing section, I will talk about the galactic concept of planetary healing and working with Earth's feedback loop system using the technique of holographic healing. In holographic energy, one part represents the whole, and the whole can be accessed through that part. In holographic healing, you only need one healthy cell to generate and communicate to all the other cells. Of course, you need the right approach and right energy. In planetary holographic healing, we have emphasized that the planetary cities of light can hold a higher, fifth-dimensional energy that can be the basis for sending healing energy and light throughout the planet. One cell can affect all other cells; therefore, one city of light can affect the whole network of cities across this planet.

When you do planetary healing and work with the feedback loop system, many of you focus on what is wrong and what needs to be corrected. I understand that and I honor that approach. I know you only do biorelativity and planetary healing to correct something. But the basis of planetary holographic healing also says: "Work with what is right. Find beauty and send healing energy from that beautiful and in-balance place to other places." One healthy cell can change everything.

In planetary holographic healing, we do biorelativity exercises working with what is beautiful and perfect, because we know that power can be disseminated over the planet from healthy energy. This positive exchange was done, for example, in Lago Puelo, Argentina, when the Argentinian Group of Forty members sent beautiful healing light to Earth from that very balanced and powerful spiritual center. I encourage you to work from some of the beautiful and healing places you know. The feedback loop system likes your compliments.

The Earth says: "Yes, I accept and like that you appreciate the beauty I produce for you." This perspective has many important ramifications I will discuss in future chapters.

Chapter 4

The Intersection of Dimensions

Juliano and the Arcturians and Tomar

Juliano and the Arcturians: Many rapid changes are occurring on Earth; it is a very dramatic time. You might be having difficulty calibrating your energy field to the changing environmental, social, and political situations. Just when you think you are on top of things and have adjusted to a new situation, another shift happens. While we and other guides and teachers predicted very dramatic polarizing and Earth changes, you have the desire and need for stability. You want to say, "It will be okay; I can adjust to this," but then another layer activates more chaos and polarization.

We begin this chapter with a subject we have visited before — the intersection of the dimensions, which is the intersection of the fourth and fifth dimensions with the third. This is a major occurrence that accounts for several different changes on the planet. First, the intersection of dimensions allows extraterrestrials to visit Earth. You probably have learned by now that distances in space — between planets and stars in this and other galaxies — are enormous. It is impossible to travel these large distances in a lifetime, even if you go at the speed of light.

The only method for interstellar, interplanetary, and intergalactic travel is through dimensional corridors. Sometimes I refer to dimensional corridors as hyperspace, which is a term that describes a place beyond space and time. It is a place that does not conform to the normal space-time continuum. In the third dimension in which you live, space and time are inextricably woven together. You cannot talk about time without talking about space. Hyperspace has no space that you can compare to the third dimension. This is very difficult to describe, because you are so used to space and time. In hyperspace, you are in a different state of being and consciousness. Travel is at the speed of thought, and what you think and where you project your thoughts is where you go.

Hyperspace Travel

We have developed very advanced technologies to bring our starships into hyperspace. Many other beings live in this galaxy and in the cluster of galaxies known as the local group, which includes the Milky Way.[1] Dozens of these galaxies are called dwarf galaxies. Our friends in the Andromeda galaxy also belong to this local cluster. These galaxies are extremely far away in third-dimensional terms.[2]

You can travel through the Milky Way galaxy and the local cluster through these hyperspace dimensional corridors. But how do you know where to go? The Milky Way galaxy is as wide as 100,000 light-years. Imagine how many star systems and planets that includes. How do you find other planets with life on them, and how do other advanced beings find Earth? When you reach a certain level of advanced evolution and consciousness, you disburse a signature energy field into hyperspace. If you want to travel through hyperspace and find a planet with life, its signature energy can lead you in the approximate direction.

Maybe you want to travel to the Pleiades. All astronomers and most of the starseeds now have an image in their minds of where that star system is located, because the Pleiades is a well-known constellation in the night sky; it is already in your thought field. Therefore, if you want to travel to that place in hyperspace, you can thought-project there. But what if you don't know where any biosphere life is in the galaxy? You can think: "Tune me in to all biospheric energy

1. The local group is the name for a group of galaxies that includes the Milky Way and the Andromeda galaxy. It comprises anywhere from 40 to 54 galaxies.

2. The local cluster is 10 million light-years in diameter, and the Andromeda galaxy is as far away as 2.5 million light-years.

impressions in the left sector of the Milky Way galaxy." Projecting this thought into hyperspace it is like raising an antenna that reaches out and picks up signals.

Extraterrestrial and higher-dimensional beings entering hyperspace and the hyperspace corridors of the Milky Way galaxy send out radar-like energy to all planets with life forms. Planets with life forms emit a signature of their life forms into hyperspace. Earth emits such a signal. Advanced beings can find you on Earth, and you can find them, because they also emit this signal. It is a matter of knowing this formula and how to raise the antenna and send the signal through hyperspace to find biological or biospheric planetary systems.

Earth has emitted a biospheric signature into hyperspace for centuries. Several groups of extraterrestrials have picked up this biospheric signal and found and visited Earth. Many philosophers and researchers have documented this, including UFO researcher Erich von Däniken. In his book *Chariots of the Gods*, he explores evidence of extraterrestrial beings coming to Earth for centuries for a variety of reasons. Some reasons have been benevolent and humanitarian, while others have been self-centered. Another UFO researcher, Zecharia Sitchin, has suggested that extraterrestrials came to the Middle East centuries ago to enslave humans. Other theories posit that extraterrestrial visitors to Earth mixed their DNA with human DNA.

The point is that one way to talk about dimensions and access to third dimensions is through these dimensional corridors, and a primary dimensional corridor is hyperspace. Extraterrestrial beings use hyperspace corridors in the Milky Way galaxy to follow the signatures of the biospheric life forms emitted into hyperspace. A large number of visitors from other galaxies have come to Earth within the past twenty to thirty years, including beings from Andromeda and galaxies beyond the local cluster.

The Third- and Fourth-Dimensional Intersection

Now let us look at the concept of the intersection of the dimensions as it applies to the fourth and fifth dimensions. Intersections exist from the fourth dimension to the third dimension. The fourth dimension contains the astral plane, the body or energy field around Earth. The astral plane contains energy, spirits, and beings still locked into Earth's incarnational cycle. These beings are not yet free from Earth karma and, in some ways, are in lower states of consciousness. The fourth dimension also has layers, so I cannot say that the fourth dimension is all lower energy; there is also some higher fourth-dimensional energy. The important thing to understand is that the fourth dimension is locked and connected to Earth's incarnational cycles, and beings in the fourth dimension can and will reincarnate on Earth.

Higher dimensional beings, including those in the fifth, sixth, and seventh dimensions, can visit the fourth and third dimensions. The higher on the dimensional ladder, the easier it is to visit and interact in lower dimensions. For this discussion, when I talk about the fourth dimension, I mean the lower fourth dimension, which is home to spirits who are ghosts or mischievous beings.

How does the fourth dimension intersect with the third? Interestingly, some intersections with the third and fifth dimensions occur on certain holidays. For example, a Mexican celebration called the Day of the Dead essentially opens a corridor for those beings who are on the fourth dimension and those who want to communicate with them.[3] It is also true that the lower fourth dimension has positive beings; when someone dies, they often first go to different places on the fourth dimension.

We are talking about lower fourth-dimensional beings who seem to be stuck and in a fourth-dimensional place of repetitive movement and experience. This has been described, for example, by author Mary Summer Rain who writes about No-Eyes, an extraordinary Native American shaman woman.[4] No-Eyes describes people who got caught in a forest fire, were unable to escape, and died. They became trapped in the fourth dimension and continually relived their Earth experiences, unable to extricate themselves without help. No-Eyes describes certain ways spiritual healers can help release stuck

3. Day of the Dead, or Dia de los Muertos, is celebrated throughout Mexico. It focuses on praying for deceased friends and family members to help support their spiritual journeys.

4. No-Eyes is a shaman who has visions of major and unsettling future changes coming to Earth. See *Spirit Songs: The Introduction of No-Eyes* by Mary Summer Rain.

fourth-dimensional beings. Many of you in the Group of Forty have the sensitivity and ability to do that much-needed spiritual work.

In this time of polarization and rapid change, the veil between the third and fourth dimensions has undergone dramatic changes. In many parts of the planet, the veil has become corrupt or loosened. There are healthy ways to interact with fourth-dimensional energy and beings, but a corruption of the veil between dimensions can cause what I have described as the bleeding of the dimensions. Energy from the fourth dimension can seep or bleed into the third dimension, for example.

When lower-dimensional beings see that seeping taking place, they might go through the holes and attach to vulnerable beings on Earth who are susceptible to attachments. In other words, lower beings come in, unwanted, and stay as long as they want. Part of this is due to the weakened energy field around many of the people on this planet. Due to an unhealthy person's energy field, holes form in the aura that lower fourth-dimensional beings can attach to. These beings can then cause mischievous and sometimes painful and harmful interactions that can escalate into wars or violent tragedies and events, some of which have been taking place on Earth over the past several years.

The Fifth- and Third-Dimensional Intersection

Now let's look at the relationship between the fifth and third dimensions. Just as links and corridors exist between the third and fourth dimensions, they also exist between the third and fifth dimensions. These corridors bypass the fourth dimension, so if you want to go to a higher dimension, say to the fifth dimension, you do not need to go through the fourth. You have free choice; you can go through the fourth to the fifth if you want. But for the purpose of our planetary work, we recommend going from the third to the fifth.

I do not use the exact word "bleeding" when I describe the relationship between the fifth and third dimensions, because the energy that comes from the fifth dimension is totally different from the energy that goes from the fourth to the third. The energy from the fifth dimension is a higher vibration that creates high activity and feelings of enthusiasm, joy, balance, harmony, and love. Feelings associated with lower-dimensional energies include jealousy, hatred, self-centeredness, selfishness, and other energies that could be described as coming from the lower self.

In some ways, there has always been a reasonable linkage and corridor between the third and fifth dimensions. The intersection of dimensions is difficult to explain, because you have no real visual image of a dimension or of the universe. You could, for example, compare a dimension to the universe and say that the existence of the universe is the third dimension, but the shape of the universe is still unknown. Scientists used to think it was a sphere, but when you say the universe is infinite, that means there is no outer edge. How do you visualize a sphere with no outer edge, that is always expanding?

The third dimension is in alignment with the shape and structure of the universe in that it is isotropic. "Isotropic" means that each part is the same, so all parts of the universe have the same physical laws, such as gravity and density.[5]

For the purposes of this chapter, I am going to make the dramatic assumption that this third dimension is a sphere with strange properties that include infinite expansion. The fifth dimension is another universe that has the shape of a sphere. At certain points in Earth's revolution around the galaxy's Central Sun, corridors or portals appear through which Earth can experience the fifth dimension intersecting with the third.

At that intersection, tremendous downloading of higher dimensional light takes place. Some have called this downloading of energy the ascension wave. It accelerates psychic abilities and expansion of consciousness. But in order to receive this higher, intersecting energy from the fifth dimension, you must tune to the right frequency, the right energy field. For example, your FM radio has a station that plays great music. You need to know the frequency number — such as 106.3 — to receive it. What if your radio does not go up to 106.3 FM and only goes up to 105? You will never hear the station without that higher frequency.

5. In cosmology, "isotropic" means having identical properties in all directions. Thus, the properties of the universe are the same to all observers, no matter what part of the universe they are in. Or, simply, the universe is the same everywhere!

This comes back to the important principle of the preparation of the vessel. Prepare to receive and expand your frequency range so you can go into the higher range of the fifth dimension. Many Arcturian starseeds gather at Stonehenge, which is a place specifically established as a dimensional intersection point. We have also set up twelve etheric crystals around the planet, where you can experience the fifth-dimensional intersection in a powerful way. These etheric crystals are stationed for you to receive and download this energy and transmit it around the planet.

Some refer to this intersection of the dimensions as the ascension wave, because the energy can accelerate ascension. You cannot ascend using normal, third-dimensional energy; you would have to be at an extremely high state of expanded consciousness. Only a handful of prophets have ever reached that state in planetary history. I am not undermining your spiritual abilities. I am only saying that, realistically, when we look at all souls on this planet who have incarnated, only a handful accelerated spiritually and used the energies effectively for their ascension.

It is in your genetic codes to ascend, but an ascension wave during an intersection can augment your abilities. It can help you be in touch with your higher self, your higher consciousness, and you can download and use this energy in a variety of different ways. Being on the planet during this intersection of energies is healing. I compare it to a solar eclipse, where there is an alignment.

Galactic Intersection Exercise

Let us again talk about the intersection of dimensions from the standpoint of the galaxy. We study galactic vibrations and are acutely aware of how Earth's solar system revolves around the center of the galaxy. Our system on Arcturus is close to your solar system — about thirty-six light-years away — and our systems travel around the galaxy together. Some estimates say that one revolution around the center of the galaxy takes 250 million years. Your Earth goes around the Sun in 365.25 days, which is one revolution. Can you imagine a revolution that lasts 250 million years?

During your planet's path around the Sun, seasons change, the angle of sunlight changes, and weather patterns change. Other energetic changes are still being discovered. So you have this unique relationship with the Sun. You have the unique possibility of experiencing different angles of the Sun while revolving around it. Similarly, this fantastic journey around the center of the galaxy brings many variations of energy. Higher energy coming to a planet often brings polarization and chaos, because beings without the capacity for integrating higher energy become more imbalanced.

You can use this energy for your own development. Activate, to the best of your ability, your crown chakra, because the crown chakra is specifically attuned to the intersections of different realms. You can open your crown chakra much wider than you normally do to receive this galactic light and energy. Focus on your crown chakra and say to yourself: "I open my crown chakra to the higher light coming from the intersection of the dimensions."

Open your crown chakra to these higher-vibrational energy fields already beginning to stream through your crown chakra, downloading and activating. Feel the light from the wave of ascension come into your crown chakra.

Using your crown chakra, place a white and orange shield of protection around your energy field. This is like a filter for your crown chakra so it only receives fifth-dimensional energy. Remember the radio station needing to go up to 106.3? Your crown chakra has to recalibrate in order to expand its receptivity and receive the higher frequency of light coming from the intersection of the dimensions. [Chants]: "Holy light."

Calibrate your crown chakra now. Give your crown chakra the command: "Calibrate right now my crown chakra for the light frequency at the intersection of the dimensions." [Sings]: "Now calibrate it. Expand it."

Your crown chakra is now expanded to a more advanced frequency range. When the intersection of dimensions occurs, you will be able to shimmer more easily into the other dimensions. You will be able to thought-project into other dimensions more easily. You will be able to bring back higher, fifth-dimensional energy into your third-dimensional body. Our greatest service and desire is assist you in this endeavor. I now turn over the rest of this chapter to Tomar.

Tomar's Temple

Tomar: [Sings]: "Tomar, Tomar, Tomar." Greetings, I am Tomar. My fifth-dimensional temple is known as Tomar's Temple. During dimensional shifts, new energy called the ascension wave arrives. I will lead you on an exercise to my temple, where you will find great comfort. You will want to be in the temple, partly because it feels secure.

One main feature of my temple is that it offers you an opportunity to experience your fifth-dimensional body without feeling Earth attachments. This is in accordance with some of the laws of the Arcturian stargate. In our earlier work, we would say that you cannot enter the fifth-dimensional Arcturian stargate unless you have graduated from Earth, which means you are finished with your Earth incarnations. But Juliano, our Arcturian teacher, can open the doorway to the stargate so you can experience its fifth-dimensional light, which is beautiful and overwhelming for your third-dimensional body.

I can bring you into Tomar's Temple. Your third-dimensional body and attachments will be purified and left outside the temple door. Then you can come into the temple and feel totally in your fifth-dimensional energy field and detach, temporarily, from your third-dimensional body. This is a joyful experience!

Tomar's Temple is filled with white light. A small, circular area in the temple looks like a small pond. It contains beautiful galactic crystals. Temple meditators sit around the pond at all hours of the day and night. In the temple, you feel a powerful fifth-dimensional vibration. You also feel a deep connection to the galaxy, a connection you might not feel as strongly in the third dimension.

The temple contains special windows, similar to the windows Juliano has described on our starship Athena. These windows are made of magnifying lenses as powerful as the most advanced telescopes on Earth. They can zoom in on any portion of this galaxy in great detail. It is similar to the idea of using an online map, where you zoom in on a particular place. Zooming is controlled by your thoughts. You think about what you want to see through the window, and the lens zooms in on that place.

These windows are also keyed into spiritual centers around the galaxy. You might wish to go to a lower energy field or a higher energy field. Many different planets around the galaxy have beautiful higher temples and higher sacred energies. As a visionary artist, you will receive images of these sacred places for the next ninety days. Throughout the galaxy are beautiful sacred mountains, valleys, and temples. You will receive images of these places. I hope the visionary artists on Earth can produce them for the rest of the world to see.

Take three deep breaths and feel the corridor of light I have sent you. The corridor links directly to the fifth dimension, to my temple — Tomar's Temple. Feel your astral body rise out of your physical body. Go up the corridor, traveling at the speed of thought. You come directly to my temple on Arcturus. At the front of the temple are huge circular stairs. Walk up these stairs and come to the door. I am there, greeting you. As you walk through the entrance, your third-dimensional body leaves you like a coat. You leave your third-dimensional body outside the door, and you enter my temple with your soul energy body. Take a seat on the circular bench around the center of the temple. White light and energy stream down; you feel joyful and balanced. We will go into meditation now. [Chants]: "Tomar, Tomar, Tomar." [Silence.]

You have felt this wonderful light and higher consciousness, and now you experience a recalibration within your system that will allow you to receive higher frequencies when you return to your Earth body. You rise from the bench and come to the doorway, ready to re-inhabit your third-dimensional body. Step through the door, re-enter your body in astral form, and travel back with me through the corridor to your Earth body.

Come back to the physical. Re-enter your third-dimensional physical body in perfect alignment. Your ability to receive frequencies for the intersection of dimensions and ascension wave has now expanded.

Chapter 5

Galactic Anthropology

Juliano and the Arcturians

Many of you are students of galactic anthropology, and we, the Arcturians, devote a great deal of our research and travel throughout the galaxy to understanding and working with various cultures. Anthropology is the study of cultures. There are many studies of different cultures on Earth. Galactic anthropology is the study of different cultures throughout the galaxy. We estimate that there are 5,000 civilizations or cultures on the planets throughout the Milky Way galaxy. That might seem like a large number, but when you consider that the number of stars in the Milky Way is in the billions, then 5,000 is an extremely small number.

Anthropology defines the study of culture in different sections. For example, medical anthropology is the study of how people approach disease and illness. Economic anthropology is the study of how a culture approaches the economy and earning money. You can learn about political anthropology, social anthropology, and familial (or family) anthropology, which is the study of family relations. For example, the Hopi and the Navajo tribes are matriarchal, transmitting inheritance and power through the lineage of the mother. The predominant culture in the West is patriarchal, and the inheritance of power is through the father. Scientific anthropology is the study of advances a culture makes in technology, such as jet propulsion, satellites, and weaponry.

A new theme of galactic anthropology is planetary anthropology, the study of the relationship that the inhabitants of a planet have spiritually with their planet. Many people on Earth have trouble admitting that the planet is a living spirit. They would have equal trouble trying to define what type of spiritual relationship they have with Earth. As we encounter different planetary cultures, we see a variety of ways that the inhabitants relate to the spirit of their planet. Of course, those who have more spiritually advanced cultures also have a close spiritual relationship with their planet.

It is difficult to talk about the concept of the word "advanced" because you immediately think about and compare it to the word "primitive." Yet many so-called primitive cultures on Earth have advanced relationships with the spirit of Earth. When you use the word "advanced" in relation to a culture, you think about technology. You have the internet, smartphones, television, and computers. However, you do not need advanced technology to relate spiritually to a planet. Advanced technology does not determine advanced spirituality. You are seeing this now on Earth. There are tremendous technological advancements, but Earth is totally out of balance, and the biosphere is threatened.

How can you describe the culture on Earth now as advanced if the same culture that has all these technologies is destroying the planet? We cannot equate an advanced culture with only technological advances. At the same time, you might look at some Native American cultures and say, "Well, these are primitive cultures because they have a great deal of poverty," which is true. However, we would not say that these are primitive cultures because, from an anthropological standpoint, they have an advanced relationship with the spirit of Earth. Unfortunately, they are not the dominant cultures on this planet. Such cultures do not have the power to manifest or control how other cultures relate to the spirit of Earth. I would call them advanced, however, because they understand the necessity of having a close relationship with the planet — in this case Gaia, Mother Earth.

In galactic anthropology, we visit other cultures throughout the galaxy, and that is how we came to Earth. Part of our mission is to explore and assist in the development of higher planetary culture and higher planetary advancement, including spiritual advancement.

Arcturian Spirituality

There are areas where your planet needs technological assistance, such as the eradication or destruction of radiation. We have special technology to destroy radiation, and we can do this through technological and biological means. We will not share this technology now because the ability to use biological technology to destroy radiation can also be misused in weapons. The major deficit on this planet, from a galactic anthropological viewpoint, is not technology; it is the spiritual wisdom to understand and unite all the different energies that make up a planet.

Religion is a part of any culture. Religious anthropology looks at how a culture practices, relates, and organizes any ceremonies regarding the Creator. Let us look at the Arcturian culture from that standpoint. We believe in the Creator. We even use one of the names for the Creator that appear in the Hebrew Bible — the word "Adonai," which is defined as "my Lord." This term is also used in the galaxy. Some of the higher concepts in the mystical religions have galactic origins. Some of the Hebrew mystics known as the Kabbalists communicated with extraterrestrial beings and received knowledge and information from them.

Direct experience with the Creator can be called "spiritual" as opposed to "religious." The term "religious experiences" refers to the many ways and types of organizational and ceremonial endeavors. Our planet only has spiritual ceremony and spiritual work. We do not have separate religious denominations the way you do on Earth. Furthermore, we use only one language. We use more sounds and tonal healing energy, especially when we talk about our medical culture on Arcturus. We meet for spiritual experiences in (what you call) temples. You have heard me talk about the Arcturian temple, and we have the energy of portable temples in our spaceships. Our temple structure is much different from yours because we are able to tie in to a universal Arcturian group-thought energy construct. Everyone who wishes to connect with higher light can get the same vibrational energy and feel the power increase of a group energy field.

We do not dominate anyone in our spiritual groups. You have to remember that we are in the fifth dimension. To get into the fifth dimension, you have to achieve a certain vibration; you have to be elevated to a certain harmonic enlightenment that is above hatred, jealousy, and judgment. You can engage in higher emotional energy, such as compassion, love, forgiveness, and acceptance. Naturally, when you are in those emotional states, it is easier to participate in advanced spiritual group-energy work.

Our temples are usually circular. Sometimes they are octagonal. We have a center in our temple areas that looks like a small circle or pond with crystals in it, and we use those crystals to magnify the spiritual thought powers.

Galactic Spirituality

Galactic spirituality is one of the sides of the sacred triangle. It is also an important aspect when working with and explaining our spiritual work and how we approach prayer and meditation. Galactic spirituality embraces several beliefs. The main belief is that there is an overriding cosmic energy field that universally connects to all higher beings. We call this state "cosmic consciousness." We are in the fifth dimension, but in galactic spirituality, we recognize that there are higher dimensional beings besides us who are in the fifth dimension. For example, the Pleiadians are in the fifth dimension and so are beings in what you call the angelic world, including Archangels Michael, Gabriel, and Uriel. In galactic spirituality, you strive to graduate from the third dimension into the fifth dimension. We, the Arcturians, were once on the third dimension, and so were the Pleiadians. We graduated, and we moved ourselves and our entire planet into the fifth dimension.

Galactic spirituality also involves multidimensional energy. In galactic spirituality, we say we are able to experience higher dimensions, so on the fifth dimension, we can access the sixth, seventh, eighth, and ninth dimensions. On the third dimension, you can access the fourth and fifth dimensions.

Each planet in the galaxy has a unique perspective related to the Creator; therefore, it is advantageous to visit different cultures in the galaxy to see how they experience the Creator. This is the same as on Earth when you see how different cultures approach the Creator and relate to spirit. It is a wonderful, broadening experience to visit other galactic cultures, and that's why we and other beings are visiting other inhabited planets in the galaxy.

What is the benefit of studying other cultures? You can understand yourself better and learn that there are different ways of experiencing the energy field of the Creator. We believe that the energy field of the Creator interacts with all dimensions. Each dimension, as you go up the ladder, has a greater and different ability to experience the Creator's energy field. We share the belief that it is possible on lower dimensions to have a direct experience with the Creator's energy field.

Arcturian Economy

Economic anthropology is the study of how people trade goods and use money. We do not have money on Arcturus. Money is a commodity unique to Earth. To understand the dominant economy on Earth now, you have to study capitalism. Capitalism is based on profits gained in a free market and encourages people's appetites to collect, own, and consume products. In our culture, we do not use money. We do not own material objects the way you do on Earth, and we do not engage in capitalism.

As a side note, some of you have repeatedly asked me why it is so difficult to change Earth society and how you can make it more spiritual. First, understand that the idea of capitalism is to collect wealth and goods and hold on to them. You want to protect and keep them. You do not want to give away your power.

The people in the fifth dimension realize that the collection of goods does not really benefit spiritual development. Material goods can provide comfort, but in the fifth dimension, we manifest what we need, and people always give or share. Because we are fifth-dimensional beings on Arcturus, we are above our lower selves, our animal selves. You might think that because we live without money and always share, we are socialists. We do not like to use such terms because they only make sense on Earth as a contrast to your system of ownership and money. I think that if we had to make a comparison, it would be similar to some of the energies that have been defined in the Kibbutz in Israel where people live together in a group. There are some differences, because we still understand and honor our individuality.

Arcturian Medicine

Medical anthropology is the study of how a culture relates to illness and death. For example, illness in the Chinese culture is regarded as blocked life force energy. If that is the cause of the illness, then the treatment is to unblock it. What method would you use? Chinese culture developed acupuncture and acupressure. By unblocking the energy, you become healthy again. Western culture says that illness is caused by something wrong in the body. There is an invasion of germs. You must treat the symptom of that invasion. Becoming well again requires medications or even removing the organ or part of the body that is ill.

Our culture does not have illness like you do, but we do have some health problems. Our model of treatment is based on vibrational medicine, and you are beginning to have this on Earth as well. You can see, even as I am talking to you, that there are advanced cultural concepts on Earth. It is just that they are not dominant in the general society.

In vibrational medicine, one concept of illness is that the energy field (sometimes referred to as the aura) has signs of misalignment, densities, or attachments, among other things. In the Arcturian medical culture, we look at the energy field first because what manifests in the physical body appears in the energy field. If you can treat the energy field first, the manifested body will heal. There is a vibrational component to all illness, and this component can be defined as darkness in the aura, an attachment on the aura, or a discoloration of the aura. We do vibrational healing and use various techniques.

We bring people to our healing chambers and use the spinning technique to put them at such a high-speed vibration that the lower vibration cannot stay attached to their energy fields. If you were to adopt our medical culture perspective, you would see that your body is not solid. A table looks solid, but on a higher plane, it is also energetic and vibrating. So it is with the human body. We can do vibrational intervention on the third-dimensional body. Some of our students who travel to Earth and other third-dimensional areas in the galaxy inhabit third-dimensional bodies. Therefore, we need to be able to work with them if they become ill. Helio-ah and I do what is called vibrational psychic surgery by placing certain vibrational instruments (you would call them medical instruments) in a person's aura and physical body to heal and remove dense and low-vibration cells. We also use sound vibration as a healing method.

Since there is no illness on Arcturus, why would we need to do any healing? At one point, we were third-dimensional beings, and our planet was on the third dimension, the same as your planet is. Therefore, we can bring unhealed or traumatic parts from other lifetimes to Arcturus. In our current lifetime, we seek to heal those parts of ourselves from past incarnations, which requires vibrational healing.

We are not hunters, and we are not food gatherers. We eat high substance foods. I know that in your culture, a lot of time is spent on gathering, preparing, and growing food or caring for animals. We have developed the perfect food, which has sometimes been described as liquid light. That food is referenced in the Bible's story of the Exodus, when the Israelites ate manna, which was food that came from the sky. It came from extraterrestrial sources. Manna was so perfect that it could satisfy all human nutritional needs, and there was no waste after eating it because it was totally absorbed. This description of manna gives you an idea of our food. When you eat such highly advanced food, there will be no food-borne illness. A large percentage of illnesses on Earth are digestive problems related to food that is contaminated with toxins or chemicals. If you all ate the perfect food, then these problems would not develop.

Arcturian Family Life

Every culture in the galaxy has different family patterns just as you on Earth have different cultures and family patterns. We Arcturians are all equal. For instance, neither sex is more powerful than the other. You have seen pictures of us. Our males and females look similar to each other. I call this the androgynous evolution. We have highly advanced male and female traits. We are not hermaphroditic — that is, we do not have the sexual organs of both sexes. In our study and investigation of galactic cultures, we have come across one or two planets that have hermaphrodites. On those planets, a person has breasts and is capable of becoming pregnant and also has the male organs. In the hermaphrodite cultures we visited, the division of male and female is retained because one sex is dominant in each person, so there are male hermaphrodites and female hermaphrodites.

The Arcturians are more androgynous. We do not carry the sexual organs of both sexes. We do not have pregnancies like you do. We use in vitro fertilization to create babies in laboratories. I know this is controversial in your society, but you must remember that we are fifth dimensional and do not misuse these scientific advancements. We have marriages, what I call soul unions, and soul family unions that are carried on from tradition. We do not use the terms "patriarchal lineage" or "matriarchal lineage." For one thing, we are not particularly interested in collecting goods or generationally passing down heirlooms to our children.

Our lives are much longer than yours. The average Arcturian does not have a child until about the age of 65 years. At 65 on Earth, people are preparing to retire. We live as long as 800 Earth years; therefore, 65 is very young. We can see many things about the new children coming in, such as their past lives, and we are able to talk to their spirit guides.

The Anthropology of Science

We also study how cultures relate to science and the development of technology. We study and organize scientific advancements such as jet propulsion and airborne munitions. Computer technology is another important issue, and I know that there has been a lot of discussion about artificial intelligence. We rate our technological advancements by integrating spiritual wisdom with them, so we have high levels of jet propulsion and a highly integrated system using artificial intelligence. We do not fear that artificial intelligence will take over. Our computers are very advanced. For example, if I had one of my computers focus on your aura, I would be able to see your current health. I would be able to see the outcome of any illness you have, and I would be able to see your past lives. I would be able to see when you will die on Earth. Our computers can also translate any thoughts from any language into a language we understand.

Our scientific knowledge is also related to a new concept we have developed called planetary anthropology. Planetary anthropology is the study of how a planetary culture relates to the planet, and I have talked about it before. Advanced cultures have strong spiritual relationships with their planet, and they use that relationship to control earthquakes, volcanic eruptions, storms, solar flares, comets, and asteroids. In extreme cases, a very advanced planet can move its position in the solar system to a point further from its sun if there were a sudden dramatic shift in the sun. Stars go through evolution. I realize this is not something that you have developed, but it is something that people like you now understand.

We study other galaxies. We can travel to other galaxies and other dimensions. Other dimensions are part of this universe we inhabit with you. You can go to a dimension like the fifth dimension and then come back to the third.

We have been studying the multiverse for a long time, and we have noted something strange: There is no way to visit another universe and come back! There are what I call space-time rifts. I talked to you about space-time rifts, or distortions, and how they have been created by scientific experiments such as nuclear bombs. There is also a different type of rift we call universal rifts. These are places where the universe has an opening, and if somebody goes through it, he or she does not come back. This is seen in the Bermuda Triangle; people disappear and never return. The plane or ship might be found, but the people are gone. They went into the multiverse through a rift in the fabric of this universe.

We are working to understand why people who go through those rifts cannot come back. Please understand that you can go into other dimensions and come back because you are still in the same universe. There are ways to protect yourself from the multiverse rifts, including putting a white light around you and using the cosmic egg.

Galactic Anthropology and the Ascension

Ascension anthropology is the study of how people on a planet move from one dimension to another, or how they graduate from one to another. We explore and share our technology of using the cosmic egg, methods of detaching from attachment, thought projection, and bilocation. Other ascension methods are used in different religious cultures. Some focus on prayer or the repetition of certain words. Some techniques involve isolation, such as using sensory deprivation devices or living in a cave for long periods.

We have visited different galactic cultures, and the ascension culture usually needs the assistance of outside guides and teachers. It is difficult for large groups of people to reach the ascension level. There must be some kind of spiritual intervention or direct assistance, and this is one of our goals.

Remember that we, the Arcturians, are devoted to service and to the overall evolution of the galaxy. This may sound far-reaching and difficult, but we are committed to the Milky Way galaxy's evolution. We travel through the galaxy, and when appropriate, we help planets that are open to our assistance. We do not interfere in their development.

When we talk about planetary anthropology, we try to teach the planetary stages of development and how the inhabitants of a planet need to interact with the spirit of the planet. In some cases, planetary cultures are not open to this, and they pay the consequences; in other cases, people like you are open to these spiritual ideas.

Some of you are galactic anthropologists. You have come here and incarnated on Earth. What better way to learn about the culture of a planet and assist its development than by being on the planet? It is the same as if you wanted to understand what it is like to be aboriginal. Would it not be better to live with an aboriginal tribe and become part of the group?

In galactic anthropology, you have the ability to incarnate on a planet as part of your study. Many of my students and the students of the Pleiades under P'taah have done exactly this. It is difficult because one rule of incarnating on Earth is that when you come through the Earth portal, you forget who you are. You have to reawaken.

In "primitive" cultures, people sit together, talk about their dreams, listen to children's fantasies, and encourage children to relate to spirits. But in the dominant Western culture, if you were to do this, others would think you were crazy and would want you to seek mental help. This is one technique we teach. We try to tell people how to be prepared for the darkening and the wiping out of their memories when they come to Earth. Sometimes people do not awaken until they are 30 years old; sometimes they do not awaken until they are 40 years old. I am Juliano. We are the Arcturians.

Chapter 6

Requirements for the Path to Ascension

Juliano and the Arcturians, Vywamus, Kuthumi, and Archangel Michael

Juliano and the Arcturians: Certain characteristics and requirements are needed for ascension. One protocol allows you to complete the path of ascension and — at the proper time — transmute your physical body into your fifth-dimensional body. The four aspects of this path are simple and basic. While there is much discussion about complex energies and different levels of dimensions, you might be surprised by the simplicity of what I describe.

As a way of introduction, the goal of the path to ascension is not to become more psychic, to see more colors or orbs, or to engage in a variety of extrasensory exercises. These extrasensory attributes are certainly enjoyable and often come as a side gift to your spiritual development, but do not think you must become more psychic, see spirit guides, or teleport to ascend. Throughout the history of the path of ascension on Earth, teachers and prophets have had various higher experiences, but those who attain higher psychic gifts do not necessarily ascend. In some cases, psychic gifts are a divergence, a blockage, or a digression from the path of ascension.

In this chapter, Vywamus and Archangel Michael will assist me in outlining four aspects of the path of ascension. The first task is to understand your personal and planetary mission. The second task is working in service to humanity and the planet. The third task is raising your spiritual light quotient. The fourth task is seeking grace. Each of these aspects has an important role and function in your ascension path. They might not be glorious or psychedelic, but in order to follow the path of ascension and ascend, you must do a lot of hard work. Some of the work is very third-dimensional.

I am often struck by those who are on the etheric seventh and eighth dimensions, which are wonderful and very attractive. But when thinking about these higher dimensions, please do not neglect your work on the third dimension. We do not want you to be diverted to those higher realms without doing your work here. There are still third-dimensional tasks, services, work, and grace to understand and incorporate into your path of ascension. These four elements are important third-dimensional work.

Aspect One: Personal Mission

Vywamus: Greetings, my fellow spiritual seeker on the path of ascension. My name is Vywamus, and I am a soul psychologist. I see the personal mission and the planetary mission as part of your soul development and your soul history. I see both of these aspects as important. It is no accident that you incarnated on this planet at this time during these circumstances. Your soul chose a time, a place, and even a family. There are no accidents, and coming here is not a random event. The circumstances on this planet, including conflicts and polarizations, are no accident. This is the long sum of a series of events. Some of these events have even occurred on other planets, and those dramas and unfoldments have been brought into the current situation on Earth.

You have to realize that your soul has a different perspective than that of your ego consciousness. Ego consciousness is related to animal consciousness, which is focused on survival and a narrow perception of the environment that sustains the biosphere. In some sense, the ego is self-centered and focused primarily on its survival. In the midst of this energy, you came to this planet for personal lessons. Your soul knew this lifetime would offer specific opportunities to receive the important lessons it needs. Your soul is focused on evolution and on graduating from this planet and its incarnation cycles.

To graduate, you have to complete your soul lessons. What are the soul lessons? Some are obvious, such as learning to love yourself and others. Another might be learning how to escape from or avoid abusive relationships. Other soul lessons can include gaining self-esteem and loving yourself. These are all personal soul lessons. Another personal soul lesson might involve helping a soul mate who is also on this planet.

You come from a soul family, a small soul group you are part of. In most cases, the entire soul group does not incarnate together. One or two from a group might come together on a planet. There are also branches of a soul tree. You might not be on exactly the same twig of your soul family's tree, but you could be on the same branch or the same limb. You incarnated on Earth knowing you would come in contact and work closely with your soul group. I use the term "group" loosely to include people on the same branch, but not necessarily a twin flame.

The twin flame is a popular concept. In general, twin flames do not incarnate together. Most often, they are on different dimensions or in different realms. When one twin flame on Earth returns, they bring information and energy that helps them both. When you meet others from your soul group, it invigorates you and helps accelerate your personal lessons. Therefore, it is highly desirable to meet, interact with, and work with your soul group.

When I speak of personal missions from the soul perspective, I mean individual issues you might refer to as personal development. Personal development is a rather recent concept that has its roots in Western thought as opposed to Eastern thought. In personal development, you are aware of yourself as a unique person with individual challenges and problems that can hinder your development and growth. These blocks need to be resolved. Sometimes, the problems include physical illnesses, physical disabilities, or limitations in movement.

As an example, let's say your soul incarnates and your personality is very physical. You become involved in professional football or soccer. But continuing in that sport is not the best thing for your soul's development, as a focus on fortune, fame, and materialism will not bring higher soul lessons to resolution. Therefore, you experience a career-ending injury. From the soul's perspective, this is a helpful development, because it forces you to engage in another career. This new career helps you focus on issues other than physical energy and winning at sports.

Aspect Two: Planetary Mission

Now let us look at the planetary mission. Your soul is advanced. You would not be reading this book if this were not the case. The planetary mission comes from your higher self. Your higher self recognizes the overwhelming process of evolution in the galaxy and the universe, and it understands that planetary groups and soul groups have evolutionary processes. In fact, there is an overall purpose to the evolution of this planet, and a specific energy is only available here: free will. Why is free will necessary, when it is responsible for destruction, blockages, and contaminations on this planet? The Creator deems that the free will of a planet provides an opportunity for the development of such spiritual opportunities as ascension.

Another spiritual opportunity that develops from free will is what Archangel Michael refers to as the evolution of the *B'nai Elokim*.[1] The *B'nai Elokim* are called the sons and daughters of the *Elokim*, and sometimes I refer to the *B'nai Elokim* as prophets, saviors, and messiahs. The *B'nai Elokim* are planetary overseers with extraordinary powers of planetary intervention and salvation. Salvation is the ability to lift up a soul into a higher dimension. The development and education necessary to become a *B'nai Elokim* is only available on a freewill, third-dimensional planet.

Your experiences and work in this third-dimensional realm contribute to your overall education, development, and evolution toward becoming a *B'nai Elokim*, a son or daughter of the *Elokim*. When you graduate from this planet, you will likely have the opportunity to go to other planets at equal or even lesser stages of development than Earth. Your experiences on Earth will be valuable for you as a *B'nai Elokim* in the role of a prophet or ascended master on that planet.

Your planetary mission goes even beyond the concepts and work of the *B'nai Elokim*. Your mission also helps to heal and bring this planet into higher balance. I know you feel a lot of disappointment and despair at times, especially when you see how out of control many aspects of the biosphere and the planetary development are. Do not let despair overwhelm you.

1. The letter *k* has been substituted for the letter *h* out of respect for this sacred name. It is a name for God or gods.

Some of you have been involved in other civilizations on other planets. Some of you have even been on Earth at other times under similar circumstances, when the forces of darkness and self-centeredness seemed to overcome the workings of the planet. During those darker times, you might have despaired, given in, and decided not to continue. Part of your planetary mission now is to not give in to the despair. You must maintain the proper thought field that contributes to the successful evolution and healing of this planet.

Planetary healing involves understanding planetary evolution and learning to gain a higher perspective. One of the missions for you in personal and planetary work is to gain a higher planetary perspective. You are learning that everything from a lower perspective does not make sense. Everything occurring on this planet is not logical from a third-dimensional, more-contracted perspective. There are so many unanswered questions about why things are happening the way they are, why so much destruction and pain is occurring, and why so many people are suffering.

Aspect Three: Service

Kuthumi: Greetings, I am Kuthumi, also known in my previous lifetime as St. Francis of Assisi. My mission as an ascended master focuses on teaching the importance of service to all who seek ascension. As Juliano said, psychic abilities and psychic powers can be exciting, fascinating, and gratifying. When I speak of doing basic service to humanity as part of your personal mission, some of you are not excited or enthusiastic. Maybe you do not see how doing basic service to those in need can lead you on your ascension path. Let me give you a simple observation: The Earth, especially now, has more opportunities for service to humanity and to the planet than at any other time in recent history. The dangers of global conflicts are real. The harm done to the environment is real. People's needs are also real. A powerful energy comes to you through service.

Earlier texts of Western religious groups, and I am referring specifically to the Hebrew Bible and the New Testament, put great emphasis on service. This emphasis is sometimes described as service to God, and the recommendation for doing service is in the form of commandments. These commandments for service have been summarized in these simple statements: Treat your neighbor as yourself; love thy neighbor as thyself; do onto others as you would do to yourself or to your family. This is the core of service.

Remember that service is one of the four core principles of the ascension path. Maybe service does not seem glamorous, but I assure you it has the highest potential for resolving karma, while accelerating and favoring ascension. In fact, of all four aspects being discussed, service might be the most important, especially as this is the time of greatest need for service on Earth.

How are you to do your service? Opportunities for service come through your sphere of influence. You have a specific group of people that you can help. You have specific opportunities to reach out to certain groups in your neighborhood, city, or country. These opportunities for service might seem random and come out of nowhere, but they come to you. For example, someone might ask you to talk to a group. In other cases, your devotion to service might involve seeking out opportunities to help others. Some people go on specific missions of service and travel to other countries. It is a spiritual law of evolution in the galaxy that higher beings are always in service — service to the Creator, service to the evolution of a planet, and service to the evolution of the spiritual family and galactic families.

Service is universal. No matter which dimension you are on, you still participate in service. As you go to higher dimensions, you are more joyful and spirited, because you understand the value of service. You are also better trained and more focused in your ability to be of service. You have unique skills and unique opportunities in whatever service is available to you and that you are capable of doing. It is worth repeating: This planet has many opportunities for service.

People ask me: "Kuthumi, why do so many souls want to come to Earth? This Earth full of conflict and polarization." It is because, from a higher level, your soul knows the value of service and how doing service helps its evolution. You do not necessarily do service for the soul's evolution; you do it for the love of assistance, the love of helping. A byproduct of doing service is burning off karma. As much as I love you, I have to say that you have leftover karma, otherwise you would not be on this planet. You still have opportunities, lessons, and service to do. In teaching ascension, we ascended masters say that you have a golden opportunity to accelerate your karma through doing service. Accelerating your karma means that lessons that might have taken four, five, or six lifetimes can now be learned and processed in one lifetime or even a third or half a lifetime.

By accepting accelerated karma, you might experience many difficulties, because you agreed to learn as many lessons as possible in this lifetime so you can ascend. On a soul level, this means you accepted accelerated lessons and accelerated karma. At times, these karmic lessons can seem overwhelming and too much for you to accept or resolve. At times, these difficult soul lessons contribute to feelings of despair and disappointment. But think about this: You want to ascend. You want to be free of Earth's incarnational cycle. You have unique opportunities now for acceleration in this conflicted planet with its polarizations. You have many great opportunities to resolve karma that seemed unresolvable in other lifetimes.

The good news is that you can take advantage of higher assistance. Also, while your problems might seem insurmountable, being in service burns off karma and helps resolve problems and makes them more workable. Problems become solvable because of the good energy and higher, spiritual cooperation that comes with service. You have unique opportunities for service on personal and planetary levels. Take advantage of them. Take advantage of your love for humanity and your love for planet Earth. Follow the commandment of "Do unto others as you would want done to yourself."

Aspect Four: Grace

Archangel Michael: Greetings, I am Archangel Michael. You might be surprised that grace is one of the four paths of ascension. I will approach grace from several different aspects. The first is that grace asks for a suspension of karmic difficulties in the face of what you perceive as insurmountable energy. You might have a problem you've been trying to resolve unsuccessfully. You might have difficulties in your physical, mental, emotional, or even spiritual life that are so complex, you feel no hope of resolution. You could be full of despair and discouragement. For a variety of reasons — some of them are karmic — you might be in a position where you are not able to resolve what this problem has brought to you. There might have been times you even wanted to leave your body and give up.

This is part of the process of karmic resolution. It is also a great opening into the discussion of grace. In grace, you say something like: "Oh Creator (or ascended masters, guides, or teachers), I have tried to the best of my ability, and I do not seem to be making progress. Grant me grace so that I might pass through this smoothly and successfully without harm to myself or my family." In a sense, grace is like a reward, a suspension of karmic punishment. For example, some of your societies have the concept of pardoning somebody who is in jail. You issue a pardon and say, "I am giving you grace. You are relieved and released from punishment."

What requirements do you have to exhibit to be worthy of grace and earn grace? This is a good question. The most important ways to earn grace are sincerity, devotion to your path, and clarity. Clarity means you see that this problem really is insurmountable and you need relief; you need a gift of suspension. In some cases, it can be helpful to say that suspending this karmic difficulty will allow you to be of greater service.

I have heard people in the world of psychology call this "bargaining." That is, you can say to the Creator: "If you relieve me of this illness, then I will be of more service to the divine cause." This is a legitimate approach, if you are sincere. You do not want to make that offer to Spirit unless you follow through on your agreement to be of more service. That is why I say the most important ingredient is sincerity. Several great spirit guides can help you seek grace. They include Mother Mary, Mary Magdalene, Archangel Michael, Archangel Gabriel, Archangel Raphael, Quan Yin, and Jesus/Sananda.

The Kabbalah has a beautiful teaching that carried down into the Christian tradition, on asking for grace. It can be summarized like this: "I surrender to a higher power; it is not my will, but Thy will." Karma that seems energetically insurmountable turns into a surrender to the higher path to God's will. By surrendering, you engage in a higher spiritual energy that allows grace to transpire in your personal life.

Raise Your Spiritual Light Quotient

Juliano and the Arcturians: Now I return for the fourth and equally important task of the ascension path, which is raising your spiritual light quotient, light energy, or spiritual vibration. This is the path that I think is the most fun for you; it is the most publicized and offers many rewards. It requires a basic understanding that this third-dimensional universe is a vibrational energy field. Everything vibrates; everything is frequency. On the path of ascension, we understand that the third dimension is a contracted, lower frequency. If you want to go into higher realms, you have to raise your frequency vibration. Your aura needs to vibrate at a higher vibration.

Several exercises and methods within this path can help you achieve a higher vibration. These include experiencing the sacred energy of sacred places, working in sacred times, calling on guides and teachers to cohabitate with you, and engaging in prayer and meditation. You can also create sacred fields that we Arcturians call planetary cities of light. You can work with etheric crystals and thought-project to the fifth dimension, which can include going to the Arcturian crystal lake or the crystal temple.

While many different methods for raising spiritual light energy exist, we need to look at Earth's situation from a realistic point of view. Many parts of the planet are engaged in lower-vibrational activities that have direct, destructive results for Earth. As you raise your frequency, you raise your vibrational energy. I am sure it is painful for you to see these lower energies playing out on Earth, but you must protect yourself and insulate your energy field from lower energies. Find ways to network with spiritual groups and friends. Find other spiritual people who want to work together to create higher networks of vibrational energy healing for the ascension path. This can help strengthen your vibrational thought field for ascension.

You can meditate on thought patterns in the Arcturian virtual temple. The virtual temple is an etheric temple downloaded to Earth from Arcturus that can accelerate and amplify thought power. You can use this fifth-dimensional thought technology and download it into Earth's dynamic thought-field source known as the noosphere. One of the most important aspects of improving the thought field for ascension and planetary balance and healing is connecting and "networking" with other starseeds and holding that network. Visualize a thought field and a higher-vibrational energy field literally connecting as an energetic grid around the planet. See the grid materialize as an energy force.

Think about the planetary cities of light. A thought field of protection surrounds the cities of light so those of lower vibration cannot penetrate and do lower work. Creating a thought field can help raise a higher, spiritual vibration for the planet. This kind of thought field and network can be referred to as a thought grid. We use the grid lines and meridians to hold that thought-field energy. We visualize Earth as the spiritual being that she is.

Monitor and raise your spiritual vibration to the highest level possible. Use techniques such as the Native American medicine wheel. A medicine wheel is a type of thought field. We want you to raise your spiritual light quotient and that of your city and the planet. You can raise your spiritual light quotient by studying and engaging in teaching, learning, reading, and having peak spiritual experiences. Seek out higher light at all times.

We are at the cusp of the intersection of the dimensions. This intersection offers more light and more energy to raise your spiritual light quotient and the spiritual, vibrational energy field of all seekers of light. Being on this third-dimensional planet now is a great opportunity. Polarization is strong, but so is spirituality. Choose the path of higher, spiritual vibration and enjoy new teachings, quantum energy, and higher dimensional work from all the dimensions, including the eighth and ninth. Enjoy it and receive it. Receiving light from all higher dimensions is an important part of the spiritual, vibrational upliftment that is occurring now and will continue to grow.

Chapter 7

Holographic Healing Work and Your Home Planet

Juliano and the Arcturians

Starseeds are Earth beings who have had lifetimes on other planetary systems and have had interactions, on Earth or other planets, with higher dimensional beings from other planetary systems. Most people now incarnate on Earth are part of Earth's home group, but the starseeds have other home planets and came to Earth recently or in past lifetimes to participate in Earth's incarnational cycle.

Sometimes starseeds are born remembering where they come from. Others awaken during their adult lives and long to return to their home planets. What is the home planet? It is where you first incarnated as a soul in this universe. Frequently, other members of your soul family incarnated there with you.

Starseeds are soul travelers for many reasons. As you know, incarnating is a learning process for the soul, and there are many new and exciting learning opportunities in different planetary systems. Starseeds follow the universal principles of spiritual service.

As a starseed, you might live on a fifth-dimensional planet comparable to the Garden of Eden — peaceful and harmonious. You would feel great satisfaction, harmony, and enlightenment there. There would be no need for your service or leadership, so your soul might long to provide guidance and spiritual wisdom to others throughout the galaxy. Therefore, you would gladly choose to embark on other planetary incarnational excursions.

Such excursions come with a price. It is difficult to leave the womb and the perfect fifth-dimensional life on a higher star system. Yes, some of you left home planets where you were already in an ascended, or fifth-dimensional, state. I am sure you long to return to that home planet after your experience on Earth. However, there is a lesson: Sometimes when everything is perfect, souls do not appreciate the higher state of consciousness and the higher evolution they are in.

During this Earth experience, you will have the opportunity to ascend and return to your home planet. I guarantee that you will greatly appreciate and take full advantage of the higher-vibrational energy and evolution on that planet, but you will know that the universe is not static and not in perfect homeostasis of harmonious balance. There are always changes, even on perfect, fifth-dimensional planets. Energies are moving, and there are reasons to go beyond one's planet. There are reasons to become a soul traveler.

Include Your Emotional Body in Bilocation Exercises

You are currently practicing astral traveling, bilocating, and thought projecting, especially in anticipation of the ascension. One thing is lacking in your bilocation practice and in the ascension practice in general. Most of you are thought projecting your spirit bodies — your aura, the higher energy body — to another place. This is appropriate and very good.

But you consist of more than a spirit body. You also have a mental body, a physical body, and an emotional body. We see that many of you are not taking your emotional bodies into these higher realms. I bring this up because I know that many of you suffer emotionally. How can you not have very strong reactions, given the terrible circumstances on Earth at this time? I am referring to the sixth mass extinction, the polarization, and the contamination and neglect of the biosphere, which continue without any real global effort to control the devastation and destruction. I know that you may have to block your emotional body so that you do not feel the intense pain of watching what is going on now. It is easy to get involved, react, and become overwhelmed emotionally by current events. You are sensitive, caring, loving starseeds. For healing purposes, you must work with and project your emotional bodies to the higher level.

In the ascension, you have to take all your bodies to the higher realms. The truth is that the emotional body is the most vulnerable and can easily attach to this planet. There are many reasons that it could be difficult to sever attachments to Earth. Most are undoubtedly tied to your emotional energy, which might be expressed as sadness or any other strong emotional reaction that you have for Earth.

Being a starseed, you most likely have seen other planets go through similar events. In some cases, you might have even incarnated in Atlantis or Lemuria, and you may have witnessed a terrible destructive cycle. Perhaps you held a powerful position as a scientist, politician, or philosopher. You might have tried to bring about healing or to change the energy of that society. If you did, you were unsuccessful and might have taken it personally. You might have been emotionally drawn to feeling inadequate because you couldn't change the destructive events occurring then. In this case, you reincarnated in a time with similar circumstances.

I know you are sincere, and I know you tried in previous lifetimes to be powerful planetary healers. One reason you returned to Earth now is to deal with that experience of failure. You might try harder to be a planetary healer, or you might need to learn the lesson of not feeling overly attached to polarizations and conflicts. It is difficult to not feel attached and not have an emotional reaction to the drama on Earth. That is why I recommend you take your emotional body with you when you purify and cleanse in your ascension work. You can work on releasing the cords of attachment.

The emotional body can be reactive. We see that you have to feel what you feel. It is unreasonable to tell yourself that you will not feel something. But after you feel it, do you respond? Or do you react to that which you have observed or are a part of? Reacting can cause more devastation. It could involve becoming angry, taking sides, being jealous, or experiencing hatred. Feelings are not wrong. The determining factor is how you react to the feelings. Some reactions to feelings can harm you. Instead, have a planned response to your feelings about Earth drama.

Negative emotional reactions can be unconscious. Imagine that you are on the freeway and someone cuts you off. Do you react with anger? You know how dangerous it can be because many people on the freeway are on the edge of exploding anyway. A common reaction to being cut off is anger. You might even want to swear at the other driver. However, respond in a measured way: Slow down, stay calm, and do not express anger. When you respond that way, you might still feel the emotion, but you choose not to express it.

Remember that the experience on the freeway could still influence you. You might need to do something relaxing to discharge that negative energy. As a starseed, all you see and experience in Earth drama affects your soul energy. You might want to do a purification exercise to release any accumulated negative energy you carry.

Purification is one of the benefits of the Arcturian crystal lake. Water and crystals can accept and purify all emotional energy that you release. I encourage you to take your emotional body to the crystal lake in your bilocation exercises.

The Holographic Self

The holographic self is an important part of the ascension process. It is said that even the brightest people use only 20 percent of the brain. What happens to the other 80 percent? Where is all that brain energy going, and why do most people never have access to it? Remember that, in holographic terms, the self is much more than the Earth ego-self you see and experience now.

In the holographic self, you have your past-life selves, your future selves, and your multidimensional selves. You have your spirit self, your emotional self, your mental self, and your physical self. It is difficult to understand the multidimensional self, but think about your mind as not just existing in this reality.

The mind has electromagnetic energies and responds to different multidimensional stimuli to form different reactions. The mind (or brain) is as complex as the galaxy and is a physical manifestation of the self in this reality. However, it has other dimensional experiences that are simultaneous to this experience.

You may have heard about starseeds who say they are captains of starships in their multidimensional reality or that they are healers or commanders of star fleets. Some could be members of another planetary confederation. Such reports are popular, especially pertaining to the Ashtar Command. Many members of that system (the Ashtar system) are simultaneously living on Earth.

I use the term "holographic self" to encompass all aspects of the self. Without the proper belief system and training, you might easily become overwhelmed and lose your balance on Earth. It is difficult enough to maintain balance and harmony on Earth without having to coordinate your multidimensional self on a starship! However, when you experience your multidimensional nature, you can access far more advanced information and energies than most people do. You could speak with ascended masters. You might have healing energy and light to work with, and in some cases, you might access new quantum technologies that are just developing on Earth.

Advancements in these quantum technologies need to be downloaded into Earth's system. As a multidimensional being on another planet or a ship, you are in a position to be a conduit for such downloads. Doing so is spiritual service.

Dreams Are Multidimensional

We continually study ways to help you maintain your awareness about multidimensional realms. One important avenue is through your dreams. They offer great experiences and messages. Dreaming occurs during REM (rapid eye movement) sleep. In that state, you can become more aware of your multidimensional self.

It is peculiar that Western society disregards the importance of dreaming. Culturally, no value is placed on dreams. I know that dreams are often difficult to interpret. I assure you, the ascended masters and guides in the multidimensional world can easily access you through your dreams. Ask them to come into your dreams, and then prepare to engage in multidimensional travel, awareness, and consciousness there.

You can tell your subconscious that dreaming is an access road to your multidimensional self. In your normal consciousness, your access to your multidimensional self is restricted by your culture and priorities. However, you are starseeds. You are sensitive. You can open the door to your multidimensional experiences through your dreams by giving yourself instructions or commands, which will be every effective.

Remember, when we talked about the cosmic-egg aura exercise, I said you can command your aura to be in the shape of a cosmic egg, and the unconscious will respond to that. In the same way, you can command your dream self to provide access to your multidimensional self and to your higher spiritual guides and teachers. You have a dream guardian (sometimes referred to as the dream censor) who oversees the input that comes into your dream awareness. Talk to that guardian. Say that you are ready to be more open and to have more direct experiences with your multidimensional self in the dream time.

Use the *Merkabah* Vehicle

The *Merkabah* vehicle is a special holographic and protective vessel that allows you to travel interdimensionally and through hyperspace. I like to compare it to a computer-controlled automobile. Imagine you are in such an automobile in a specific part of town and you put your destination address in the computer. Then the computer maps your possible routes on the screen. You choose the route or let the computer choose it for you. Then you sit back and let the automobile take you to your destination. We will now do an exercise using the *Merkabah* vehicle to go to your home planet.

> Visualize your *Merkabah* as a seat in the center of a giant bubble. This special *Merkabah* vehicle is surrounded by a beautiful, tetrahedron-shaped bubble. This is a holographic vessel. Your spirit and emotional bodies enter the vehicle. Leave the physical and mental bodies behind. Your emotional body is an etheric double of your energy field. See the two layers, or bodies. [Tones]: "Oooohhhh."
>
> There is a device in the center of the vehicle that looks similar to a joystick. You also have access to a small galactic map and a keyboard. To indicate your destination, type in these words: "Take me to my home planet." There is a button on that joystick labeled with the word "begin." Press that button now. The etheric computer in your vehicle will automatically program the *Merkabah* to take you there. Your *Merkabah* vehicle knows exactly how to get there interdimensionally. [Tones]: "Tatatatatatatata, oooohhhh."

You are traveling through hyperspace at the speed of thought. You come to the outer boundary of the planet. Satellite *Merkabah* vehicles immediately let you into the home planet's temple. You step out of the *Merkabah* vehicle, and your soul-family brothers and sisters greet you. You feel relieved to be home. You interact and experience the wonderful energy of being with your soul family on your home planet. You are in a state of ecstasy because you feel well understood and well received. Your emotional body is with you.

There is a small pond similar to the Arcturian crystal lake in the temple of your home planet. It may be only 100 feet in diameter. There is a powerful crystal on top of the pond. With your emotional body, slowly enter the pond. It is only 1 or 2 feet deep. The crystal-infused water now purifies your emotional body. All the trauma, polarization, and worries that had attached to your emotional body are now cleansed. You are purified. [Tones]: "Oooohhhh, oooohhhh."

It is beautiful to watch all the layers of trauma fall off the emotional body, and the pond absorbs them and sends them up into the light. The pond receives a high-energy, quantum download. Bathe in this pond as the emotional body continues to purify and release trauma. [Tones]: "Oooohhhh." When you are on your home planet, releasing emotional trauma is much easier. You are in the most supportive, energetic, and sympathetic atmosphere with your soul family members. You are almost done with all these wonderful discharges. [Tones]: "Ooohhh."

Now your soul family surrounds you, and you step out of the pond to merge with your spirit body. You embrace your soul family and receive encouragement, upliftment, and (of course) healing energy from them. After this beautiful embrace, you know it is time to return to Earth. You climb back into your *Merkabah* vehicle filled with joy and healing energies, and you know that you will have the opportunity to return to your home planet. Returning to your home planet is part of your multidimensional self.

You are in your *Merkabah* vehicle. You program the vehicle to return to Earth. Put in your Earth address. Say goodbye to your home planet for now. Say goodbye to your soul family for now. Press the "begin" button. You fly away from the temple, escorted by small starship satellite vessels, and enter hyperspace, traveling back to your home on Earth at the speed of thought with your spirit body and your cleansed emotional body. [Tones]: "Tatatatatata, tatatata, tatatata, tatata."

You arrive in your home on Earth. You sit in the vehicle as you process and integrate what you have experienced, knowing that you will feel more enthusiastic, devoted, talented, and focused on your great mission as a starseed on Earth.

Step out of the *Merkabah* vehicle, and reunite with your physical body in perfect alignment. Take three deep breaths, and know that you can return at any time to your home planet for rejuvenation and purification. At the time of ascension, you will easily return to your home planet if that is your desire. It is wonderful to know that your soul family is waiting for you and can help you now if you need them. Do not forget that you give valuable information and energy to them as well.

In the light of Adonai and the *Merkabah* energy field, I, Juliano, bless each of you with my love and guidance.

Chapter 8

How to Cope with Dramatic Changes on This Planet

Juliano and the Arcturians and Chief White Eagle

Juliano and the Arcturians: Everyone is being affected by the dramatic changes occurring on this planet, which are causing you to feel doubt and despair. One of the members said because everything is so polarized and there are so many problems emerging, certainly this means that the ascension is close. I agree, and I think this is an interesting and positive perspective on how to deal with the dramatic changes.

Some of the earlier predictions of global warming and higher temperatures put this kind of change a decade or two in the future. No one predicted that the global changes would happen this soon — that there would be so many fires or record-breaking temperatures. There are many Earth changes happening now. The information regarding these Earth changes might not have been correctly tabulated.

It would be interesting if someone were to open an Earth Change Center so that people could receive earth change reports from all over the globe. Earth events could be reported, and then the data could be statistically tabulated. If such a center existed, then it would be overwhelmed with reports of the dramatic events happening.

These dramatic events are going to increase. There will not be a lull or a plateau where everything suddenly seems stable. Rather, shifts in temperatures, storms, and geological adjustments will increase. What might even be more frightening is that the sixth mass extinction will become more apparent. There will be more dramatic reactions in the oceans along with many fluctuations in the jet streams.

As a starseed group, you have tremendous sensitivity and incredible spiritual energies and spiritual powers. You have a vast history of planetary discovery and experiences, and some of you have been on other planets that have gone through such crises.

Do not think of yourselves as victims of this strong shift. You are not powerless. Planet Earth is vulnerable and fragile, but I also know that you have extraordinary powers. The most important power and, I would say, the most important perspective in coping with these Earth changes lie in your connection with the fifth dimension.

What distinguishes the starseeds from the rest of the population? Well, the starseeds understand and are establishing and improving their connection to the fifth dimension. This strong connection is revolutionary in terms of religious and mystical experiences described by the masters throughout the history of the planet. There has never been a movement of spiritually evolved people who have joined specifically establish corridors, etheric crystals, planetary cities of light, and planetary ocean reserves of light.

Global networking has an immediate and profound effect on the collective consciousness and the collective unconsciousness of the planet. That is only the beginning of the power that has evolved in the fifth-dimensional process of connecting the higher realms to the third dimension. You are doing the best you can, and I want you to understand that the fifth-dimensional energy, corridors, and downloading are also establishing a protective energy field around you.

The fifth-dimensional work is not solely for protecting Earth or individual areas. It is also set up to protect you. You have protection in the most basic way from any type of catastrophe you are near or upheaval caused by Earth events. Any of these things have the potential to be personally upsetting and harmful to you. But working as a starseed with the Arcturians and maintaining your global connections intensify the protective energy field around you. Know that calling on your fifth-dimensional guides, teachers, and the Arcturian energies will protect you.

Protect Your Energy Field with Resiliency

Fifth-dimensional energy has multiple powers, which include filtering and repulsing onslaughts of dynamic negative energy that could come from personal and planetary energetic "darts" from lower vibrations. You need to be especially careful at this time because of the toxic political environment in the United States and other parts of planet. You have to protect your energy field.

One of our most dynamic and powerful fifth-dimensional protection exercises is based on the Chinese energy concept called resiliency, or pung. It helps create the ability to repel lower-vibrational energies from your energy field. Remember, everything is a vibration.

In Earth's feedback loop system, there is a series of stages and levels on which directions and communications about how to react are sent into the spirit of Earth. Unfortunately, negative feedback is continually being downloaded. Some of it is from negligence or lack of knowledge. Much of it is attributed to the lower evolutionary scale of many of the world leaders and people in power.

Starseeds are an evolved representation of humanity. We've talked about the omega human, which is the next stage of the evolution for *Homo sapiens* and is represented by you, the starseeds. You have greater sensitivity and ability to relate to the spirit of the planet to understand the feedback loop system. The feedback loop system reacts to input based on whatever is entered or downloaded into it.

I have compared Earth's feedback loop system to the human subconscious, which in many ways is a blank screen like a computer. How you program the computer determines what will manifest on your screen. The computer and the subconscious do not discriminate whether the input is good or bad. They just set themselves up based on the input.

The workings of the human subconscious and the planetary subconscious can be compared to the personal unconscious. We use the words "subconscious" and "unconscious" almost interchangeably. Technically, the subconscious is right below the unconscious, and information from the subconscious can be retrieved through some conscious thought and recollection. But the unconscious is not retrievable during the waking consciousness. The only way the unconscious can be reached is through dreams, art, or hypnotic and trance work. During such work, the consciousness is expanded, which allows it to access the unconscious.

Gaia's subconscious is being given directions randomly without higher thought from people who have lower-evolutionary thinking. For example, business people might say: "Let us clear this forest; we need to use the wood." They are not thinking about how Earth will respond to the removal of all plant life on a piece of land. They also might not think about asking permission from Earth to take out only a few trees and leave the rest to protect the land from flooding.

There is a large systematic program of forest destruction on Earth. It is a sad observation, but there is a force in society moving the planet toward negativity and biosphere destruction. I have heard some people refer to this force as Satan. But we, the Arcturians, do not believe Satan is a real entity. We do see that there are darker forces in operation throughout this planet that do not have higher consciousness. For unknown (illogical) reasons, the darker force is pushing this planet toward more destruction and chaos, and there is almost a welcoming of the chaotic response.

There are some people who are misguided and think that inducing chaos throughout the world will lead to positive change. This argument has been used on other planets. Yes, there must be cleansing and clearing, and we need to help promote the removal of darker forces to bring in higher energy, but the belief that chaos always brings in harmony is mistaken.

Your planetary history shows chaos can lead to more chaos. A good example is the Russian revolution, which was initially based on the higher principles of universal brotherhood and equality. But this revolution wound up in the hands of one of the worst dictators in the history of humankind, Joseph Stalin. The Russian revolution started powerfully, and it focused on clearing away the old monarchy. This revolution did not result in a utopia for the Russian people. There are other historic examples where initial chaos led to worse consequences.

Though this belief has been proven to be mistaken, there are forces that believe it and are working toward creating chaos. We cannot pretend that the darker forces do not exist on the planet. You are witnessing them directly, and you are seeing the results of this lack of relationship to Gaia.

Fifth-Dimensional Energy Download

As the starseeds, you are not victims; you have great spiritual abilities. Visualize your aura. It is beautiful. Visualize your aura as a cosmic egg, and visualize a line around your aura that unifies your energy field. Focus your energy on the cosmic egg. [Chants]: "Oooohhhh. Oooohhhh." At the top of your cosmic egg is the crown chakra, your highway to the fifth dimension — the opening that allows the fifth-dimensional light to enter your energy field. Allow this multidimensional protective light to enter your energy field. As it comes in, you expand; you fill up like a balloon with higher light, oxygen, and specially fortified air. I am standing above you, directing this fifth-dimensional light into your aura.

You are processing and receiving this higher light beautifully. This multifaceted energy provides several functions. Your aura expands like a balloon now as it is filled with this light. The pung energy in your aura is the resiliency — the bouncing back and the pushing away of negativity. It also helps you to expand so that you have space within your energy field. This is like you have layers of protection, and then you have the space of you.

There is much negativity around the globe, particularly in the political and economic arenas, as well as with weather patterns. You can repel the effects of negative energy by the elaborate, dynamic expansion of your aura with this fifth-dimensional download. [Chants]: "Ta, ta, ta, ta, ta, ta." You have a marvelous, protective force field around you. Let this high-powered energy that fills your aura now permeate your physical body.

On one level, this energy is expanding your aura, and on another level, it is healing your body. Direct the energy to the areas of your physical body that need healing. There is plenty of this energy around you. This is a quantum, multidimensional energy. Do not worry about health problems you were told could not be healed. Do not think like that because that is the third-dimension paradigm. In the fifth dimension, all things are possible, and miracles occur. Let this multidimensional energy permeate your physical body and go to all areas for complete healing.

There is much of this higher light and energy. Send a gigantic, impenetrable bubble around your home. Allow this multifunctional, multidimensional energy to fill your home, your environment, and the energy around your land so that you are protected in all ways. Let that process begin now. There is enough protective energy to build up the auric field around your house. [Chants]: "Aaaayyyy." Sense the shimmering of your energy field and the energy field around your home now. [Chants]: "Shimmmeeerrr. Shimmmeerrrr. Shimmmeeerrr."

Remember that shimmering also is a way of protecting yourself, your home, and even the planetary cities of light from negativity because it raises the vibrational charge. Shimmering creates a higher frequency, which repels negativity. It also creates an electromagnetic charge in your aura and energy field. Everything is electromagnetic, even thoughts. The heart is electromagnetic. All your organs have a certain frequency. They all respond to more balanced and harmonious charges that are created by shimmering. [Chants]: "Shimmmmeeerrrr. Shimmmeerrrrr. Shimmeerrr. Shimmer. Shimmer. Shimmer. Shimmer. Shimmer. Ta, ta, ta, ta, ta, ta, ta, ta." Feel the electromagnetic charge from the shimmering move through your aura and into your physical body. [Chants]: "Shimmmmeeerrrr, Shimmmeerrrrr. Shimmeerrr. Shimmer. Shimmer. Shimmer. Shimmer. Shimmer."

This is a harmonic rebalancing, an energetic charge. Think of yourself as a battery with a low charge. The shimmering recharges your battery — your internal energetic body — that keeps you going on Earth. This charges your whole body and your energy field as well as the energy around your home. You are illuminated as a starseed.

As a starseed, you emanate light — electromagnetic, multidimensional, balancing, healing light. Blessings.

Earth's Crown Jewel

Chief White Eagle: Heya ho, heya ho! Greetings. All my words are sacred. I am Chief White Eagle. The starseeds have a special relationship with Mother Earth. You have come from other planetary systems, and you remember the importance of forming this bond to the planet. Juliano has talked about your home planet and how eager you are to return.

It is important to point out that your soul is deeply connected to this Earth. There is an imprint on your soul, a bond you have with this planet. Maybe Earth is not your home planet, and maybe there is a higher, more evolved planet for you to return to after this incarnation and the ascension.

Each starseed has a connection to Gaia. It is why you came here, and I want you to honor this connection. You may not think this is an advanced skill, but believe me, it is very special. One of your special abilities is to connect spiritually and interact with the spirit of Mother Earth, Gaia. Unfortunately, the majority of the population does not know how to do this. Using the medicine wheel will help to increase your spiritual connection with the planet. The planet wants guidance.

It is true that humanity is the crown jewel of Earth. A planet that is able to have higher-conscious beings has evolved; therefore we can say that humanity is the crown jewel, the crowning accomplishment, of the planet. Earth will survive, but we do not know for sure whether humanity will.

We are bonded to Earth with a special energy. Many of you have asked me about the ascension of planet Earth, and the question continually arises: "Well, Chief White Eagle, does the planet have to be ready to ascend? How can the whole planet ascend when there are so many parts that are of lower energy?" After consulting with Juliano and other masters, we think that the highest beings of light (like you), will ascend, but the planet will not completely ascend. It will ascend in separate sections.

This may seem odd. However, we are talking about a holographic world and a holographic universe. The fifth-dimensional Earth has a lightbody just as you as third-dimensional beings have lightbodies. You are not going to bring your lower animal self, your worries about money, or your jealousies to the fifth dimension. Your lightbodies do not want them, and you cannot merge with your lightbodies with such focuses. It is the same way with Earth.

An Earth lightbody already exists on the fifth dimension. Those parts of higher light on Earth, such as the planetary cities of light, will ascend to the fifth-dimensional lightbody of Earth. The higher parts of Earth will merge with Earth's fifth-dimensional lightbody.

Gaia is receptive to the fifth dimension and, naturally, is multidimensional just as you are. Gaia knows every plant and animal that has ever existed on her. She has the records of all life forms, all interactions with extraterrestrials who have visited, and all interactions with the external energies of the galaxy.

Know that Earth responds to your prayers and your focus on the fifth dimension, and Earth responds when you send her fifth-dimensional energy. Gaia needs the fifth-dimensional energy download as much as you do. Without a fifth-dimensional energy download, you would have a much more difficult time coping with what is happening on the planet. Earth also benefits from fifth-dimensional energy and light.

Do the exercise for Earth's energy field and aura. Help to open up the North Pole, which serves as the crown chakra for the planet. Help download higher energy into Earth's energy field. Work within your medicine wheel, because Earth loves when you talk to her; Earth loves when you honor her in sacred space.

One of the great gifts of the starseeds is the ability to create and work with sacred space and sacred energy. You, the starseeds, have the ability to make more sacred energy on this planet. This is one of your missions — to balance and hold sacred light on Earth. There is a need to create more sacred spaces on planet Earth.

Blessings. I am Chief White Eagle. Ho!

Chapter 9

The Philosopher King and the Council of Elders

Juliano and the Arcturians

Let us look at the well known statement "as above, so below." In many ways, this is a summary of New Age philosophy and an important observation. One cannot understand all causes and effects of the third dimension by looking at the energies. There are hidden dimensions and energies above this world that influence the development and unfolding of the cosmic drama you and I observe.

Generally, you assume that higher energies are always in perfect balance and that only lower energies, such as the third-dimensional Earth energies, are suffering and out of balance. You only have to look at the Arcturian Tree of Life to understand you are living in a holographic world and universe, and that means what happens on one part of the universe affects the other part. In the same way, what happens in one small part of the universe is a microcosm of the whole universe. Therefore, what happens on a higher energy level affects the lower energies, and what happens on a lower energy level affects the higher levels.

About 5,000 planets have life forms with higher consciousness in this galaxy, and each planet has a specific operating principle. Earth's operating principle is based on duality and free will. Earth is part of a grand plan to develop a world that provides the optimal learning experience for soul development. You can see how a planet like Earth, which has uncontrolled free will, also presents problems.

When free will is allowed without restrictions, those who are negative or of evil intent can choose to express their free will. This presents a problem because those in power, who control many of the resources, are not focused on spiritual wisdom or spiritual balance. Unfortunately, they have the free will to act only in alignment with their self-centered needs. Earth is a demonstration that free will can also be out of control on a planetary system.

I, Juliano, and the other Arcturian guides and ascended masters often compliment Earth for providing the experience of free will. I have described how souls line up waiting to come to Earth just for this. Manifestation on the third dimension allows you certain experiences that will accelerate soul development. It may seem contradictory to you, but Earth's free will provides the perfect opportunity for soul learning and development. On planets that are more regimented, the opportunity for soul growth is limited. Unfortunately, the experience of free will on Earth is threatening the planet and can lead to the destruction of the biosphere.

Higher beings and higher energy sources guided the set up of this planetary system. These higher beings and energy sources are studying and working to develop systems and planetary experiences that are in alignment with soul development. It is clear, though, that this freewill system on the third-dimensional Earth is in a major crisis.

Experience Unity Consciousness

Perhaps you believe that it's the third dimension on this Earth that is out of balance. But Earth is part of an interacting system. What happens on the upper planes affects the lower planes and vice versa. I think this is a rather revolutionary concept, and in some ways, it is also rather shocking. How many of you would even consider that what you are doing here and what is happening here affect the higher realms? I am sure most of you do not think that your actions have any effect on the higher realms at all.

The dimensions are a holographic system, and what happens on Earth affects many energy fields in the galaxy. This is the main reason so many fifth-dimensional guides and teachers have come to the planet. They have expanded the limits of intervention to bring in a new balance that is needed on this planet. Higher consciousness is required to shift and resolve this planetary crisis.

All higher consciousness is part of a great unity field, and this unity field has existed at one point within a great oneness. You were part of this oneness. You were part of a great, unified consciousness that existed before space and time. This is very difficult to explain, but unity is part of who you are, and you have an inherent wish to be reunified. You feel the calling to return to unity. Many of you are working toward this goal and looking forward to a return to higher unification of consciousness, which you have previously experienced in your soul history.

If you feel alone now, there is a part of you that remembers the unity you experienced. Once you have interacted with unity in this universe, then you always remain affected by those energies. All it takes is one experience, and no matter where you go in the universe or in the galaxy, you remain energetically connected through thought. You remain connected because you long for a return to unity.

There is a concept in modern physics called entanglement. When there are two subatomic particles that have been in contact or have interacted, they remain forever bonded. This concept gets more expansive because in the new theories, entanglement means that those particles, no matter how far away they are, still have a bond and can affect each other at great distances. This is a mystical idea. How would it be possible that particles so far apart could still affect each other? The reason is they bonded, and that bond transcends space and time.

You might feel isolated today, but you are part of this greater unity, which is an immeasurable distance away from you. The experience of unity predates the existence of this universe. It predates space and time as you know it. Over the course of the development of this universe, soul energies were dispersed into many planets and many areas of the galaxies and the universe. You have become separate from the unity, but the unity consciousness still exists throughout the universe. The bond of unity within your soul has not changed with the expansion of space and time. You have the memory of that unity, and you long to return to it.

Your experience on Earth as a third-dimensional being is definitely about separation from unity. Fifth-dimensional energy is more oriented toward unity. When you go to the fifth dimension, you will feel and experience a much stronger sense of unity. You will have no sense of being alone, as you might have right now.

The ascended masters carry a large part of the unity consciousness energy on Earth. Humanity has a difficult time experiencing this unity, but there are many opportunities on Earth to do so. Some of you have already taken advantage of these experiences — meditating, enjoying a beautiful sunset, or having heightened experiences at sacred energy sites. Some of you have experienced the cohabitation of higher, advanced spirits such as Jesus, Mary, or Kuthumi in your energy field. They have brought their energy into your energy field to help you to experience this unity.

Unfortunately, it still can be very difficult to sustain unity thinking or the unity experience on Earth because of this planet's duality. If the core operating system of this planet is duality, then you would have to work hard to overcome that feeling and move into higher consciousness and unity consciousness. I am happy to say that many of you have done that. These advanced experiences of unity show that the ascended masters and their work are affecting you and the planet.

Expanded Consciousness Is Necessary

Remember that with entanglement, once you and another are together at any point, no matter how far apart you become, you still have the ability to be affected by that person. To maintain entanglement with the higher masters and teachers, you have to expand your consciousness and reach out. Up to this point on planet Earth, expanded consciousness was not a necessary characteristic for survival. In the past, the necessities for survival might include the ability to build fire or a safe dwelling, craft weapons and tools, and travel or move to different locations easily in order to change climates.

In those times, higher consciousness was not a basic need. In the early primitive world, higher consciousness was not useful. If you were living in a forest or another primitive environment, going into higher consciousness would remove you from perceiving the dangers around you. Those who could step into higher consciousness might risk death. Eventually, as societies developed, certain people were given the title of shaman and allowed to go into higher consciousness. These societies protected their shamans. This acknowledgment helped establish that higher consciousness was needed for the health and welfare of a culture.

The survival of the biosphere and the planet require the evolutionary stage of development called higher consciousness to come into fruition. It is clear to us, the Arcturians, that humanity cannot survive in this current state of low consciousness. Without the evolution to a higher consciousness, this planet's biosphere will collapse. You, as starseeds, understand this message and know that there is a necessity for higher consciousness.

These are the questions that need answers: "How do we ensure that this higher consciousness is immediately downloaded into this planet? How do we ensure that all the leaders of this planet have the ability to make decisions based on this higher consciousness?" This is the problem, and this is what the higher realms are working on.

It's not just a problem on Earth. It is also a problem in the higher realms because the imbalance and the disunity being experienced on Earth affect the other realms. To put it another way, the death and destruction of the plants, animals, and now humans, are happening on a large scale. The number of lost souls coming from Earth to the other side is quite extraordinary. These souls require great efforts on the other side to be rebalanced and repaired.

During the history of Arcturus, we also suffered from conflicts and were almost destroyed. There are a few of you who have very strong Arcturian memories, and you may have some core memories of the destruction of one of the Arcturian planets. This occurred during a time of great conflict similar to what you experience on Earth. We, the Arcturians, did evolve.

In our early history, we were polarized, filled with hatred toward others, and had some major conflicts. The Pleiadians had similar experiences. There is a history of planetary warfare among the Lyrans, with whom we share some common ancestry. The Lyrans are one of the core ancient groups and the oldest developed civilization in this part of the galaxy. They are the ancestors of the Pleiadians and humans on Earth.

The nature of the universe is filled with violent events. The universe is in balance, but there are exploding stars and planets that crash into each other. There are gamma rays that kill other life forms.

There are asteroids striking planets and many other violent galactic events.

The Arcturians had to develop a balanced system that would be able to counteract violence. We have proposed to you the idea of creating what we call a just society. Part of creating a just society involves creating planetary cities of light, which will help in creating a new and more balanced planet. There has to be some kind of solution to the problems creating imbalances, such as poverty, disease, hunger, and homelessness. Some of these problems have been made worse by climate change. There are core third-dimensional problems tied into technology and pollution that greatly contribute to the imbalances.

It so happens that in a freewill zone, people often choose the wrong person to lead a country. Those in power might not have the best interest of the whole planet at heart. To have a leader who has a planetary perspective is unusual, and most of the time, when somebody has this kind of perception, that person is not successful in maintaining a grip on power. How did we, the Arcturians, deal with that issue?

The Concept of a Planetary Leader

There is a concept that is galactic in origin but came to Earth through the teachings of the famous Greek philosopher Plato: the philosopher king. Plato explained that a ruler of a country — a ruler of a planet — should have the wisdom and perspective of a philosopher. Plato's definition of a philosopher king would have to be broadened to include a planetary perspective as well. He or she would need knowledge of biorelativity and planetary healing. The philosopher king would need to know the other dimensions and how they interact with the third dimension. In addition, the philosopher king would need to understand the planetary stages of development, including the conflict between spirituality, technology, and pollution.

Who would elect a philosopher king? People in the business of making money from Earth's resources might not want a philosopher king running the world. The philosopher king might not agree to use oil as the basis for the economy. Such a king might say that oil usage is leading to too much carbon emission and contributing too much to climate change and that we have to stop using it. Of course, anyone who would rule on Earth now from that kind of viewpoint would not be allowed to stay in office.

On Arcturus, we developed a system called the council of elders. We have offered that system as a prototype for the Group of Forty. The council of elders is an advisory group capable of embracing an advanced perspective. Thus, they can make recommendations for important decisions regarding the overall welfare of the planet. On our planet, the council of elders chose the philosopher king for our planetary system.

On Arcturus, we have a system in which people are trained from a young age to do the work they are destined to perform. For example, the Dalai Lama was chosen and trained to become the next leader of Tibet. The council of elders on Arcturus has ancestral groups of potential leaders who are trained to be philosopher kings. When they choose a new leader, everyone accepts the decision. We know that the council of elders does not come from the standpoint of ego or self-centeredness but from that of the greatest good for all — the unified energy field of Arcturus.

The council of elders selects a philosopher king based on attributes most in alignment with the energy needed at the time on Arcturus. This means that the council of elders can install a philosopher king and also replace him or her, depending on the different conditions or leadership characteristics needed. Placing a leader into power is not done with ego. The removal or replacement of another philosopher king is not viewed negatively. Nobody feels bad when they are removed from a leadership position, and there is no incitement or violence because of leadership changes.

Plato obtained the concept of the philosopher king during a time of higher thinking when he was able to connect with the galactic masters. However, the resolution of Earth's problems is going to depend on the capable leadership of this planet.

The Anointed One

There is a long history on this planet regarding the coming of the Messiah, and the word "Messiah" comes from the Hebrew word *Mashiach*. This is translated from Hebrew as "the anointed one." It was tradition among the ancient Israel tribes to anoint their kings.

Their first king was Saul. The Israel tribes believed that their king would be chosen by God through a prophet. The prophet Samuel anointed Saul, and he put olive oil on his forehead, meaning that he was the king.

The anointed one was expected to rescue Israel. Later, the idea was expanded so that the anointed one would rule over the whole Earth. The philosopher king also operates from the highest principles of higher wisdom. The philosopher king brings divine order back to the biosphere. Of course, they did not use the word "biosphere" in ancient times because they did not have that concept.

The idea of a Messiah and Savior coming to rule the world is also grounded in mythology and unconscious thought forms in Native American teachings. Look at the teachings of White Buffalo Calf Woman. You will find some interesting parallels to the energy of the Messiah and the philosopher king. One of the main differences is that White Buffalo Calf Woman is a feminine energy. I support the feminine energy coming into power on Earth. Masculine energy has dominated Earth for thousands of years and has led distortion and excessive aggressiveness on the planet.

White Buffalo Calf Woman is a figure who has the power to bring back a new balance and order to Earth. She possesses great strength. White Buffalo Calf Woman is not portrayed as a weak woman; she is someone who can victoriously instill proper order on this planet.

So here we have one of the greatest religious concepts offered to Western civilization, which is the coming of the anointed one. The idea of the philosopher king has similarities to that of the Messiah. The Messiah is a higher, fifth-dimensional thought form, just as the energy of the philosopher king comes from the higher realms. It is clear to the Arcturians and the fifth-dimensional masters that in a freewill society, it is extremely difficult to elect a philosopher king to run the world in a way that brings balance to the planet. You and I probably will agree that this is exactly what is needed. The philosopher king is also a person with the highest perception who could come to reorder everything and bring it into a new balance. He or she would need the power to stop all wars, nuclear weapons, and pollution. He or she would need the power to ensure clean energy and equal distribution of all foods.

In the Arcturian Planetary Tree of Life, you see the Messianic light and energy — the sphere in the middle of the tree. We do not have any conflicts over our rulers. There are no problems with the distribution of energy, wealth, food, or land. There is an expectation that the Arcturians and the higher dimensions can help instill that kind of leadership ideal for this planet. We can help instill a higher planetary perspective.

First contact has to be based on a higher thought form and a higher implementation of a more enlightened rulership over the dominion of this sacred planet known as the Blue Jewel. I am Juliano. Good day.

Chapter 10

Harmony and Balance

Juliano and the Arcturians

In this time of polarization and Earth changes, many variables can intrude on your desire to be in harmony and balance. Some intrusions come from external, electromagnetic sources. Others come from major Earth changes, such as extreme weather and earthquakes. Increasing geopolitical polarization can also contribute to disharmony. One of the main challenges is how to maintain your balance and be in harmony.

For your personal development and work toward ascension, you are pushed on many different levels to accelerate your growth. Remember that in the ascension process, you are given the opportunity to complete Earth lessons and soul lessons in an accelerated manner. What might, in different times, have taken four of five lifetimes of soul work and soul lessons can now be achieved in one lifetime.

The ascension process has this rule or regulation: You must try to learn as many life lessons as possible in the time you are here on Earth. As a seeker of ascension, this has a powerful meaning. You are not here for a vacation or to be lazy and laid back. You are here to do soul work. Being on Earth is an opportunity to increase your soul-lesson completions, and you want to complete as many as you can. This process and commitment help you ascend.

I have emphasized many times that ascension requires preparation. You do not just sit back and wait; you prepare and do the necessary work. This attitude of intention and commitment can provide you with great grace for your ascension. Remember, it is not imperative that you complete every lesson or that you reach 100 percent perfection in your soul and personal work. Effort and intention are also important.

Find Balance

This challenging time makes it difficult to stay in balance and harmony and work on your soul lessons. Keeping your electromagnetic energy field in balance can help. You can do this through exercises that balance the polarities in your aura. These can include energy work of the cosmic egg and with crystals to ensure your energy field is protected. Balancing yourself and staying in harmony involves working with both your lower self and your higher self. You cannot take your lower self — your animal self, the part of you with instincts and desires for food, personal gain, and wealth — with you on your ascension. It is not going to the fifth dimension.

How do you harmonize the lower self and the higher self? You raise the energy level of the animal self. I have noted that praying or saying a blessing before a meal is a common practice among religious groups. Thanking the Creator for satisfying your animal self is one of the great contributions offered by religions and spiritual practices. Blessing food before eating raises the energy level of the lower self, as you unite the instinct of hunger with higher energy.

This is an important example of balance, because other aspects of your lower self besides eating need to be energetically raised and brought into balance. For example, sexuality needs to be in balance with love. There is also the balance that comes with finances and economy. Accumulating money has to be in balance with giving to charity. Other balances have to do with exercising and taking care of blockages in the body.

These aspects of the lower self are not bad. If you want to be in better balance, then bless those parts you identify as the lower self, elevate them, and seek to bring them into integration and balance with your higher self. Uniting the lower self with the higher self is one of the greatest secrets for being in balance. Accept and identify those parts of your lower self that are problematic. When you identify them, we do not ask that you reject them; we ask you to elevate them, because part of the soul lessons have to do with elevation of the self. This includes purification of the lower self.

Another method of achieving balance is focusing on your higher self and devoting time and energy to activities that promote your higher self. This can include charity, meditation, *Merkabah* travel, connecting with Arcturian guides and teachers, and healing others. Maybe you see yourself as a potential healer. Developing your healing powers also helps develop aspects of your higher self. When you connect, identify, and interact with your healing self, you naturally come into greater balance and harmony. Working with the higher self in this manner is not a negation of the lower self, but rather what you might call setting priorities. You set a priority to do ascension work and spiritual work for your soul's evolution.

Here is a simple example: Time is short. We cannot say how long you will be on the planet. So when you look at your priorities, you will naturally find that you do not want to waste time. You do not want to be involved in lower energies or with people who are blocked and focused on negative energies.

Planetary Healing

This leads us to general planetary healing. We see dramatic Earth changes and polarizations. Hurricanes and earthquakes are great examples of planetary imbalances. I remind you that our fifth-dimensional planet does not have earthquakes. Other balanced planets we have visited in the galaxy do not have hurricanes, volcanic eruptions, or pollution. A fifth-dimensional planet is in a high state of consciousness achieved through the spiritual work of the planetary healers of that planet. You might ask: "How can I bring Earth into balance and harmony, especially in the face of overwhelming catastrophes and tragedies?"

We make no prediction that planet Earth is going into a fifth-dimensional balance soon. Let me make the comparison between evolution and personal work and evolution on a planetary basis. Personally, you can bring yourself into greater harmony by identifying and working with parts of your higher self. Likewise, in working with the planet, you can bring the planet into higher harmony and balance by focusing on the higher parts of the planet. We have given you the tools for doing this through our discussions of sacred cities of light, biorelativity, and creating corridors along sacred energies. Identify the most positive parts of this planet and work to bring those areas to a higher point.

You might think this energy work with the planet is not making a difference; it is still out of balance and Earth changes continue. So what good is planetary spiritual work? That is not the correct attitude. The correct attitude is to identify and work with higher energy, higher sites, and sacred energy. Working with higher energy points on the planet contributes to the higher evolutionary cycle of Earth and helps it continue on its path to the fifth dimension. You are responsible for your sphere of influence, regardless of what else happens on Earth. You still work toward your goals for planetary and personal healing. If you see "sickness" on the planet, you still work with higher energy. You do not stop your work.

It is the same with personal sickness. When sick, you seek connection with your higher self to bring all parts of yourself, especially those affected parts in the lower self, to a higher energy. You do not stop and say, "No, I am not going to do that because the negative energy or the blockages are too strong." Through your planetary work, you are creating a great foundation for fifth-dimensional Earth.

Healing Technology

This leads me to the main idea of this chapter, which is balancing yourself and balancing the planet in fifth-dimensional harmony. I will describe this planetary healing technology in as much detail as possible so you can understand how to use it. The two concepts that I will introduce are familiar to you. One is the hundredth monkey effect. In the 1950s, anthropologists in Japan claimed they had observed a monkey washing its food, which was a new behavior. Other monkeys copied the same behavior. When the number of monkeys washing their food reached one hundred, all the monkeys on the island — estimated at five thousand — did the same. This showed a manifested, measurable event from consciousness.

This study was done as an anthropological survey and has not been statistically or scientifically proven, but there is a relationship between this effect and spiritual work: When a group of spiritually minded starseeds reaches a critical number, this can cause a major shift on the planet. We have been working toward this critical mass and have identified as many as 1,600 devoted and strong Arcturian starseeds. It is necessary that all 1,600 have high levels of commitment and spiritual energy. There might be 40,000 members in a spiritual group, but if only 500 really do the work, then the rest are not contributing to the critical mass needed for change. Those 1,600 starseeds include committed and hardworking members. Starseed group consciousness has been building on this planet for at least the past twenty to thirty years. It will be responsible for a major spiritual shift on this planet.

How will that spiritual shift manifest? A few predictions have been made:

- Shifts will occur in government attitudes toward becoming better caretakers of the planet.
- A greater groundswell of starseeds will continue to create and protect sacred areas and sacred cities of light.
- Starseeds will start a movement causing a shift in the thinking and energy for the entire planet.

The important point is that you contribute and connect with a starseed group known as the Arcturian starseeds that is working toward this energetic, planetary-healing energy field. What does it mean to belong to this planetary-healing energy field? To explain, I will introduce another concept of modern physics called "entanglement." Entanglement describes two subatomic particles that at one point touched each other in the same space and time. Then, due to various physical reasons, the particles separated and in some cases moved vast distances apart. But they still maintained a connectivity, communicated, and were affected by each other.

Energetically, starseeds are part of the same Arcturian starseed energy. At one point in your soul history, you were all united with the Arcturians and other ascended masters. This entanglement can have positive impacts. In entanglement theory, what affects one particle affects another, and when two particles are entangled, they can be entangled with a group of particles. A united group of particles increases the group's power.

I have defined the measurement of thought power in terms of a thought field and the unit of measurement of that power as arcan power. The descriptive notation to measure the units of power can include group or individual thought energy. I compare this measurement to watts. A ten-watt light bulb is brighter than a five-watt light bulb. A starseed doing thought work equivalent to a ten-arcan power is stronger than someone doing five arcana of thought. When you are connected to and conscious of the entanglement energy you have with other Arcturian starseeds, you can use the connection to raise your arcan thought power. Entanglement with Arcturian starseeds helps raise your thought vibration. You benefit from the group's energy. You do not give up your individuality when you use group energy. You happily and productively join this entanglement, which leads to higher healings for the planet and higher personal development for you.

The Ring of Ascension

With this introduction, I will now discuss the ring of ascension and how it can be used for personal and planetary balance and healing. The ring of ascension is a spiritual and etheric halo surrounding Earth. You can connect corridors of light from the ring of ascension to your house. The ring of ascension receives energy and light from the ascended masters on the fifth dimension. They download higher light in a form you can access on the third dimension. You can easily travel to the ring of ascension from any corridor. It is a real energy field and energy force.

Many things are now in place for ascension. There are planetary cities of light, and many corridors of light are active. You have helped activate many sacred sites for fifth-dimensional work. The ring of ascension is in place around the planet. A primary way to stay in balance and keep Earth in balance is to have more interactions with the ring of ascension. The ring of ascension is also related to the collective noosphere. The ring of ascension is an accelerated energy field in which healing thoughts and evolutionary thoughts can be downloaded, accelerated, and manifested. If you personally are in need of healing, you can connect with the ring of ascension and download special healing energy and light for yourself.

Hundreds, maybe thousands, of higher-energy thought forms and higher-dimensional light from the ascended masters have already downloaded into the ring of ascension. The ascended masters provide a tremendous service to Earth by creating and working with this ring of ascension. They want you to use it for both personal and planetary development.

I like to compare some concepts regarding the ring of ascension with modern computer technology. You are probably familiar with software updates. For example, computer operating systems need updates every few months. As a computer user, you might not know when an update is downloaded if you use an "automatic updates" function. To use this function, you set the computer program to automatically receive and download updates that make the program more effective.

Let's use this computer analogy for understanding how the ring of ascension can help you and the planet. Ascended masters and others, including myself, continually put new programs and thought forms into the ring of ascension. These updates help keep this planet in as high a spiritual vibration as possible. To receive an update into your spiritual body, you can give permission for it to be downloaded when it's available. Another choice is to set the internal valve in your spirit body to automatically receive updates. When you give approval for the automatic update function, you receive updates without needing to be conscious of the process.

I ask you now to consciously make the choice, and say this affirmation: "I give permission for the ring of ascension to download automatic updates into my spiritual body. These updates will contain new information on Earth balancing, personal balancing, and ascension, as needed." I will repeat that affirmation: "I give permission for the ring of ascension to download updates into my energy field as needed, even without my awareness." Remember, you do not give your computer permission for each download, because you have faith and trust that your computer is only connecting with the highest good from the computer maker. At least, we hope that is the case.

Ring of Ascension Exercise

Let us reestablish your connection to the ring of ascension. Visualize a corridor of light around your room and around your body. [Chants]: "Oooohhhh." Visualize this corridor going straight up, miles and miles above Earth to the ring of ascension. Say this affirmation: "I now connect through this corridor to the ring of ascension around Earth. I thought-project my spirit body through the corridor into the ring of ascension." As you do this, you experience a great energy field of light from the fifth-dimensional masters, specially calibrated for your integration.

Visualize yourself in spirit form — your etheric doppelgänger or the etheric self you have thought-projected. See that self sitting in a comfortable position in the ring of ascension with a fantastic, powerful energy swirling around you. You have the highest ability to absorb and download whatever you need for yourself or for the planet. Again, you are sitting in the ring of ascension, having arrived through the corridor of light. Now we will go into silent meditation as you experience the swirl of this wonderful energy field known as the ring of ascension. [Silence.]

While you are there, give permission again. Say: "I give permission for automatic downloads from the ring of ascension to be integrated and delivered to my third-dimensional energy field." Give that permission now.

At this moment, receive the most up-to-date download from the ring of ascension into your energy field, containing the most current information on Earth changes, creating more sacred space, etherically connecting using the hundredth-monkey effect with other Arcturian starseeds, and how to use this ring of ascension energy for your personal balance and harmony. Again, we will go into silence. [Silence.]

I, Juliano, now download arcan power to you as you meditate with me. You can use arcan power for your personal healing and planetary healing. Let us first use it for your personal healing. You are in a state of meditation in the ring of ascension. Your thoughts accelerate as you benefit from this group energy. Visualize now and think healing thoughts for yourself and project those thoughts to any physical part of your body you want healed or brought into balance. Silently say these words: "With this energy from the ring of ascension, I hereby send balancing, harmonious healing light to the part of my body that needs healing." We will go into silence. [Silence.]

Now look at your energy field from a higher perspective. Bring your energy field into balance. Your energy field is an electromagnetic polarity containing positive and negative energy. Put these polarities into balance. Your vibration is of optimal harmony, and through your arcan power you can send a golden halo to your energy field. This helps place your energy field into harmony. Remember, the ring of ascension is a halo. The halo is composed of golden light that produces a higher harmony when it comes into contact with you. Halos of harmony and golden light circle the heads and shoulders of the ascended masters. The ring of ascension is a halo with vast amounts of golden light.

Absorb the golden light into your energy field as you sit and meditate with us in the ring of ascension. Many higher souls are in the ring of ascension now, including starseeds from the Arcturian group and other ascended masters. Fill your aura again with golden light from the ring of ascension. [Silence.]

Make the commitment to bring back to Earth this golden light you have accumulated and absorbed. Bring that light down into your physical body and into your physical energy field. When it comes into your physical energy field, it will go into your physical body. Along with that is the great bond of light, the great bond of energy that you feel with all starseeds who are together now. [Chants]: "Oooohhhh."

Let the golden light from the ring of ascension fill your etheric doppelgänger or your etheric double. Now align your doppelgänger or etheric double with the corridor between you and the ring of ascension you established at the beginning of this exercise. Bring your etheric double down through the corridor in perfect alignment over your third-dimensional body. Your etheric double merges with your energy field on Earth and fills your energy with the golden light of the ring of ascension. Let us go into silence again. [Silence.]

Rapid Changes Require Frequent Updates

You are connected in a deep way — perhaps I can say an entangled way — and in a most positive way with the ring of ascension. You have authorized continuous updates to occur from the ring of ascension to your energy field. These updates will download to you periodically even without your conscious knowledge and even if you are in a contracted state of consciousness due to stress.

In such times of rapid Earth changes, new updates are needed. Even the understandings of ascension and other planetary changes you had five or six months ago need to be updated. We see the need for continual updates. For example, climate scientists said that if the current level of greenhouse gases continues, all coastlines will be inundated by 2080 with catastrophic coastal events. Several months later, climate scientists changed their prediction and moved coastal catastrophic events to 2030.

We work with you to connect the sacred areas you have designated with the fifth dimension. The ascension of a planet does not include every area of a planet. You are preparing for ascension, but you are a small minority on the planet. There might be 7 billion people on Earth, but only 100,000 can ascend in the first wave. Spiritual areas on Earth, which I call enclaves, are preparing for ascension, but they represent only a small portion of sacred, higher-spiritual areas that can ascend into the fifth dimension.

In conclusion, take a deep breath and say again: "I accept and integrate the latest updates from the ring of ascension."

Chapter 11

Sound and Vibrational Healing

Juliano and the Arcturians

Everything in existence is in a vibrational state, and everything that vibrates can resonate with sound. Sound is one of the most healing methods for inducing subatomic shifts. The composition of all matter is in a frequency, and that frequency can be described as vibration. If you know the resonant or harmonic frequency for healing an energy body, you can tone that frequency, and the sound will very likely set up a healing process. Vibrational toning can also change or create an opening in the energy of a blocked cell. This can have a powerful healing effect.

You might think that healing from toning should occur immediately. From a quantum perspective, everything occurs in the now, but from a linear perspective, vibrational toning sets up a beginning, a shift, a movement. Some healing activations might take a couple of days or even a week. The important thing is that vibrational energy helps shift blockages in the body. It is a major energetic success when you can shift energy with a tone that sets a series of healing events into motion.

I like the word "plaque" that describes problems in the circulatory system of the human body, including problems with the heart, lungs, and arteries. Plaque build-up is also involved in the neurobiology of the brain and is one of the symptoms or causes of Alzheimer's disease. Plaque occurs around the human aura and can have several effects, including slowing the aura's vibration. In some cases, the weight of this plaque — even though it is on a subatomic level — is measurable and can cause contraction of the aura. Using specially calibrated healing tones or sounds can break up this plaque.

Calibration is an important concept in tonal healing, vibrational medicine, and planetary vibrational healing. Calibration means adjusting the frequency of the tone to the receiver. If the tone is too high or not calibrated correctly, it can harm the receiver. Toning generally does not cause harm. Vibrational healing of the body is a new art. Using the wrong tone might not have a beneficial effect, but it should not cause harm to the receiver. If the tone is too low, the blockage will not be affected. You must calibrate and adjust the tone to the person you are working with. Calibration of tone is perhaps the greatest skill for sound healing.

Planetary Healing

These descriptions and methods of tonal healing can also be applied to the planet and planetary healing. How can tones and sounds affect the planet? Certain planetary healing sounds can be calibrated specifically for healing Earth and bringing the planet back to harmony. From a narrow, linear perspective, this planet's situation looks quite dire. Some of you might be pessimistic about what's happening on Earth, and with good reason. Earth imbalances can dampen or block Earth's aura. As you know, Earth has an aura, and many of the problems I described for human auras are similar for Earth's aura. In particular, I refer to the build-up of plaque and how that can slow a person's vibration. Likewise, plaque that builds up on Earth's aura can slow down the light frequency or spiritual light quotient energy in Earth's energy field.

Removing plaque, especially through sound healing, can help a person return to a normal or healthy vibrational frequency and a higher balance. Certain drugs, especially opioids, slow the vibrational frequency of the aura, which can be a problem for spiritual work. People's auras can have a variety of other problems, including holes and attachments from unwanted entities. As a planetary healer, you want to release plaque from Earth's aura so it can vibrate at the highest possible frequency. It is good news that we can calibrate chanting to the needs of the planet, especially when we want to do tonal interventions.

Let me speak a little about the electromagnetic frequency of Earth. Electromagnetic frequencies interfere with the energy fields around the planet. Some of these frequencies are produced by cellular phones, cell towers, radiation, and a military radar called HAARP, which stands for High-frequency Active Auroral Research Program. This is a military project of the United States government. A series of radar-like antennas create ultra-high radio frequencies that are sent great distances into the atmosphere. The radio frequencies can be used to jam electromagnetic transmissions originating in a particular area. In certain cases, this jamming throws electromagnetic energies in that area off balance, causing humans to experience disorientation.

If you were a soldier in an area with such unbalanced electromagnetic energy, your cognition — your mental abilities — would become deficient. You would become confused, disoriented, and lack the ability to make sound judgments. In some cases, you might even lose your ability to speak or walk. This might sound surprising, but remember that you are an electromagnetic being of light. You are a sensitive multidimensional electromagnetic being, and the fragility of the electromagnetic balance in your body is still being explored. Some of the electromagnetic energy in the brain is extremely sensitive to radio-frequency influences.

Electromagnetically, your brain is very complex. Comparisons have been made of the number of neurons and pathways in the brain to the number of stars in the galaxy. Some estimates place the number of star systems in the Milky Way at 200 billion. There are an equivalent number of neural connections in the human brain. Even the most advanced computers cannot come close to how effective your brain functions. Because your brain and the electromagnetic frequencies within it are fragile, it does not take much to disrupt the electromagnetic energy balance of the brain. When that field becomes disharmonious, deficiencies in behavior and thinking result.

Let us look again at the human aura. Spirit attachments from negative entities can sometimes attach to people, and these attachments can create an imbalance in the electromagnetic energy field, resulting in disoriented and confused behaviors. The opposite effect occurs when a positive spirit visits. A positive spirit can enhance the electromagnetic energy in your system. It can also open portals within the brain and the assemblage point. In modern psychology, the assemblage point is known as the reticular activating system. This is a valve that can be opened in the brain to experience higher perception in alignment with fifth-dimensional perception.

Earth's Vibrational Frequency

Let me return to the idea of the frequency of Earth and balancing chanting frequencies for healing Earth. In modern electromagnetic theory, a very low radio frequency is known as an ELF (extremely low frequency). Gaia emits an ELF, known as the Schumann frequency, estimated between 3.5 and 7.1 hertz. To give you an idea how low a frequency this is, radio frequencies in commercial FM radio can be as high as 90 megahertz.

People have speculated about the importance of Earth's electromagnetic frequency. Is this Schumann frequency part of Earth's feedback loop system? The Earth's feedback loop system, described in biorelativity, is a self-regulating system Earth uses to regulate global temperatures, weather patterns, and other important variables related to climate, volcanic activity, and earthquakes. Unfortunately, investigation or research into Earth's complex feedback loop system is minimal.

What kinds of activities influence the Schumann frequency, and are Earth changes shifting the rate? If the rate is shifting, can we, as planetary healers, affect the Schumann frequency? Can we help bring it to a higher level, and will that help bring Earth into balance?

Earth scientists speculate that the Schumann frequency is influenced by electromagnetic energy such as storms and lightning. There have even been discussions about whether the frequency is influenced by extraterrestrial sources from other planets within the solar system. For example, when the Shoemaker-Levy comet struck Jupiter in 1994, it created huge storms on that planet that emitted tremendous electromagnetic energy. A portal in Earth's energetic system received and processed that energy, which possibly shifted Earth's frequency.

The accumulation of unbalanced energies from global warming — including shifting ocean currents and military and nuclear experiments — can also shift this core frequency. The noosphere can shift it as well. This frequency can be positively influenced by Arcturian starseeds on Earth. There are ways to communicate with Earth that can influence this frequency. There are also ways to influence Earth's aura and bring Earth into a better electromagnetic balance. I am interested in raising the spiritual light quotient of the planet, which involves rebalancing its electromagnetic energy.

Frequencies in the atmosphere can be measured electromagnetically. We can understand the characteristics of a planetary environment and its spiritual level by measuring the frequency of that planet's atmosphere. Let me give you another example. If you go into a sacred place on Earth — a temple, synagogue, church, or an energetic vortex such as Grose Valley, Australia, or Sedona, Arizona — you can feel the intense electromagnetic energy. You can feel the higher vibration. When you are in that area, your personal vibration also rises, and you respond by feeling euphoric or more psychic. Your frequency rises because you are open and can process that higher vibration.

Let us return to the subject of HAARP, a military project that emits high-frequency electromagnetic energy. Generally, people exposed to that intense electromagnetic energy will have a hard time dealing with the frequency overload. In terms of spirituality, you can also get an overload of high spiritual frequency. Even if you are spiritually advanced, you can overload on higher frequencies and pass out. If somebody goes to a higher-frequency physical place, such as Sedona or Grose Valley, and they are not prepared or able to process or integrate higher frequencies, they could also become overloaded.

Let us return to the planet and the concept of chanting, specifically mantras. The word "mantra" is a Hindu word describing a type of chant.[1] Mantras are a great example of using vibrational toning to achieve higher states of consciousness. Certain words in Sanskrit are power words with high vibrations, just as Hebrew has certain higher-power and energy words. Hebrew and Sanskrit are sacred languages on this planet. Other languages on Earth have power words, but these two languages have vibrational tones and sounds that were created in

1. A mantra is a sound or group of words, such as Om, which in Sanskrit is believed to have spiritual powers. Mantra chanting and meditation can help induce altered states of consciousness.

alignment with the basic core-vibrational frequencies of the universe and galaxy.

Toning words in these languages can have immediate effects on your consciousness. The channel has used special Hebrew words, such as "*kadosh, kadosh, kadosh, adonai tzevaoth.*" This phrase emits sacred tones that can be used as a mantra. When the words are toned correctly, you can achieve a higher shift in your electromagnetic energy frequency. [Chants]: "Kadosh, kadosh, kadosh, aaaa aaa ado adooonaiiidonai tzevaaaaooooth."

Toning Exercises

Let us go into meditation and allow these tones to accelerate the speed of your aura. Feel an electromagnetic shift in your aura; feel the upliftment. Now let us tone and use the basic Sanskrit word "Om." Everyone knows Om, and that word can be calibrated and used to rebalance the Schumann frequency that is part of the electromagnetic spectrum emitted by Gaia through the core of Earth.

Toning must be integrated and calibrated to the receiver of these sounds. There are different levels of toning. Special lower-frequency tones can be used to resonate with the electromagnetic frequency of Earth. Some places on the planet are higher in light and resonance, while other places on Earth have more distorted Schumann frequencies. Listen to the toning of Om. [Chants]: "Om."

Visualize and thought-project the most balanced frequency for the entire planet and see the electromagnetic aura of the planet come into balance. [Chants various sounds using Om.] In planetary healing work, we seek to bring together 1,600 people chanting Om at the same time. We can use the group's arcan power to communicate directly with the spirit of Earth/Gaia and bring the Schumann frequency into the most appropriate resonance for the planet.

Tibetan monks who are connected to their ancestors realize the importance of toning. They work with special tonal frequencies to help hold the energy of Earth. Some of these tones are made with specialized long horns that look like long trumpets.[2] The Tibetans use those frequencies for healing. The didgeridoo of Australia is in this same genre. Aborigines understand the concept of using tones to interact with Earth's frequencies. Interacting with Earth frequencies using these types of instruments is especially useful if the user has the knowledge and right intention to heal and balance Earth.

The Schumann frequency is influenced by electromagnetic energy from lightning and other electromagnetic global events, including Earth changes. Interestingly, a characteristic Earth frequency can be transmitted through the didgeridoo that can help bring rain to an area. An opposite tone can be used to block storms. But it is only recently that people on Earth have developed the means of doing worldwide chanting. Let us do this chant again. [Chants]: "Om."

Tones to Accelerate Auras and Remove Plaque

Let me also share with you the Arcturian frequency and tone for accelerating auras and removing plaque. First, use the special tones from this chant for yourself, so your aura and energy can vibrate in a much more resonant way. [Chants]: "Ta ta."

Visualize your cosmic egg and the outer line of the egg pulsing. [Chants]: "Ta ta." As I make the elongated sounds, any buildup of plaque on the aura will break up. [Chants slower]: "Ta ta." When you hear the channel raise his voice, that means a particular area of plaque in your energy system must be broken up. Sometimes it is necessary to use a higher sound to do that. [Chants in higher tones]: "Ta ta."

Visualize with me the aura of Earth. It can be extended miles outside Earth's atmosphere and beyond the ionosphere. The aura is electromagnetically connected to the Schumann frequency. Earth's aura also fills all the areas of the planet, including the ground and oceans. How are we to encompass the whole Earth in our planetary

---

2. This Tibetan horn is a long trumpet called the *dungchen*. In Tibetan Buddhist culture, its sound is compared to the singing of elephants. It has also been described as a haunting wail.

healing work and in our chanting? I have introduced the concept of the ring of ascension. It is difficult to visualize the whole planet but easier to visualize this etheric halo-like ring around Earth. This ring of ascension responds to your interactions and healing thoughts for Earth. Through your visualizations and projections, you can send or thought-project your self into the ring of ascension.

When you are at the halo around Earth, tone these sounds: [Chants]: "Ta ta." The ring of ascension now vibrates, Earth's aura vibrates, and the plaque in Earth's aura loosens. [Chants]: "Ta ta." This Native American healing chant is also helpful. [Chants]: "Heya ho." The Earth responds to these tones.

Let this low, Schumann frequency come into the highest alignment so Gaia can hold a higher spiritual light frequency for the entire planet. We all agree that this planet needs to go into a higher spiritual frequency. [Chants faster and then slower]: "Heya ho, na na." Let us go into silence again. [Silence.]

See Earth's aura and your personal aura vibrate with greater and higher frequencies. [Chants faster and then slower]: "Heya ho, na na."

Dramatic changes in Earth can occur through global mantra toning. This mantra toning can be applied using the very powerful Hebrew word "shalom," as well as the Arabic word "salaam." Both contain high energy vibrations, but "shalom" has within it the core frequency of Om, which relates to the vibrational energy of Earth's core. Let us chant together. [Chants]: "Shalom."

The word "salaam" also has a very powerful vibrational energy. [Chants]: "Salaam." Let the energy of shalom and the energy of salaam put peace, harmony, and balance into Earth's aura. See these words projected around the ring of ascension: Shalom — S-H-A-L-O-M — or Salaam — S-A-L-A-A-M. Let these words appear like a marquee around the ring of ascension. The vibrations of these words, the tones of these words, now go around the entire ring of ascension. Everyone on the planet receives this vibration.

Let us go into meditation again as you visualize and chant. [Chants]: "Om." This type of chanting is called electromagnetic-frequency modulation toning, and it is extremely important now for rebalancing Earth. You can also use this toning to rebalance yourself.

We are quickly moving into the era of vibrational medicine and vibrational healing. We are quickly gaining an understanding of the vibrational energy of the universe, and with this understanding comes the ability to quantumly rearrange and rebalance yourself and the planet. You can say this affirmation: “I allow myself to be quantumly and vibrationally rebalanced in the highest spiritual calibration now.” Feel your vibrational energy come more in harmony with the highest light. [Chants]: “Om.”

Chapter 12

Electromagnetic Assimilation

Juliano and the Arcturians

The topic for today's lesson is electromagnetic assimilation, and I will be teaching you how to assimilate this energy in order to neutralize it. Even though you receive a lot of electromagnetic energy from your environment, you can process it in your own electromagnetic energy field.

You are actually an electromagnetic being — a multidimensional, loving, electromagnetic being of light. "Electromagnetic" refers to the energy fields of your mental, emotional, spiritual, and physical bodies. All four bodies have electromagnetic fields, and each has a certain electromagnetic charge.

Electromagnetic energy is one of the primary sources of life. There is even electromagnetic energy in your heart. Emotions also have an electromagnetic charge, and so do ideas, prejudices, and belief systems. You store this energy in your muscular system from this and other lifetimes. These experiences also carry a charge.

I have talked about the protection of your energy fields in the past, and I have also described in detail about how you can protect your energy field through the use of Arcturian technologies, such as the cosmic egg, and the development of what the Taoists call a pung energy field. (A pung energy field refers to a resiliency in your energy field that can push back and help you reject unwanted energies.)

Not all unwanted energies can easily be pushed away. You probably have already noticed that you are affected by what is occurring on this planet — including polarizations, climate change, and even by cosmic energies. In addition, your energy field is affected by the widespread use of electromagnetic radio waves from computers, cell phone towers, smartphones, and other electromagnetic radioactive waves generated from a variety of sources. These sources include medical treatments and military projects.

The military uses electromagnetic waves in the High Frequency Active Auroral Research Program (HAARP) project, which is the use of high frequency auroral radial propagation waves for shifting energies in the ionosphere. This is done for multiple purposes. This type of project directs high frequency electromagnetic waves into an area, and the people who live there might not even know that they are being exposed. This is a good example of how people receive electromagnetic energy without their knowledge.

Unwanted Electromagnetic Energy

Receiving unwanted electromagnetic energy is a new experience on Earth. In other incarnations, you did not have to deal with high levels of electromagnetic energy. While there are many positive benefits from technological advances over the past fifty years, receiving higher doses of electromagnetic energy definitely presents a challenge for maintaining your health, especially when a great deal of the electromagnetic energy comes into your four bodies.

You receive electromagnetic energy below the level of your conscious mind, and you would need heightened or expanded consciousness in order to be aware of receiving it. Many people who are empathic and highly sensitive report that they feel this energy being sent to them.

Recently in the state of Arizona (and probably other states), the electric company placed new electronic meters on homes in order measure home electricity usage. The old analog electric meters had to be personally read, which meant a meter man came to your house and read the meter to record your usage. These new meters transmit an electromagnetic radio reading to a source perhaps five to fifteen miles away so that your electricity usage can be electronically reported. This might be a good time-saving device, and perhaps it is more accurate, but the fact is that this meter is a radio transmitter potentially interacting with your personal energy field.

Radio transmissions are sent through antennas. Antennas that are vertically polarized radiate in an omnidirectional pattern. "Omnidirectional" means that the radio wave is transmitted and radiated 360 degrees in all directions. Transmitters can also use antennas that are directional as well, which means that the electromagnetic radiation signal predominately radiates in one direction.

The electric meter transmitter on your house most likely uses an omnidirectional antenna. This means that some of those low-powered radio waves being transmitted toward the electric company's receiver can also come into your house. If that meter is close to your bedroom, you might receive those electromagnetic waves at different times of the day or at night when you are sleeping.

I am using this example to explain that your energy field is receiving electromagnetic energy waves from many sources. I want to be clear that the frequency and the wattage from these electric meters is in the milliwatt range, which means that they are extremely low power. Modern scientists believe that the wattage from such a device is so low that exposure to this field is not harmful.

On one level, that is a powerful argument because most people can tolerate low levels of exposure to electromagnetic radio waves without being affected. However, how such exposure affects you dependents on your sensitivity. If you are extremely sensitive, exposures on a milliwattage basis might affect your aura, and it is possible that you could feel it. In some cases, exposure might cause physical or other health problems. (There are shielding devices even for these electronic meters. You do not need a complicated shield to block one-tenth of a watt.)

Also, one-time exposure to a milliwatt can have a limited effect, but continuous daily exposure is another matter. Your cell phone might have as little as one-tenth of a watt of transmitting power. While I could tell you that one-tenth of a watt is not going to hurt anything, if you are using the cell phone for three or four hours a day, it could be harmful. I know that many of you carry your cell phones with you and have them in continuous contact with your body. You are being exposed to the omnidirectional radio waves that are sent from the phone to a tower.

There is not yet definitive research on harmful exposure levels to electromagnetic radiation energy. Some research indicates that cell phone use is not a problem. Other studies have found that continued cell phone use is harmful and may cause brain tumors. One of the principles of electromagnetic radiation is that the closer you are to the source, the more intense electromagnetic radiation you are receiving.

If you are holding the phone to your ear, then your brain is receiving a lot of this electromagnetic radiation. If the phone is five or ten feet away, there is a decrease in intensity and harmful effects to your brain. The further away you are, the better, and there are probably special shielding devices that you could use.

I am not suggesting that you throw away your cell phone, and I am not suggesting that we no longer use these new electronic meters. No matter how hard you try, in a modern society you cannot escape the electromagnetic field of computers and other sources continually transmitting around you. The only possibility of blocking exposure is to live as a recluse away from society without any such device nearby.

How to Safely Assimilate and Discharge Electromagnetic Energy

The term "assimilation" could be replaced by "integration," but I have used the word "assimilation" for a specific reason. While on Earth, you will have to assimilate many experiences into your mental, physical, emotional, and spiritual bodies. Since society will continue to develop electromagnetic technology, and it is impossible to avoid it, I will teach you how to safely assimilate this energy into your system by strengthening your aura.

The most beneficial shape for the aura is the egg shape. Meridian lines run both vertically and horizontally on the surface of your aura, also known as the cosmic egg. These meridian lines go into the cosmic egg. The aura can also be filled with pung energy. This is a special etheric and internal energy that has great resilience in helping one protect the energy field.

The aura can expand a certain maximum distance away from the physical body. The further it expands from the body, the more potential protection there is. For example, if the aura is only able to expand one inch away from the body, then there is not much protective space.

An intrusion could potentially reach the physical body. But if the aura extends eight or nine inches away from the body, then there could be enough resiliency (or pung) in the aura to enable you to resist intrusions. With an expanded aura, you have extra room so that the energy will not touch you physically.

Star of David Energy Protection Technique

In order to safely assimilate this energy into your system, visualize your aura as a cosmic egg. See the Star of David, which consists of intersecting triangles with six points, in a horizontal position on top of your crown chakra in the cosmic egg. This star has special meaning related to divine power and protection in the Kabbalah and Hebrew mysticism. This is also a galactic symbol and signifies the intersection of the third and fifth dimensions.

Now activate the two large intersecting triangles that represent the intersection of the third and the fifth dimensions in you. This gives you the most powerful energy protection and activation. You are immediately energizing and shielding your aura and your energy field. You now have a shielding power that is far beyond what you would normally be able to use. Your ability to block harmful energy coming toward you is increased at least 10 to 30 times. In some cases it can even be increased 100 times.

When the Star of David is in the horizontal position and connected to your crown chakra, it radiates a protective electromagnetic shield through all the meridians and throughout your aura. It also sends a healing electromagnetic, vibrational current throughout your whole outer aura. The electromagnetic current is not like a normal energy current. It is an interactive current with the third and fifth dimensions. This is a quantum energy current, and even though it might be very low wattage, it has intense powers.

Think about this for a moment: What better way to neutralize any type of electromagnetic force coming toward you than to use a counter-quantum healing current in your energy field? The healing current that is created by the Star of David around your aura is the right frequency, vibration, and resonance to block most of the harmful electromagnetic energy field that comes to you.

The energy created by the Star of David will help you assimilate the forces coming at you. Let me explain this. Sometimes it cannot totally block them, because total blockage may require a different energy, and in some cases, it may require a stronger energy than you would be able to hold. Earlier I used the example of the electric meter on your house transmitting energy waves while you sleep. After a while, your force field may break down.

When you are sleeping, your force field becomes more vulnerable, but the Star of David over your crown chakra and above your cosmic egg creates a beautiful, protective current that assimilates, resonates, and integrates any exterior current — any exterior force — so that it becomes harmless inside your system.

The discharge of these energies is another important aspect of this aura protection work. With assimilation, you can hold on to a certain amount of energy that is aberrant or not especially healthy to your system, and later discharge it. Now we will practice the Star of David technique, and then I will explain how to discharge the energy.

First, we will clear all energy. [Chants]: "Oooohhhh. Oooohhhh. Oooohhhh." Take three deep breaths. Command your aura to go into the shape of the cosmic egg. Expand your aura so that it is now eight inches from your body. [Tones]: "Ta, ta, ta, ta, ta, ta, ta."

See twelve vertical lines coming down the aura from top to bottom. Then visualize twelve horizontal lines going around your aura and body. Now visualize the Star of David coming down horizontally and resting on top of your crown chakra. As that Star of David comes into contact with your crown chakra, you will feel that there is an immediate electromagnetic charge through your whole aura.

This is a balanced and healing charge. You should also find that it is a very pleasant charge. It assimilates all the energies into harmony and balance. Let us go into meditation now as you experience the Star of David charging your aura. We will go into silence. [Silence.]

To the best of your ability, see this charge going through the twelve vertical lines, the twelve horizontal lines, and the meridians. As these vertical and horizontal lines are charged, the charged field expands around the whole aura. Next, you can make sure all the quadrants of the aura are now carrying this charge. With this completed, you are totally protected. [Chants]: "Oooohhhh. Oooohhhh."

We have now completed the general charging of all four bodies — the mental, emotional, physical, and spiritual. With this exercise, your energy field will be able to assimilate external electromagnetic energies in your outer aura and the four bodies. Now, it is necessary to release all unwanted energy, because you carry a lot of it. Some of this energy has been stored in your aura without your knowledge.

To discharge this energy, visualize the Star of David rising five feet above your head. As it rises, it emits beautiful white light. This is healing purification light that acts as an etheric shower above your aura. This white light washes and cleanses your energy field of any unwanted energy. It is like taking an energetic shower.

Remember, you can hold on to this negative electromagnetic energy or the unwanted energy, but now you are making a conscious effort to release it. Visualize again the cleansing white light from the Star of David five feet above your crown chakra washing over you. Now this energy is just disappearing. We can see it is going into the ground so that Earth can absorb it. Let us go into silence again as you visualize this process. [Silence.]

The exercise that I just led is a general one in which all four bodies are integrated. For more in-depth work, we recommend that you do this exercise for each of the four bodies. I will do a separate exercise for the emotional body as an example of how to do this with the individual energy bodies.

The emotional energy body, like the other three bodies, has an etheric representation of itself within your aura. When I look at you with my eyes, I just see you as one body. If it were possible for me to examine your energetic bodies, I would see there are four bodies interwoven. Now I want you to separate the emotional body in your mind.

Star of David Technique for Healing the Energetic Body

Visualize the emotional body in the shape of you. Complete the cosmic egg exercise around the emotional body. The emotional body carries a high electromagnetic charge. Everyone has both positive and negative emotions, and no matter how hard you try, you will always have emotional reactions. You cannot be on this planet now without having some strong emotional reactions.

Place the Star of David on the crown chakra of the emotional body's aura. Visualize twelve vertical lines and twelve horizontal lines on your cosmic egg. Send an electrical charge through these lines in order to protect your emotional body.

Raise the Star of David to a position five feet above your emotional body's cosmic egg, and then experience this great stream of cleansing light washing down over your aura, helping you discharge all the charged, polarized, and unwanted energy that you have been carrying in your emotional body. Feel that cleansing now. [Chants]: "Oooohhhh. Oooohhhh."

Your emotional body is now balanced, and unwanted, negative energy is washed away. Let the emotional body remerge back with the other three bodies.

Heal the Electromagnetic Charge of Trauma

You are on a soul journey, and this lifetime on Earth is just a small part of it. However, you have the task — either now or later when you are in the other realms — of assimilating this experience. It can be a challenge because you might be having many unwanted experiences. I am sure that you knew that you had the possibility of experiencing certain traumas in this lifetime and that you were going to witness traumas on this planet.

There is a method for assimilating these personal and planetary experiences. I want to speak briefly about the concept of the self from the perspective of soul psychology. There exists in psychology the concept of the unwanted (or disowned) part of the self. These are experiences that you have had in this lifetime or in other lifetimes that you did not assimilate or integrate as part of you.

You have pushed those experiences away from your consciousness because you do not want them to be part of you; they are your unwanted parts. The conscious mind thinks that if these parts are pushed away, then they are not part of you. The same process has occurred many times in your soul's history; there are traumas you experienced in past lives that you have disowned.

Through assimilation, you can integrate all these experiences, even the painful ones. There is a method that will help you assimilate the traumas by integrating or releasing their charge. If you do not assimilate the energy, the charge stays with you, and you carry it from lifetime to lifetime.

One of the great opportunities on Earth relates to the starseed consciousness many of you have. You now have the mental abilities and the expanded consciousness to assimilate — and eventually heal — all the unwanted parts of the self. One of the great advantages of being on Earth is that you have a great opportunity for soul assimilation and soul integration, and you can do this in a conscious way. This ability is of major value in the third dimension.

You might also carry charges from traumatic experiences on other planets. Often the strongest charge is carried on the emotional body. Of course, the physical, mental, and spiritual bodies can also carry the charge.

When you are ready, you will be able to recall repressed traumatic memories from either this or other past lifetimes. If you give permission to your mind to allow the retrieval of these memories, then they will come up in your consciousness. This is an opportunity for you to assimilate them because you want to integrate the disowned parts of yourself. This is part of your ascension work.

Ultimately, this same healing technique can be used on the planet. There are many traumatic events occurring now on planet Earth that must be integrated into global consciousness. Integrating these events requires a much larger energy field and greater global participation.

Blessings to you all, lightworkers around the world. Good day.

Chapter 13

The Concept of Messiah Group Energy

Juliano and the Arcturians and Vywamus

Juliano and the Arcturians: Let us look at the *I Ching*, known as the *Book of Changes*. It is based on the Chinese philosophy known as Taoism, which contains the concept of universal yin and yang energy. The only constant in the universe is change. I want to use that brilliant observation to look at the world situation, your personal situation, and your ascension into the fifth dimension.

Every person resists change. One of the characteristics of aging is the desire to maintain your status. When you were a child, starting about the age of eleven or twelve, you probably could not wait to grow up. You were happy to change and might have become bored if not for change. But now, as a wiser adult, changes may become overwhelming. Perhaps you even look for ways to stay the same.

When we look at the planetary situation, change continues at a rate too rapid to integrate. The models for predicting changes often no longer work. Take, for instance, climate change. I am sure you have heard predictions of Earth's rising temperatures that will cause a rise in sea level. Scientists have estimated that if everything continues without changes, many coastal cities will be under water by 2050. A year or two later, the estimate was moved up to 2030. Then you will hear it again with yet an earlier date.

Rapid Changes

This rapid change on the planet compares to what occurred 50 to 55 million years ago in the Yucatán Peninsula region of Mexico when an asteroid strike led to the fifth mass extinction. The impact immediately resulted in the death of all the dinosaurs and many other plants and animals. An estimated 85 to 90 percent of all life forms died during that planetary event.

You are presently experiencing the sixth mass extinction. The ecological changes currently occurring are equally as rapid as when that asteroid struck Earth millions of years ago. Compared to the overall age of Earth, approximately 4.7 billion years old, even 50 or 100 years is an extremely small percentage of the overall time we are talking about. So this is a rapid change from the perspective of Earth's age.

We, as planetary healers, want to slow down or stop this rapid change. This requires swift and positive intervention, which leads me to the evolutionary change of humanity. During rapid change, whether on a personal or planetary basis, a crisis occurs.

Some of you may have experienced life-threatening events that forced you to change your old patterns of thinking. This includes habits that might have worked fine when you were younger. For example, if you became ill, you might have had to change your diet, or you had to move because of toxins in your environment. The ability to change is one of the key ingredients of survival.

On a planetary level, that crisis confronts all species with the choice to change or perish. You are being challenged to make rapid changes in your belief systems and your perceptions about Earth and the third dimension. Humanity must adopt fifth-dimensional consciousness in order to survive and save planet Earth.

Go with the Flow

The Tao has specific indications of how different time periods have different energies. In order to adapt to the times, you must understand the energies of the time and how to flow with those energies. This adaptation also includes instructions for world leaders.

The Bible encapsulates the change agent for the third dimension in the concept of the messiah, or the warrior-king. The emphasis on warrior and king may surprise some of you. In ancient times, during the period recorded in what you call the Old Testament, the messiah was considered a peaceful king and also a warrior. In the biblical Hebrew language, the messiah (*mashiach* in Hebrew) means "anointed one." This refers specifically to when the high priest poured oil on the forehead or head of the king, which was called the anointing. The ritual symbolized the entry of the anointed person into his reign as king.

Once anointed, the messiah had the power to change the political, social, and natural environments using the higher spiritual laws of the Creator. In Old Testament times, one person would carry that energy and cause the change. In 2019, the energy of the messiah can be passed on to groups of people.

The Path of Higher Consciousness

Today you struggle with the question: "How is it possible for someone who has high spiritual consciousness to use that energy to change this reality?" In biblical times, the person who had higher consciousness also had the power of the warrior. Many of you have been warriors in past lifetimes. I am not suggesting that you adapt the warrior way and get ready to go into battle. There is a new way, and perhaps some have identified this correctly as the way of the spiritual warrior.

What is important for you to understand is that the beings of higher consciousness also possess personal power equivalent to the warrior. The personal power of the spiritual warrior manifests through a higher way. Jesus/Sananda taught the path of higher consciousness to change the world. This path of higher consciousness aligns with peace and spiritual harmony.

The combination of the energy of the messiah with the energy of the warrior spirit produces what can be called the energy of the warrior-king. This power can be carried by group consciousness. You, as starseeds, can participate in this group messiah energy. It will open you up to personal change and offer a force for planetary change.

Fifth-Dimensional Power

Let's look at fifth-dimensional beings, sometimes referred to as extradimensional beings or extraterrestrials. When you think of the Arcturians, or any other higher being who comes to this planet, you probably consider them as having great powers. How could an Arcturian spaceship come into this reality and not be protected?

Higher beings lack the giant, muscular physiques personified in the gods of Greek mythology and perhaps expected in the earthly warrior-messiah/warrior-king role. Arcturians, for example have slim figures with minimal muscle. Our might resides in our mental powers. Telepathy, teleportation, and other higher powers come with fifth-dimensional consciousness. These powers are superior to any type of brute strength. We, with our mental powers, can control even the most advanced radar techniques and laser beams directed toward us. We would not come close to a planet like Earth unless we knew that our technology outperformed yours. We can easily protect ourselves from any type of military attack on the third dimension.

I want to assure you that, as fifth-dimensional beings, we have never imposed ourselves on humans. We would never perform chip implants on anyone or abduct anyone. Beings who do this are of a lower echelon. Abducting someone or implanting a chip into people violates their free will and is considered karmic interference in a planetary system.

A good model for understanding higher-dimensional beings is the comic book character Superman. With Superman, we are, again, talking about an extraterrestrial being coming to this planet and, by the nature of his own development, using fifth-dimension powers to bring better order.

The Israelites and ancient students of the Tao knew that higher beings from other realms could manifest on this planet and have Superman-like powers. This does not mean that the higher beings would fly through the air wearing a cape. But it does mean that they would be able to change aspects of this third-dimensional reality.

Having the power of the warrior-king requires great responsibility and superior ethics. That is why only fifth-dimensional beings can obtain the power to change this reality. We are working with you to establish the foundation for, and receptivity to, the download of the messianic light needed to shift this planet.

Hominids Ready for Alchemical Change

It is good for you to understand that your current state as *Homo sapiens* is only a link in a long lineage. Your more primitive expressions include Neanderthal man, Cro-Magnon Man, Peking man, and Australopithecus. You do not represent the last manifestation of this line. You will continue to evolve. The changes in your consciousness will help move humanity to the next level. I have designated the next level of evolution for humanity as the omega man or woman.

The omega man or woman has great personal power and higher consciousness. The omega man or woman has fifth-dimensional consciousness, and he or she will use the laws of alchemy to change this planet. I purposely chose the word "alchemy," because this Middle Age philosophy attempted to demonstrate that metals could be coordinated and mixed to turn lower metals into gold, the most precious metal on planet Earth.

Experts in alchemy created personal power through the accumulation of wealth. Symbolically, those who could do this could become rich. This process demonstrates the ability to transform lower energy into higher energy. Today, you can do alchemical exercises to activate personal and planetary change.

Meditation for Warrior-King Energy

I want to lead you in a meditation for the evolution of humanity and for the gathering of the warrior-king energy. We want to merge that energy into a group focus for planetary change. The coming rapid changes necessitate great concentration and focus to hold the energy for higher evolution. To develop this energy, say this affirmation: "I open myself to the warrior-king messianic energy." I want you to understand the warrior energy as the energy of personal power that will help you affect this manifested reality.

When you say the affirmation — "I open myself to the warrior-king messianic energy" — take three breaths and feel a great opening in your crown chakra as your spirit rises out of the physical body and floats to the top of the room. As you go, you leave the room and continue upward from Earth into the ring of ascension.

Once in the ring of ascension, enter a special doorway I have opened that enables you to see the future of this planet. Sit in a meditative position by this special doorway in the ring of ascension. This fifth-dimensional etheric ring has the greatest energy for higher planetary light.

From this position in the ring of ascension, look down at yourself back on Earth, sitting there in your room. Observe your past experiences in this lifetime. Some have called this perspective the life review. You can see yourself even as far back as your birth, when you came into your body. See yourself and realize that you come to a higher, more evolved state.

At the same time, look toward your future to see how many years you might have left in this physical body. As you look forward, add the energy of the fifth-dimensional warrior-king to your future time on Earth. Say this affirmation: "I project the warrior-king messianic light into my future self on Earth." This will give you great advanced powers of healing and the ability to manifest positive planetary change.

Now, see your future time on Earth with this ability for spiritual manifestation. Unite with all the Arcturian starseeds in the ring of ascension and feel a strong group connection. Say this affirmation: "We, as a group, manifest the warrior-king messianic light onto planet Earth in the future. We, as group energy, manifest the warrior-king messianic light onto this planet." Feel the group energy link from this power, and hold this deep group connection.

Vywamus will now speak on the subject of resistance. I am Juliano. Good day.

You Can Accept Change

Vywamus: Greetings! I am Vywamus. I am a soul psychologist. Juliano has asked me to talk with you about resistance to change. When you connect your higher energy fields in the ring of ascension, you enter a heightened state of understanding. It is easy to talk about change, but in order to institute change, you must have the ability to deal with resistance to change.

Most people can see what is wrong with others. The true art dwells in understanding what you need to do to change and help yourself and other people deal with resistance to change. Even as a student of the ascension, you will resist the changes you must make to obtain a higher consciousness because of a fear of the unknown. You fear giving up old ideas and the old selves you have brought with you from your childhood, including your inner child, and other lifetimes, referred to as remnants of your reincarnated self. The old ideas have become your identity. The way to change lies in identifying with your fifth-dimensional self, not your older self, for true healing.

This can be difficult to implement. You need to learn how to surrender attachments to your old beliefs. Here is a good affirmation to help you do that: "I hereby release all old beliefs of my self that are not in alignment with my higher self. And so it shall be."

You see the resistance every day. Denial, one of the strongest forms of resistance, is a powerful defense mechanism. Denial allows you to avoid the pain of change. Some people resist accepting climate change and global warming are happening; they are in denial. Denial dulls the pain one would experience if one accepts climate change.

Turn and Face the Strange

Who wants to give up their power? Who wants to give up their control? Who wants to give up their ability to dominate this planet? Only those who have things to lose will want to hold on to the old system, and that desire for control and power contributes to the denial. This is another part of resistance. There is an old way of doing things on this planet that has been successful. This planet has experienced rapid unbelievable technological advancements in the past fifty years — for example, advances in the computer world, lasers, digital technology, and space travel. Mastering time travel and the ability to travel interdimensionally loom just over the horizon or already exist.

The technology to control the whole planet exists. A handful of powerful people now exert that control, and the resistance to change lies in the fact that they do not want to give up their power.

Healers must find a way to overcome their fear of change and of losing the self. It is natural to want to hold on to what you have. The Taoist philosophy teaches that everything changes. To embrace this paradigm means you cannot remain rigid and fixed. Hold on to the value that everything changes, and direct those changes toward healing. Use healing affirmations and connect with the spiritual groups focused on planetary and evolutionary change.

A Meditation for the Higher Evolution of Humanity

To continue Juliano's meditation that brought you into the ring of ascension, say: "I am here to contribute to the evolutionary change toward the omega man or woman." It is a great personal mission to be able to contribute to the higher evolution of humanity that is represented as the omega man or woman and the warrior-king messianic light energy. Hold that affirmation now in your meditations.

Let yourself return from the ring of ascension back to your physical body in your room. Hold and download that powerful energy back into your physical body. You can accept change. You can change and participate in the evolutionary shift that we all know is so necessary now on Earth.

Call on me, Vywamus, to help you overcome your resistance to change. You are here to prepare for greater awareness and a greater downloading of your higher, fifth-dimensional self on this planet. I am sure of it.

I am Vywamus. Good day.

Chapter 14

Time Travel Can Aid Planetary Ascension

Juliano and the Arcturians

We are going to look at planetary ascension, time travel, and how to prepare a planet for ascension. The idea of ascension on a planetary basis is closely connected to the concept of a planetary messianic intervention. In reviewing the religious teachings on messianic energy, we can note that there are two conditions that would cause a messianic intervention.

The first condition relates to the evil and corruption on a planet. In this scenario, the only way to rescue the planet is through a messianic intervention. In other words, since things have gotten so out of control due to evil, lower consciousness, and corruption in this world, there is no hope that the planet will be able to recover on its own. Therefore, a Messiah or messianic energy is authorized from the Higher Council to intervene and save the planet. The second condition for a messianic intervention relates to (what in religious circles is called) the number of righteous men and women on a planet. In this view, no matter how much corruption and evil exists on the planet, that planet can only earn or be designated for a messianic intervention if there are a certain number of righteous people.

What does it mean to be a righteous person? What does it mean to be able to categorize and count the number of righteous people on a planet? That idea of needing a certain number of righteous people on a planet before a messianic intervention also sounds conditional. You need 2,000 righteous people on the planet for it to be saved. Planet

Earth has 8 billion or more on this planet. Two thousand is certainly a small number. Can 2,000 righteous people tip the scales to allow for a messianic intervention?

Starseeds for Planetary Healing

From the Arcturian perspective, we have altered this concept of righteous people and changed it to mean starseeds and planetary healers. Do not let this go to your heads when I say that the planetary healers are righteous. "Righteous" does imply a high level of holiness. The truth is that you — in your roles as starseeds and as planetary healers — seek and gather holy light and holy energy. Your planetary healing work with biorelativity, planetary cities of light, and ocean reserves of light certainly qualifies you as righteous.

Arcturian starseeds stand for the protection of the biosphere and for the elimination of all causes for the sixth mass extinction. You stand for connecting with the fifth dimension and promoting the evolution of humanity to what I call the omega man/woman — a person who has evolved beyond the lower self and into higher consciousness. It is important that the strength and power of your thoughts are focused.

There are more Arcturian starseeds than just in the Groups of Forty. Also, other starseeds are working for planetary healing besides the Arcturians and the Groups of Forty. One thousand and six hundred starseeds are necessary for planetary intervention to hold concentrated thought power and concentrated energies for planetary healing. This is a collective effort, and there is a collective brotherhood-sisterhood energy.

In addition to the power of 1,600 and the power of 40, the tools for planetary ascension that we teach have unique power. We have also provided twelve etheric crystals and ladders of ascension to enhance your thought power and your planetary healing power. We are teaching the unification that is designated as the sacred triangle, which greatly enhances the arcan power of your thoughts. Working to unify galactic spirituality with mystical, higher consciousness and Native American spirituality creates a completely new, powerful energy of planetary healing.

Prepare for Personal Ascension

Planetary ascension can occur when there are righteous people on the planet, but these righteous people need to be involved in preparation for the messianic intervention and planetary ascension. It is not enough just for the righteous people or planetary healers to be on the planet; they must be actively involved in preparation for intervention.

This presents an interesting analogy with personal ascension. Theoretically, there are great similarities between your personal ascension and the planetary ascension. The most obvious similarity is this: When you are working on your personal ascension, you prepare for your personal transformation. There are people who have said, "I am going to ascend, so I am just going to relax and not work on myself anymore."

Part of your ascension work is to seek out and complete — on an accelerated basis — your life lessons and soul lessons. Another way to put it is you need to work on your unfinished soul lessons. We hope you might say, "Okay, I am ready to finish my soul lessons." Some of the soul lessons present baggage and burdens and, in some cases, illnesses or conflicts. Completing soul lessons is not as simple as taking a course in graduate school. It can be painful at times.

Ultimately, personal ascension is a process centered energetically on your energy field and your aura. This is why we do a lot of preparation with aura training, including accelerating vibrations and experiencing higher aura energy. We have given many exercises in aura work, including the shimmering and cosmic egg exercises. The cosmic egg exercise puts the aura in its optimal shape. We have talked about the need to heal or close any holes in the aura and remove parasitic attachments from the aura. Also, you need to remove hooks that might be from other lifetimes or any negative entities.

All this work with the aura is an important part of the preparation for ascension. Your work does not have to be 100 percent perfect, but your effort and intention are powerful and important. The fact that you are aware of your energy field, and work with it, purify it, and make it vibrate faster contribute to a very positive outcome for your ascension.

During ascension, your aura pulses at an accelerated rate that allows you to transform. I often refer to this transformation as alchemical, because it seems you start working with physical energy and then somehow that mysteriously transforms into an etheric, multidimensional energy. That transformation is so complete that the physical body, in its ascending transformation, disappears from the third-dimensional reality and is transformed into its fifth-dimensional form.

The Planetary Ascension

Earth also needs preparation for her ascension, and Earth cannot ascend without the righteous people or planetary healers on it. The energy of ascension is a higher vibration, and there is a rapid acceleration of higher consciousness coming into the planet. These forces provide an opening that allows ascension to occur. There has to be a certain dynamic and higher-dimensional energy field that is downloaded into Earth for ascension.

While it is important to prepare for ascension, connect energetically, and work on higher consciousness, this by itself is not enough. You also need an external, higher-dimensional force that provides a corridor of light and energy. This light will be the final stimulation for the energetic transformation known as ascension. Now, this is the same opening that provided the messianic intervention and messianic light. This means that the ascension is also potentially a time for messianic light and messianic energy.

There will be three waves of planetary ascension. Everyone will probably want to go on the first wave, especially when we talk about the corruption, evil, and the possibilities of further extinctions on the planet. Why would people choose to bypass the first wave and wait for the second wave? The answer is simple: The ascension light from the first wave is going to provide a powerful healing energy for the planet. The first wave will provide an introduction of messianic energy for Earth; therefore, it will provide an amazing upliftment and consciousness, potentially causing tremendous healing for the planet. It may not bring about total planetary healing, but it will certainly be a healing that is miraculous on many levels. Experiencing that energy is worthwhile and might be enough to convince some people to stay until the second wave.

Ascension and Intervention

Questions have come up numerous times about leaving family members. For example, someone will say: "My family members are not really into this type of energy or work, and I cannot leave them behind." Another will say: "I cannot leave my dog behind." Or someone will say: "I cannot leave my wife behind or my children." Know that there will be very positive effects from the planetary ascension. One positive effect will be the downloading of messianic energy and light onto the planet. The messianic light's strength and the number of people who will go in the first wave are still not clear.

Others question when ascension will occur. Everyone wants to know what date, and that date is often correlated with a catastrophic amount of corruption, evil, and destruction on the planet. The general consensus has been that as that increases, it brings us closer to planetary ascension. What a paradox! Who in their right mind would want to see more deterioration? At the same time, wouldn't you like to see a messianic intervention as soon as possible? Know that planetary ascension and the messianic energy intervention can occur together. You can focus on and ask in your prayers and meditations for an immediate ascension and a messianic intervention because of the deterioration of the biosphere.

Use Shimmering to Heal Earth's Aura

Just as personal ascension requires aura healing, planetary healers need to prepare Mother Earth for her ascension by working with Earth's aura. Planetary aura energy healing work requires more people in different parts of the world to work together; 1,600 planetary workers are certainly enough to do this kind of Earth aura energy healing. The personal basic aura exercises that I have given you for your use — the cosmic egg, shimmering, and healing and closing the fabric of the aura — also apply to the planet. This work provides a great energetic boost.

For example, shimmering will raise the planet's vibration.[1] Shimmering is based on the concept that an aura has a certain vibrational speed that can be accelerated using toning. This is why

1. Shimmering is an exercise that raises the pulsing speed of an aura.

I often use toning. [Tones]: "Ta, ta, ta, ta, ta." I want to demonstrate that the vibrational pulsing of your personal aura can be increased through the exercise of increasing toning sounds. Let us experience this now.

Shimmering Exercise

Take three deep breaths. See your aura, and command it to go into the shape of the cosmic egg. Become aware of the outer pulsing of your aura, and let us use toning to increase the pulsing speed. Try to correlate that to the toning that I am doing. [Tones]: "Ta, ta, ta, ta, ta, ta, ta." [Repeats the toning with increasing speed.] Use your imagination and thoughts to accelerate your aura as fast as you can, even if that it is in nanoseconds. [Tones again]: "Ta, ta, ta, ta, ta, ta, ta." Once you activate a speed, you can hold that speed for long periods of time.

To activate the shimmering speed of Earth's aura, do a similar exercise: Visualize Earth's aura, and thought-project yourself to 10, 20, 40, and then 50 miles outside the planet. Use your imagination to visualize a line around the outer edge of Earth's aura. Chant to begin to shimmer Earth's aura.

The shimmering will also help to raise the spiritual light quotient of the planet. When the whole energy field of Earth is pulsing — and I mean pulsating in unity through group effort — then many people on this planet will feel that healing energy. Many people will feel the effect of the shimmering.

Use the Iskalia Mirror to Shield Earth

There is a long history of rifts in Earth's aura caused by military experiments, nuclear explosions, and other devious methods that have been done for personal and military gain. Some of the rifts are located over areas that have experienced warfare. There are bad rifts over Iraq, Syria, and other places in the Middle East. There are also rifts caused by nuclear experiments. There are rifts now over

Fukushima, the North Sea, and parts of Antarctica and the North Pole where nuclear waste has been dumped.

These rifts need to be healed and require what I call "planetary stitching" of Earth's aura. This technique requires you to identify where the hole exists in Earth's aura in order to sew up the rift. Use remote viewing and remote travel — energetically and etherically — to find these rifts and repair them.

Sometimes cosmological events create rifts. Your solar system is traveling through the galaxy at a phenomenal speed. One revolution around the entire galaxy can take as long as 500 million years or more. Each year, Earth passes through new angles to the center of the galaxy. In some areas, Earth receives stronger radiation and cosmic energy that has never before come to Earth. For example, the expulsion of certain new neutron stars gives off cosmic radiation. If that radiation is very strong, it can penetrate Earth's aura and cause rifts.

Cosmic events can be dealt with by shielding. The Iskalia Mirror[2] provides protection for Earth from damaging cosmic events and strengthens Earth's aura. This shielding provided by the Iskalia Mirror can be compared to a shield made by Native American shamans in their spiritual practices. These shields can provide protection against negative forces.

When you use a shamanistic shield, it is not the size of your whole body. It has etheric and energetic properties that protect you. It is important to shield Earth from cosmic energies that are potentially harmful. Also, you can shield Earth from the evil intent of lower extraterrestrials.

The Karmic Chain of Events

In the future, everyone has ascended. I am not putting any timeline on it. People might ascend in different periods, but ultimately, as one famous teacher said: "We are all on one road, and it leads to the same mountaintop." Some of you are going through different canyons

2. The Iskalia Mirror is an etheric mirror placed over the North Pole by the Arcturians. It helps amplify positive energy coming to Earth from the Central Sun and provides planetary healing energy.

and valleys, but the bottom line is that you are all going to ascend, and Earth is going to ascend as well. We can time travel to access future time and future energy of the ascended Earth and bring that future energy back to help the current Earth and your present self.

When we work on your personal ascension, we help you to thought-project yourself to the Arcturian crystal lake. It is also possible to thought-project a whole planet using time-traveling techniques. There are places in the fifth-dimensional world where planets can be thought-projected for healing. These special places cleanse and heal a planet's aura. Imagine that there is an Arcturian cosmic or galactic planetary lake where you can thought-project a whole planet. It would have to be immense to hold the etheric energy of a planet.

There are also ways in which the future energies of a healed planet can be brought back down into the present. You might have already heard stories about people in the future traveling to the past. There are science-fiction movies that imagine what would transpire if a future time traveler came back into the present, such as *Back to the Future*. Is it possible to travel to the future?

Well, before I answer that, let me explain an Arcturian term, known as the law of the karmic chain of events. This occurs when somebody from the future comes back to the past and changes events. For example, imagine that after an unsuccessful assassination attempt to kill Hitler, someone from the future travels into the past to make sure that assassination attempt is successful. Or imagine when Hitler was wounded on the battlefield in World War I. Someone from the future travels back into the past and helps to move that bullet that hit and grazed Hitler. Now, instead of being seriously wounded Hitler is killed.

According to the law of the karmic chain of events, many events would change dramatically. It's very complex. What does that mean? Would Hitler's early death allow for another maniac to come into power? Could the murder of Hitler lead to another chain of events that brings nuclear destruction to the whole planet? Is it possible that Hitler's early death would lead to a more positive overall chain of events?

Think of how complex weather patterns can be. Nobody knows with complete accuracy how to predict the weather or what the results of global warming will be. There are interesting models, but it is still very complex. The karmic chain of events is far more complex than Earth's weather patterns; one almost needs a supercomputer to predict how history could change due to the intervention of time travelers. Because the karmic chain of events is so complex, any future time traveler who comes back to the present Earth has to take an oath not to interfere with Earth events.

Time Travel Methods

To travel into the future, visualize Earth from the perspective of outer space. One rotation of Earth on its axis equals one day. If you want to go a week into the future, visualize the Earth rotating on its axis seven times. If you plan to go ninety days into the future, then visualize Earth making ninety rotations. Now, if you want to time travel a year into the future, then visualize the revolution of the Earth around the Sun, which takes one year or 365 days. If you want to go five, ten, or fifteen years into the future, then visualize a specific number of revolutions around the Sun.

To go back in time, follow the reverse procedure. Visualize the rotations of Earth in reverse so that you go in a backward direction. If you want to go back a week, visualize the reverse rotations of Earth seven times. If you wish to go back a decade in time, then visualize ten reverse revolutions. This method requires a great deal of concentration.

This visualization exercise is not the sole part of this time travel procedure. I have only given you part of it; other parts of the time-traveling exercise are still secret. It also requires corridor work along with work on Earth's electromagnetic energy and aura fields. Remote healers have used this method for military purposes to go forward in time.

Bring Back Positive Information

Gaining knowledge from the future can be extremely helpful to create change. You can put pressure on certain forces on the planet when you know there is a good opening in the future. It is also helpful to know who will have the power to work with you. There might be certain knowledge in the future that you could obtain that might convince people to change their ways.

While the law of the karmic chain of events is such that future time travelers are not permitted to change the past because of unknown outcomes, people in the present can go into the future and bring back knowledge and information that will help in the present. There are certain safeguards activated that allow you to go into the future and bring back information and still be free of karma. The basic rule is that you bring back positive information for the greater good of humanity.

Planetary Healer Exercise

Visualize Earth's aura while it is spinning. To the best of your ability, see Earth on its journey around the Sun. Thought-project yourself to a position above the North Pole of this planet. You are in a protective corridor of light. Make this affirmation: "I am a planetary healer, and I am a righteous person." Let us pause to hold that visualization and meditation as the first step toward time travel. [Pauses.]

Starseeds like you have this planetary awareness. Now you know there are ways of thought-projecting the whole planet to a healing lake in another part of this galaxy. Planetary healers can work with Earth in the past, future, and present. They can also heal and work with Earth's aura through shimmering. These are all great tools that you — as righteous people and planetary healers — can implement.

I hope that together, we will be able to travel into the future to obtain technological and social information to help create healing and new balance for Mother Earth. I am Juliano. Good day.

Chapter 15

Let There Be Light

Juliano and the Arcturians and Archangel Michael

Juliano and the Arcturians: Greetings, this is Juliano. We are the Arcturians. There is so much to say about light, and there is much need for more light on this planet. This talk is about the history of light in the galaxy and universe, including instructions for how each of you can take advantage of being a lightworker by receiving and sending out light to others.

Light is stronger than darkness; therefore, where there is light, there cannot be darkness. This seems obvious. Much of the discussion today will seem simple, yet simple is good. Sometimes it is important to go back to the basics of spirituality, and the basis of all spirituality is light.

In the creation of the universe, there was the "word," and the word was spoken. The first words spoken as recorded in the Bible were, "Let there be light" [Genesis 1:3, NIV]. This is instructive on two levels. The first level is that there was a pre-existence before light, and the creation of light occurred after the words were spoken. This also tells you of the importance of light in the creation of this universe.

There is a close connection between sound vibrations and light frequencies. There are fascinating characteristics of light in the galaxy and in the universe. It was discovered that light travels at the phenomenal speed of 186,000 miles per second. Most people cannot even imagine that speed of travel, but you have heard me say numerous times that thought is capable of traveling faster than the speed of light, because thought is of a different texture and frequency.

Your thoughts can also interact with light frequencies. Once it is understood, this interaction will be an important development in space travel and time travel. When I refer to space travel, I mean intergalactic and intragalactic travel. When I refer to time travel, I mean the ability to travel through corridors and hyperspace (the space between the dimensions). In hyperspace, thought controls where and how fast you go.

The Evolution of Humankind

We can talk about Neanderthals, Cro-Magnons, and now *Homo sapiens* as part of a line of development from earlier species. It is a well-known anthropological observation that the present humans are not the last — or the best — manifestation in this chain of evolution. I think you will agree with me, especially considering how humans are destroying the planet.

The majority of the destruction on Earth now is due to humanity. All life — including all aspects in the biosphere — now is in human hands. Never before in the history of this planet has one species been able to dominate all aspects of life.

The next stage of *Homo sapiens* is the omega man and woman. Humankind will then be much higher than the Cro-Magnons, higher than the Neanderthals, and higher than their current evolution. Believe it or not, humanity is close to a huge, evolutionary leap.

Omega Light

The first vibrational light frequency we want to discuss in more depth today is omega light. Omega is the last letter of the Greek alphabet, and in spiritual technology, the last represents the best. It also represents the light that is of the highest evolution for each person and the highest frequency that will be attained in the spiritual world. In addition, I use this terminology to describe the highest possibility of spiritual evolution for humans.

When we call on omega light, this frequency will bring out the best in you and activate the omega energy within you. It will activate the best part of your DNA codes. It will also activate and unlock the codes of ascension that are in your reticular activating system — the part of your brain related to higher consciousness. In addition, the omega light will activate your assemblage point. This point is used by shamans to represent the opening of higher, evolutionary consciousness.

The Group of Forty members have been using the term "omega light," and some of you send letters or emails and sign off with the phrase, "With Omega Light and Love." You might not completely understand that you are referring to the highest activation of light — the highest evolutionary possibility of each person — and thus you sent omega light and energy to them.

Even pronouncing the term "omega light" is an inner reminder to your secret codes that you can open to your higher self and your higher energy now. Part of that higher energy relates to participation in the evolution of *Homo sapiens* to the next level, and the other part relates to higher consciousness and fifth-dimensional consciousness.

Now, some have even described the omega light and the evolution of humanity as representative of the ascended masters, such as Sananda, who is representative of the highest evolutionary point that can be achieved.

Following is a way we can work with you to activate the omega light within you to participate in the omega light activation of the entire species. What better contribution can you make to humanity than to help activate the evolution of omega energy?

Omega Light Activation

I, Juliano, will now send down omega light to each of you. Receive this light in your crown chakra. We will use it to activate within you the highest evolution and energy — the best evolutionary energy — and the best spiritual light within you. [Chants]: "Omega light." Let the omega light come into your crown chakra, and fill your auric energy field. It fills your crown chakra with an activation that brings out the best and the highest within you now. [Chants]: "Omega light." We will pause for meditation. [Pauses.]

When you send light, you also receive light. This is an art. It requires practice. I would like to use the analogy of looking at the Sun. You may need to use special glasses to look at the Sun. Even if you are not looking directly at it, you should wear sunglasses, because the Sun has intense rays of light. This means your eyes are not evolved enough to look directly at sunlight. If you were to look directly at sunlight for any amount of time, you could permanently damage your eyes. This is especially true during the dangerous time of the solar eclipse, when Earth still receives the Sun's rays as the Moon passes in front of the Sun. During the eclipse, you might have the false belief that you cannot be damaged by looking at the Sun.

Spiritual work requires an ability to receive higher light, and this comes from practice. It is similar to training to run a race. You have to practice and build up to your conditioning. You don't expect to run a race without training, and so it is with lightwork. You have to practice receiving light and distributing light throughout your body.

We begin the practice of receiving light by sending light to your crown chakra. It is then distributed to all parts of your energy field. There can be a buildup of etheric plaque on the aura that slows down the vibration of the aura's frequency. The plaque on the aura is like a governor on an engine; it will not allow your aura to go at a higher speed. This means that if a higher frequency such as omega light is coming into your aura, then your aura may have trouble integrating and vibrating at the speed of that new light.

This is not all bad; it is also an inherent protection of your energy field. While you want as much light as possible coming into your aura, you still have to be aware that you can only assimilate a frequency of light that is compatible with your ability to receive. To increase that ability, you must train.

Iskalia Mirror Light

The Iskalia mirror has the unique ability to focus light from the Central Sun onto Earth. Some high light frequencies — like the Central Sun energy — require an amplification of light so that it can be put in a form that can be processed by humans. The Iskalia mirror is a special mirror that filters light from the Central Sun to be used and processed by the human aura.

This relates back to the history of light in the universe. The original light in the universe was so diffused and high that only an ascended being would be able to interact with and use that light. The light was so intense that no normal living being — especially no third-dimensional being — could possibly have seen or interacted with that light and survive.

This phenomenon has also been observed in relation to Divine light. There is a reference to this experience in Exodus [20–22, ESV] from one of the ascended masters, Moses. Moses wanted to see God's face, but God's face had so much light that God explained to Moses that he could not look directly at him and live. God instructed Moses: "'You cannot see my face, for man shall not see me and live.' And the LORD said, 'Behold, there is a place by me where you shall stand on the rock, and while my glory passes by I will put you in a cleft of the rock, and I will cover you with my hand until I have passed by.'"

This biblical story gives you an idea of the intensity of the light from the Creator. However, there are ways of building up your ability to look at light. Ascended master Moses was trained to look at the shadow of the Divine light, even looking at the shadow is such an intense experience that only a select few people would ever be able to experience that. In other words, it is a great spiritual advancement to be able to see and experience the shadow of the Creator.

The Central Sun light is the focus of all spiritual light in the galaxy. All the great beings, including all ascended masters who come to Earth, have studied and experienced the Central Sun light. It is a very high frequency of light that was initially described in the intersection of your Sun with the Central Sun on December 21–22, 2012. At that point, the intersection of Earth's solar system with the Central Sun was comparable to an eclipse. This was a special alignment that allowed the Central Sun light to come through from thousands of light-years away and set up a new activation. That activation was correctly identified by the Maya and by the lightworkers as the 2012 activation light. There were many expectations of what that light frequency would do. Part of the idea of the Iskalia mirror was that the ascended masters would help you align and interact with that light in a usable way.

You might ask the same question we have asked: "Did the activation of that higher spiritual light occur in 2012, and was it sufficient to change the evolutionary cycle of Earth and put it on a different path?" The answer is unclear. In many ways, the spiritual technology and activations from the 2012 light interaction with the Central Sun were successful. Many starseeds opened up to their deeper missions and received new guidance on their planetary missions, and there was a great upliftment of new energy for the ascension. There were also activations of many old and sacred sites around the planet. New corridors were established. New light frequencies spread out across the globe, and there was a huge increase in spiritual light frequencies on Earth.

In other ways, it was not successful. Major changes and shifts in the political, economic, and social fabric of this planet did not occur. There were high expectations that the spiritual energy from these light frequencies coming from the Central Sun would be enough to solidify the transformation necessary to move Earth toward higher evolution and toward the omega man and woman.

This did not occur, partly because of the need for global preparation. When there is not enough preparation to receive these higher frequencies, then the frequencies pass over or are not integrated. In some cases, they are rejected.

Remember, there is a self-protection mechanism in the human aura. You cannot receive a higher light frequency than you can tolerate. The Iskalia mirror is still etherically above Earth and downloads Central Sun light. The Central Sun light needs to be spread continuously throughout this planet. It contains further instructions and further discoveries about how to ensure that higher frequencies — such as omega light and the Central Sun light — can become true tools for the activation and the evolution of the *Homo sapiens* into the omega man and woman.

Arcturian Blue Light

The next type of light I will talk about is the Arcturian blue light. Each of you is receiving our Arcturian blue light. We continually work with this blue energy and blue light, sending it to all of you who are requesting it. The blue light has a special spiritual frequency unique to the Arcturians.

Blue is a very healing color. For example, think how warm and how healthy you feel when looking at a blue sky. Then, use that image to picture the Arcturian blue light coming into your aura and down into your crown chakra. This will give you an idea of the feeling of well-being and the healing aspects of Arcturian blue light. We also use the blue light in our psychic surgery. We work with people using spiritual and medical technologies. For example, we can send strongly focused blue energy into an infected organ or another part of the body that has been damaged. We have great success in being able to repair diseased organs.

The Arcturian blue light contains a special mixture of alchemical frequency light energy. We have been studying and working with the blue light for many eons. The Arcturian blue light has special healing properties. When receiving this light, you can receive a dynamic, fifth-dimensional healing. It also has special spiritual activation energy, and it can interact in a specific way with your aura. If there is plaque on your aura, the blue light knows how to interact with the frequency of that plaque in order to remove it and allow you to vibrate at the highest frequency possible within the parameter of the blue light frequency.

We have different frequencies of blue light. Sometimes it is necessary to transmit the light in a general way, and other times we use it in a specific chakra focus to treat people. For this transmission, we will send down blue light in a general way. (We would use it in a focused way if we were working with you individually.)

Arcturian Blue Light Transmission

I am sending down to you now the Arcturian blue light. [Tones.] Receive the Arcturian blue light into your crown chakra now. [Tones.] The blue light is called *azul* light in Spanish. The word "azul" captures the Arcturian frequency of blue. [Tones]: "Azul light. Azul, azul, blue light." Let us go into silence now as you receive and integrate this light. Direct it to wherever you wish within your body. [Pauses.]

The Arcturian blue light's special formula interacts with your aura and dissolves any plaque that is slowing down the vibration of your aura so that you can interact and use this light. [Tones.] Let the omega light come in with the blue light through your crown chakra.

Quantum Healing Light

In some ways, quantum healing light is a combination of the omega light and blue light. The word "quantum" refers to little packets of light. They are so small and difficult to observe, detect, and predict that a huge mystery has developed around how quantum energy functions. At the same time, the quantum world has completely revolutionized modern society and computer technology that you benefit from in some ways. It has also led to other discoveries, such as the development of nuclear energies.

Philosophically, the discovery of quantum energy has shifted traditional scientific thinking. It has led to a discovery that the world is not run like clockwork. The third-dimensional subatomic world operates on other principles that are unpredictable. This unpredictability sets up a vast array of choices and challenges that also transcends normal logic.

Quantum healing carries the same spiritual energy and light, and that means there are aspects of this world that can receive healing that transcends logic. For example, in the third-dimensional world, there are diseases that people may not be able to overcome; they appear to be incurable. When using quantum healing light, we bring down an energy of unpredictability that transcends logic and normal expectations. Healing with quantum energy creates positive unpredictability for curing illness. We are bringing down energy and light that is transcending normal medical logic.

The concept of quantum healing is also important in relation to healing the planet. There is an air of hopelessness about the planetary situation. We look at the accumulation of pollution in the oceans, the destruction of the forests, and the changing weather patterns. You might wonder how all this can possibly be corrected. And even if it could be corrected, it may take 50 to 100 years. This correction could only occur if we immediately stopped coal and nuclear energy production and ceased pollution of the ocean. None of that is happening now.

I can tell you that in quantum healing theory, there can be divine intervention, including messianic light. This is a type of quantum healing light. Call now on the quantum healing to come to you, and in further lectures, we will talk about sending quantum healing light to the planet and to the noosphere to shift the consciousness and set in motion a newer energy in alignment with the omega light.

Quantum Healing Light Transmission

Receive quantum healing light now in your crown chakra. [Tones.] Quantum healing light frequencies are now entering your aura. We will go into silence. Receive quantum healing light now. [Sings]: "Quantum healing energy and light." [Pauses.]

You are now receivers of this light. You can use this light now. It is a brilliant, white light with golden parts and golden, sparkling energy. Gold is a symbol of harmony. Let there be a halo around each of you now — a golden halo.

Now I am going to ask Archangel Michael to speak with you. In the Arcturian blue light, this is Juliano. Have a good day.

Divine Lights

Archangel Michael: Greetings, I am Archangel Michael. First, we will teach you about zohar light. Zohar is a mystical light, and the word "zohar" in Hebrew means "brilliant," "splendid," or "splendor." This is an unusual description of light, but the description tells you that this light frequency is so high that it can be compared to the concept of splendor. How would you imagine splendor? Maybe you think of diamonds. Think of the most beautiful, sparkling diamond you can imagine. The light that emanates from the diamond is filled with splendor. Maybe you have a certain crystal that gives off a light frequency. We would say this is splendor.

This word "splendor" is a superlative. It is a higher designation of brilliance that is not often seen on the third dimension. Most people live in cities and do not see the brilliance of the night sky. The skies in the city are not dark; they are not filled with the light of galaxies and stars. Humanity has lost a lot from its disconnection from the universe and inability to experience the splendid light of the night sky. Just as sunlight, the zohar light is a splendid light. The difference is that the zohar light comes directly from the Creator.

Zohar light is a pure light. Remember, Moses was not able to look at the face of God because he could not experience the Creator light directly. Try to imagine that there is a thread of light through the whole universe that comes from the Creator. The Creator is so overwhelmingly powerful that only a small essence of the Creator light could be tolerated in this universe. That thread of light now exists in the third dimension. That thread of light becomes available under special circumstances. It is a splendid light, and that splendid light is called the zohar light.

When you have any connection to the zohar light, you can ride the light throughout the universe. You could ride the light back to the beginning of time. You could ride the light into the future. The zohar light also directly leads back to the energy of the Creator. It is a secret mystical light that is ritually purifying to experience. [Tones]: "Zohar light."

In the Hebrew language, holy light is known as *Aur Ha'kadosh*. Holy light is sacred light. It has special powers, so in order to experience holy light, you have to be in a special vibrational frequency. You also should be protected from third-dimensional energy when you experience holy light. I am going to sing the words *Aur Ha'kadosh*. Just call on and receive holy light into your crown chakra. [Tones]: "*Aur Ha'kadosh*."

The light from *Aur Ha'kadosh* is very close to the light of *Ruach Ha'kadosh*, which is the Holy Spirit. Many of you know about the Holy Spirit from Christianity. The Holy Spirit emanates holy light, and the state of mind of the Holy Spirit or *Ruach Ha'kadosh* is considered enlightenment. When you are in that enlightened state, you can experience the holy light continually. Even though there are polarizations and densities in the third dimension, the underlying energy of this whole galaxy and planet is still holy light and the Holy Spirit. [Tones]: "*Ruach Ha'kadosh*, Holy Spirit."

The Light of Bahir

Just as people of the Arctic have many words for "snow" because assessing snow is critical for their survival, we evaluate the nature of spiritual light, because it is an important tool in our work. In the spiritual world, we have many different descriptions of light, including healing light, holy light, sacred light, omega light, quantum light, and zohar light. There is another type of light in the mystical tradition — the light of bahir, which is another word for brilliance.

The light of bahir can be described as overwhelmingly bright. Some of you have been to higher realms in your dream world or astral travel to the fifth dimension. Maybe you have seen gardens, skies, or colors that were brilliant. Some of you have come back and observed that colors from the fifth dimension are not normally available in the third dimension. The colors on the fifth dimension are more brilliant.

Do you need sunglasses to experience the brilliant light? Your crown chakra and your third eye filter the brilliant light so that you can integrate it. Activate your ability to see brilliant light. [Tones]: "Light of bahir. Bahir light. *Ha'kadosh. Zohar.*"

It is written in the Kabbalah that the first person of higher consciousness was Adam. This first man had special abilities to see light and distinguish the variances of light. The first Adam was able to open his eyes and see zohar light across the whole universe. It is very hard to imagine how somebody could see light across the whole universe. You have telescopes now that gather light from almost the beginning of the universe and that primordial light is traveling back to Earth.

May the light of zohar and bahir and the holy light, *Aur Ha'kadosh*, be with you now and for the remainder of the time you are here on planet Earth in the third dimension. Know that you will be able to interact and use this light for highest healing purposes.

Blessings. I am Archangel Michael. Good day.

Chapter 16

Methods to Protect Yourself

Juliano and the Arcturians

We have many new lessons and ideas to cover in this chapter related to the acceleration and rapid changes taking place on planet Earth. The first subject is protecting yourself during this time of dramatic change and crisis. In truth, it can be difficult to know the safest places to live on the planet. It is important that your third eye remain open, because one of your most valuable assets during this time of dramatic change is your psychic ability, which can be defined as multi-talented or multifaceted.

Your primary psychic skill is the ability to see into the future and know or intuit coming events. Frankly, it is not always possible to move to another location. You might learn about the potential for a future event in your area, but it is not practical to leave. Psychic abilities are still very useful, even in those situations. Look at how you can best accelerate and enhance your psychic abilities so you can sense potential crises that might affect you. This ability is the best insurance against the dangers of Earth changes. If you know a building is going to fall, you won't enter that building, correct?

A second aspect to psychic ability is something I like to call creating sacred space. Creating sacred space is an important activity in planetary evolution and planetary ascension. I talk a lot about the future evolution of humanity, and I refer to the next link in that future as the omega man/woman, but Earth is also evolving. The next link in Earth's evolution is the fifth-dimensional link. One of the most rapid ways to encourage Earth's evolution is to create more sacred spaces. These include planetary cities of light and planetary ocean reserves of light. Creating individual sacred spaces in your home and neighborhood are also helpful. One or two of you living in a house can create sacred spaces in your house and on your property. When you enhance the sacredness of your land and home, you add another layer of protection.

Everything is electromagnetic, including the universe and every object and living being on the planet. Perhaps one of Albert Einstein's greatest discoveries was that fields exist around objects, including planets, suns, and your body. The space around your home, city, and country have electromagnetic-energy-field signatures. The good news is that you can influence and activate the electromagnetic energy field around you, your property, and your loved ones, including your pets.

We already know about thought fields and how important it is to create a constellation of thoughts. This includes individual thoughts combined in a group, which can create thought fields with more power for manifesting. In the same way, you can create electromagnetic energy fields of protection for yourself.

An accumulation of thoughts and energy from meditations can go into a thought field. I will describe some of these meditations in this chapter.

How to Protect Yourself and Your Property

Your third eye perceives and interacts with your thought field. Many things that occur energetically around you are below your consciousness. This has been shown by scientists in relation to the human body. Many functions of the human body, such as digestion, heart rate, and blood pressure, are below your consciousness. These functions continually work within the body without your awareness. You might only become conscious of them if something is wrong, and they call your attention to a problem.

Your energy field is the same: It continually functions and picks up many things without your awareness. How aware and tuned in are you to your energy field? How much can you influence your energy field? Are you trying to make your energy field a better shield? Are you placing an energy field around your house and car? One way to enhance the energy field around your house is to place crystals in the cardinal points around your house or yard, then activate that area. This is actually similar to how we activate the planetary cities of light during the planetary-city-of-light activation. Before the activation ceremony, people place crystals at the four cardinal points that anchor energies and strengthen the electromagnetic energy field.

You want the electromagnetic energy field around your property to have a function the Chinese refer to as pung, which means elasticity and the ability to repel energies that could be of a lower nature. You want a shield to act as a filter: It should let higher energy and higher light enter your energy field and repulse lower, darker energy. I do not recommend setting up a shield like a wall, because a wall can also reject higher light and higher energy. Higher light and higher energy can strengthen the field around you and your property. With your mind, you can direct the energy field to have more pung or elasticity and more ability to repel lower energies.

Where do you get the ability to develop the proper shielding, if it is not within your mind or repertoire of spiritual tools? We Arcturians are committed to helping you and protecting you even during events such as earthquakes, volcanic eruptions, and severe storms. It is our prediction that these events are increasing and will continue to do so. We are able to download higher light, such as blue Arcturian light, into your designated energy field. For example, if you designate a need for energy around your property, set up the four crystals and call on me, Juliano, to bring down the special Arcturian light. This special Arcturian light will have pung energy, which repels lower, darker energies but does not block higher light. This is a good way to protect yourself.

You can also ask for Arcturian protective light when you work on your individual aura. The spiritual tool for working on your aura really begins with the cosmic egg. You can place crystals around the room where you meditate if you want to strengthen the room's energy. Generally, it is effective to work with the cosmic egg and strengthen your cosmic egg.

An important tool to begin this type of protective work is your third eye, so you can be aware of your energy field and any intuitive messages that might come to you. Then you can make an appropriate response based on the information you receive. Everyone knows we are very close to the "end-time" events in this planetary crisis. But just knowing that is not protection enough. You'll want to have enhanced sensitivity and perception.

Third-Eye Exercise, Part One

I am going to lead you now in an exercise to enhance your third eye. Take three breaths and become aware of your crown, third eye, and heart chakras. It is our belief that chakras should be worked with in triads. It might be easier to say, "Let us work with the third-eye chakra," but that chakra is part of a chakra system. It is similar to the concept of the Tree of Life, which has twelve spheres. It is okay to work on one sphere, but it is better to work on a triangle of spheres and see how they interact.

Imagine these three chakras — your crown, third eye, and heart — interacting with each other. Each chakra has rotating, funnel-like energy in front of it. The funnel on the crown chakra projects three or four inches above the top of your head. The heart chakra projects the same distance in front of your heart, and the third eye projects three or four inches in front of the center of your forehead.

Place your palm above the crown, and feel the chakra's energy in your palm. Now place your palm over your third eye; you will likely feel some heat. Put your palm over your heart chakra and say: "[Your name] now unites these three chakras."

You need these three chakras to work in unison to have the highest psychic ability, which you can use to predict dangerous events. You might get a psychic impression in your heart that something is going to happen. You might get a psychic impression from your crown chakra or, in more advanced cases, receive images. The subconscious, unconscious, and multidimensional consciousness have unique ways of communicating through images. When you seek information through the predictive world, they usually come as images rather than words. For example, imagine an earthquake is about to happen. An image might come to your third eye of shaking, or a feeling in your heart tells you that something catastrophic is about to happen.

Continuing with the exercise, place your hand over your third eye, approximately three inches in front of the chakra. Imagine you have a hand pump and are about to pump up your chakra as if it is a bicycle tire. Move your hand to your forehead, then move it back again, this time about four or five inches from your forehead. This pumps up your third-eye chakra, making it stronger and stronger.

Think again of the image of the bicycle tire. In the beginning, you can push on the pump right down to the bottom, because the tire has no air. But as the tire becomes more pressurized, you have to push harder. You are not able to push all the way down on the pump because of the back-pressure. Feel this pressure on your third eye as you pump it up. This pumping is a spiritual tool for making your third eye stronger and increasing your psychic sensitivity.

Pull your hand away from your forehead. Can you already feel the energy flow? We want the energy to flow outward in a circular manner. Circle shapes are part of the quantum world, and energy in a circle is coordinated and in alignment with the basic subatomic energy waves that come into your third eye.

Third-Eye Exercise, Part Two

The next part of this exercise focuses on making small circles in front of your third eye. Your third eye has now been expanded. Hold your hand about six to eight inches in front of the third eye, and rotate your hand counter-clockwise. Going counter-clockwise is similar to winding up a spring. You are winding up your third-eye chakra.

Make nine counter-clockwise revolutions. When you are finished, lower your hand. The cone of your third eye chakra is sprung and now rapidly spinning clockwise. It is very much alive and activated.

Project a little arrow and straight line that goes from your third eye to the other side of the room. You are expanding the reach of your third eye to the edge of your energy field and to the end of the room. Send that energy line out through your whole property. You can also think of the line as an antenna that can receive information and psychic impressions wherever it reaches. You have extended the range of your third eye outside of your room and onto your property.

Take a minute and allow yourself to receive any psychic impressions. Are you receiving any images, for example? Extend the line farther. Choose a spot in your neighborhood and send the line there. You might receive images or psychic impressions over the next seven days. The images you receive about your neighborhood and property might feel stable and good. In other cases, you might receive some kind of warning; you might see an image of a large storm or some kind of disruption. Your role is to receive all images and not filter or hold back any psychic information that comes to you. We will go into silence as you do this exercise. [Silence.]

Put any images you receive into a special memory bank that you can recall at any time. Do not make decisions about what to do with whatever information you receive; simply put it in your memory bank. When you come out of this light trance, you can examine them and make decisions then.

Now, withdraw that psychic line back to your third eye. Make an etheric dome of protective blue light around your property. You might be aware of the experimental place called the Biosphere, located in southern Arizona. It was an experiment to create a self-sufficient living space. The structures are covered with huge domes, and underneath are gardens, machinery for recycling air, and all other necessities for living independently. The idea was to see if astronauts could live on the Moon or Mars in such structures.

I want you to place an etheric-blue dome around your property. This dome has the properties of pung energy: higher light will come in and push lower or dark forces away. Visualize an opening for a corridor on the top of the dome.

That corridor goes up to the Arcturian starship Athena. I, Juliano, and my team of Arcturian workers will now send protective energy and light into the dome over your property. It begins now.

Third-Eye Exercise, Part Three

In this next part of the exercise, we will work specifically with your energy field. You can include yourself and all your pets, plants, and trees under this dome. Let everything under the etheric dome be filled with the blue protective light. Incidentally, this etheric energy under the dome is a healing energy field. Think of it as higher oxygen, higher etheric energy, that you can breathe within this dome.

Bring that etheric line from your third eye back into your forehead area. Leave the etheric line at the edge of your personal energy field, approximately seven or eight inches from your forehead. See the next seven days as huge layers of energy layered on top of each other. Send your etheric line forward again from your forehead. See that line extend through those days of the week, sending light and energy from your third eye. Let the etheric line be like a beacon of light. Let it sensitize itself to any unusual energies you should be aware of during the next week. Maybe you will travel or someone will visit you. Receive any impressions for the coming week. We will go into silence again while you do this part of the exercise. [Silence.]

Bring that etheric line back toward your third eye, and let it extend just to the outer edge of your aura. Say, "I now activate my sensitivity for my third eye so I can receive all information from my energy field about future events." Now when you send out this line, you will receive pictures, energy, and information that can help you can make corrections and adjustments in your daily life concerning potential problems and future events.

For example, say you plan to go to another city on Tuesday or Wednesday, and you will be traveling on a freeway. Send this line of thought out to Wednesday, and you might receive information that there will be a big traffic jam on the route you planned on taking. You might psychically see an accident. After receiving this information, you might decide to take another route, cancel the trip, or be extra careful as you drive. You can say to yourself: "I am not going to speed the way I usually do." Your third eye is now really activated, and it will give you information that can help you make decisions.

Finally, imagine the bubble again around your house. See yourself in a protective cosmic egg, and receive the blue light of protection from the Arcturians. Let this blue light come into your energy field, bringing you health and vibrant energy on all levels. You are protected. You have the ability to expand perception, and you can evaluate and discern images that you receive through your third eye.

Reacting versus Responding

We are going to switch themes now and look at the concept of the evolution of Earth and how Earth responds to humanity. In reality, this planet is still young. Even though 4.5 or 4.7 billion years might seem like a very old planet in human years, the age of a planet is not always measured linearly. You might be seventy years old but have the body and mind of a thirty-five-year-old. Your linear age is based on the year you were born, but your metaphorical age is based how your body acts. The Earth is a living spirit, also called Gaia or the Blue Jewel, and it responds to traumas.

The Earth is experiencing a trauma. The biosphere is greatly contaminated; many of its meridians are blocked. Many aspects of Earth are out of balance. This is no secret. Anyone who is at all sensitive, especially a starseed, knows that Earth is out of balance. Imagine a child is out of balance. That child is going to act out, possibly with anger. It is the same with Earth. The Earth is being abused. How would you respond as an abused child? You might withdraw and contract, angrily kick and punch, or destroy things around you.

Earth shows some of these effects of trauma, including contracting. As the planet contracts, it releases energy in the forms of storms, earthquakes, and volcanic eruptions. When we work with you, we also speak with Earth; we try to suggest there is another way to respond.

In my teachings on the psychology of planetary development, I talk about reaction versus response. Let me explain. Imagine you are driving a car and somebody cuts in front of you. You are very angry and react, raising your fist and swearing at the driver. You do not think first; you just react angrily. In this stressful age, any type of reaction can be dangerous, because somebody could respond or react back in a violent way.

Response is different. In a response, you might feel the desire to react angrily and lash out, but you hold back this impulse. You say to yourself: "No, it's not a good idea to become aggressive. There are a lot of crazy people in this world, and if I raise my fist and yell at that person, I have no idea what he or she will do. My aggressive reaction could escalate the situation very quickly." Instead, you respond by hitting the brakes, slowing down, and letting the person pass. That is a response rather than a reaction. Reacting involves no intervening thoughts; there is no control; it is all unconscious. I call this subconscious, as it is below consciousness.

Part of the role of humanity, and of evolution, is to evolve from reacting to responding. This can be difficult because humanity is still close to its animal nature, and animal nature is more closely aligned with reaction. In the animal world, animals usually do not have time to respond, and reacting is necessary for self-protection. Part of the evolution of humanity is to transcend the animal reaction from the subconscious to a higher response.

Earth's Response to Humanity

Let us take that model of responding instead of reacting to the planetary level. What is Earth's repertoire of reactions and responses? Earth has a limited way of communicating to humanity and to the world. What you now see, in many cases, is Earth reacting. In our work as planetary healers, we want to elevate Earth to respond. That requires good communication and heightened energies of interaction between humankind and the Spirit of Earth.

To improve the interaction between Earth and humankind, we work with the concept of the planetary subconscious and the planetary noosphere. We are starting to download higher thought forms into the planet's subconscious and the collective subconscious. The collective subconscious has dramatically increased its power, mainly due to new technology. New technology includes the internet and images on television and all media, including smartphones. These images download into the planetary subconscious, and many contain aggression and violence. This increases the possibility or violent planetary reactions, which I would say are increasing. Unknowingly, humanity is placing these primitive images into the planetary subconscious.

The saying "As above, so below," was originally based on some spiritual teachings. It means that what happens within the higher energies also happens within the lower energies. I want to modify this and say: "As below, so above." In other words, whatever happens in the planetary subconscious will manifest on the third dimension. There are still higher energies in the higher realms, but those do not necessarily manifest on Earth. "As above, so below" makes it seem that if something is wrong with the higher dimensions, their energy messes up the third dimension. I believe it is the opposite. The lower, collective subconscious energies of the planet influence and manifest much of the violence and destruction.

We, as planetary healers, and you, as individual healers, can help change the collective subconscious of the planet. That is a big task, but it can be done with such activities as global events, global meditations, medicine wheels, and gatherings at sacred sites. You have the power and energy to change the planetary collective subconscious.

At this time, Earth reacts to the planetary subconscious, which includes continual input of what I call "planetary abuse." This is why crisis events on the planet are accelerating. But Earth will respond to your spiritual work, which can strengthen the collective subconscious in a positive way. Send Mother Earth messages of evolution, kindness, and love, and she can rebalance and respond instead of react.

Chapter 17

Practice Living in the Fifth Dimension

Juliano and the Arcturians

It is difficult in the linear mind and the mind of cause and effect to understand the multidimensional self. Basically, in your mindset on the third dimension, you see things in a linear fashion. This means there is a past, a present, and a future; and this timeline is on a straight line.

When you think of your future self, you see it on a linear line after the present self. The multidimensional self can be defined as a self that exists on several different dimensions at the same time, or simultaneously. This means when you experience the multidimensional self, or the consciousness of the multidimensional self, you can be here and conscious of yourself in the third dimension and at the same time be conscious of yourself in the fifth dimension. In some cases, it is also possible to be in the fourth dimension at the same time as being in the third dimension.

I want to emphasize that experiencing the multidimensional self can be done from a higher, expanded state of consciousness. It is a sign of higher evolution. In the future of humanity, especially when we talk about the omega man or woman, we can say these more-evolved beings have a multidimensional consciousness. This means not everyone is advanced enough to experience or participate in multidimensional consciousness. It requires what is known in the Kabbalah as the big mind, or the expanded mind. You would not be able to experience multidimensional consciousness with the small, or contracted, mind.

Here, There, and Everywhere

How is it possible to exist on two different dimensions at the same time? To begin to understand this, we must transcend linear time. So we have collinear time and circular time. "Colinear" means there are two parallel timelines. You can imagine this as a railroad track progressing on a long roam. Colinearity is a useful concept to understand the multidimensional self.

Dreaming is a way to understand how it is possible to have a self in two different dimensions. When you dream, you are confined to the sleep state. You may be asleep for seven to eight hours, but you only dream when you are in a deep state of sleep during rapid eye movement (REM), sometimes referred to as the third state of consciousness. It has been observed that when you are in this deeper sleep state, you inhabit your dream body.

This dream state is a good example of multidimensional experience or presence. While dreaming, you are in your physical body in the third dimension. At the same time, you inhabit your dream body. It so happens the dream body changes. You have the wonderful ability to shape your dream body into any form you wish. You can make yourself young, such as when you were nineteen or twenty years old. You can even choose different bodies, such as forms of people you know who could represent you in the dream.

The fact is when you dream, you are in a multidimensional consciousness. You are in a state of being in two dimensions at the same time. The difference is that we divide these states from sleep state to waking consciousness.

Many people are able to enter the sleep state or the dream state from waking consciousness in fantasy or daydreaming. Some people call this state lucid dreaming. In this state, you briefly nap for maybe a minute or two or even five. You immediately go into the altered state of consciousness, and then you begin to experience multidimensional dream consciousness. The dream state, and the dreaming experience, provide us with a good foundation for understanding the multidimensional experience.

The Other Side of the Curtain

Our work, that is the work of the Arcturians, focuses on expanding your consciousness and preparing you for the ascension. We encourage all starseeds to practice multidimensional consciousness through exercises. You can practice multidimensional consciousness by consciously projecting your astral body into the fifth dimension.

In this practice, there are sacred places on the fifth dimension to project yourself to your fifth-dimensional body. It is important for you to have the most powerful experience and protection when you travel into your multidimensional self or when you participate in multidimensional experiences. Thus, we have set up the Arcturian crystal lake and Tomar's temple. We have also setup special healing chambers on our starship, Athena, for you.

Many starseeds are already deeply experienced in multidimensional work. Some of you report that, when you are able to have glimpses of your other multidimensional states, you see yourself as a commander on a starship or a doctor or a healer or some high healer on another planet or galaxy. Sometimes I refer to the awareness of the experiences in other realms as the "bleeding between dimensions."

There is a safeguard that puts a curtain between the basic reality you live in, which is the third dimension, and any multidimensional reality you may experience, such as the fourth or fifth dimensions. At times, that curtain allows a bleed over. This means you can have awareness of what you are doing in the other multidimensional life.

This is, for the most part, a positive and desired experience for starseeds. If you are not mentally stable or you do not have the proper belief systems or understandings of the nature of multidimensional lives, then you might find the bleeding-between-dimensions experience upsetting. You might think you are going crazy if you have detailed experiences with multidimensional events.

Stay in the Golden Corridor of Light

There is a phenomenon known as abductions and abductees, and this includes people abducted or taken into starships. They report the experience with great accuracy. The question always arises about whether these people are fantasizing or part of a group delusion. In other cases, they may report specific examples of interactions with other beings. Every abductee case has an aspect of multidimensional consciousness and multidimensional experience.

If you were in a room and somebody was abducted, you might still see a corridor or a portal opened by fourth-dimensional beings that allows the multidimensional self to be captured, or abducted, and brought into starships in another realm. Abductees may report they are physically taken, and in truth, they are physically taken, because the doorway has been opened up for the multidimensional self.

I would like to emphasize the importance of protecting the multidimensional self. There are certain safeguards everyone can practice in order to ensure that your space, which includes the portals that are potentially around you, is protected. The simplest way is to visualize a golden corridor of light around you when you sleep. Visualize that this corridor cannot be penetrated by lower beings. I feel it is important for every starseed working toward his or her ascension to practice protecting the multidimensional self. Practice by sending your consciousness protective energy for your fifth-dimensional body.

I do not encourage people to practice the multidimensional experience in the fourth dimension. There are certain examples and circumstances when it is useful to practice being multidimensional in your fourth-dimensional body. For the most part, I believe that you and I work together for your ascension. Therefore, you do not need to practice going into the fourth dimension.

You often go into the fourth dimension in your dream state. Many of the events you see and experience in your dreams are part of the collective unconscious, which is in the fourth dimension. At the same time, on rare occasions, you may have higher experiences in your dream state that can compare to going into the fifth-dimensional consciousness.

You can create and shape your fifth-dimensional body the same way you can create your dream body. Most of you will choose a younger form of yourselves for your fifth-dimensional bodies. You will choose a time in your history on Earth when you think you were more beautiful or more handsome, and that is fine. You will want to choose a body form from when you were at your best. But you can still choose an older form when you are perhaps wiser and more advanced. It does not necessarily have to be a younger body.

The Art of Lucid Dreaming

Let's compare the concept of lucid dreaming to working with, and practicing, the multidimensional experience. Lucid dreaming is a concept in which you are aware, while you dream, that you are dreaming. This was discovered in the past fifty years in modern psychology. This state of lucid dreaming is vividly described in Carlos Castaneda's books, including *The Teachings of Don Juan* series.

Lucid dreaming is a desirable state of consciousness, because if you are aware that you are dreaming, you can control and direct your experiences. In the Carlos Castaneda series, it was desirable for the shamanistic trainee to practice lucid dreaming. While he was in the dream, he could do different things such as fly, jump off cliffs, and major shamanistic exercises he would not be able to do in normal consciousness.

The simplest way of practicing lucid dreaming is to meditate right before you go to sleep and give yourself instructions. In the Carlos Castaneda series, the shaman gives him an anchoring technique. He gave himself a hand signal before he went to sleep, and told himself that when he could see his hand moving a certain way in the dream, then he would get into the consciousness called lucid dreaming. A simple description is holding all five fingers with your palms facing you in front of your third eye. Practice seeing your hand in that position during waking consciousness. Next, tell your subconscious this: "When I am in the dream state and I see my hand in front of my third eye, I will enter the state of consciousness called lucid dreaming."

You could practice or meditate holding your hand in front of your third eye and stating that affirmation, and when you are in the dream state and see your hand in that position, you would go into lucid dreaming. When you do lucid dreaming, try to do different things, such as flying, becoming psychic, or healing parts of you. There are things you can do in the multidimensional dream state that you cannot do in normal consciousness. In the dream state, you have psychic powers unavailable to you in normal consciousness.

Create Your Fifth-Dimensional Anchor

Each of you has a fifth-dimensional body in the fifth dimension just like you have a dream body when you go into the dream state. You can practice accessing your higher-dimensional body in the fifth-dimensional or multidimensional state. Just like the anchoring exercise of looking at your hands, you can setup anchoring to get into the state of fifth-dimensional and multidimensional consciousness.

I, Juliano, have worked with you to anchor in that state of fifth-dimensional consciousness using tones and sounds. When you hear a certain tone or sound, it can trigger you to go into a higher state of consciousness that gives you the opportunity to go into a fifth-dimensional experience and enter your fifth-dimensional body. This is similar to holding your hand out in waking consciousness to help you practice going into lucid dreaming while in the dream state.

We can practice going into the fifth-dimensional state when you hear these tones and sounds. Some of the tones and sounds sound like this: "Ohhhh." This tone gives you the instructions and anchoring to travel interdimensionally through corridors of light to a fifth-dimensional state, and then you can enter your fifth-dimensional body.

Create Your Fifth-Dimensional Body

Let us have you shape your fifth-dimensional body. We can do this now before you go there. I want you to visualize a form of your fifth-dimensional body. If you want, you can choose yourself when you were twenty-five or thirty years old. Maybe that's the time when you, possibly, were the most handsome or the most beautiful. You can choose yourself at any time.

Visualize this body in front of you, and we will call this your etheric double. Now, project that body to the Arcturian crystal temple lake by traveling through the Arcturian blue corridor of light around you. You are traveling at the speed of thought through this Arcturian blue corridor. [Tones.]

As you travel through the corridor, you come to the Arcturian crystal lake in the fifth dimension and, amazingly, the fifth-dimensional form you created in the third dimension is already there. And you, in your fifth-dimensional body, are sitting in a cross-legged position, perhaps doing yoga or in meditation, around my crystal lake.

Find your multidimensional body. Travel over it, and then download or enter that existing fifth-dimensional body with your astral double body now. [Tones.]

You are now in your fifth-dimensional body at the fifth-dimensional crystal lake. At the same time, you are in your third-dimensional body back on Earth. This is a multidimensional experience.

You can have other multidimensional experiences besides on the Arcturian crystal lake. Remember, I am giving you these instructions so that you can practice being in the multidimensional self. At the time of ascension, I think it would be helpful for you to astral travel and enter your fifth-dimensional self here on the crystal lake, because from here, you can go to many different places on the fifth dimension.

You will be able to travel to Arcturus, or you can go to the Pleiades. You can travel to different galaxies. When you are comfortable visiting your fifth-dimensional body, then you are already ahead of the game.

The 75-Percent Solution

The ascension technique bilocation refers to being able to exist in two different bodies at the same time. It is even possible for a being who is highly evolved to be in two bodies on the third dimension at the same time.

There are similarities between experiencing bilocation and the multidimensional self. One is that you have control over how much awareness you have in each state. For example, right now you are in your multidimensional state on Arcturus, and you may be in 100 percent consciousness here at the crystal lake or 99 percent here and 1 percent on Earth. Another possibility is that you can be 80 percent in Arcturus at the crystal lake and 20 percent in your Earth body. You can control the percentage of awareness.

In lucid dreaming, you can raise the percentage of your consciousness in the dream state. I want to help you raise your consciousness in the fifth-dimensional body so that, ultimately, you will be 75 percent in your fifth-dimensional body and only 25 percent in your physical body. That means you can do more things in your fifth-dimensional body than you were able to before.

What kind of things could you do? You could do healings, you could be psychic, and you could travel to other realms. You may want to travel to the seventh dimension, or maybe you want to visit another planet. Once you become comfortable in this state of multidimensional awareness, then, just as in the dream state, your psychic abilities increase. There are many wonderful places to visit in the fifth dimension. In some cases, instead of projecting yourself to the Arcturian crystal lake, you might project yourself to Ashtar's starship or to your home planet.

Note: There are a lot of fourth-dimensional extraterrestrial beings floating around Earth. Some of these beings have bad intentions. I do not recommend that you practice your multidimensional self by going to one of these lower being's ships. We already know the stories of abductees — the pain and suffering they experienced and how it mentally unbalances them.

When you go to the fifth-dimensional Arcturian crystal lake, you do not become unbalanced. Rather, you become more present, and you receive more help in your current life. Now, that is not the case if you are abducted and brought to a fourth-dimensional spaceship against your will by an extraterrestrial not of the higher light.

Even if you want to travel to other starships on the fifth dimension, I personally recommend that you come to the Arcturian crystal lake first. From there, you can project yourself to other fifth-dimensional places.

Practice Your Percentages

You are in your fifth-dimensional body, you have left Earth, and your Earth body is well protected. There is a corridor of light around you and your home. You thought-project yourself and astrally travel with your etheric body to your fifth-dimensional body at the Arcturian crystal lake.

You are now in your fifth-dimensional body. You are at least 40 percent aware in the Arcturian crystal lake fifth-dimensional body and 60 percent in the Earth body. Try to make it 50 per cent for each body to the best of your ability.

You are now 50 percent in your Earth body, and 50 percent in your fifth-dimensional body at the Arcturian crystal lake. You are sitting comfortably in your fifth-dimensional body. You can become as tall as you want, as slender as you want, and as beautiful as you want. You can have long hair if you wish to, and you can sparkle your third eye. Most importantly, you have high psychic powers in your fifth-dimensional body. You can thought-project yourself to other places on the fifth dimension.

Let us then ask: Where do you want to go? Do you want to go to Arcturus? Do you want to go to the Pleiades? Do you want to go to my starship Athena? Do you want to go to the Andromedan Galaxy? Do you want to go the stargate? Now you can thought-project yourself to these places from the Arcturian crystal lake.

You do not need the corridor like you do going from the third to the fifth dimension, because you are already in the fifth dimension at the Arcturian crystal lake. You already are in a sacred space. Maybe you wish to come closer to the Creator. Maybe you wish to visit Sananda.

Let us go into meditation again, and we will do this second multidimensional. You can astrally travel to anywhere you wish. I will help and guard you at all times. We will go into silence.

I hope you enjoy your powers of traveling. Some of you have come to my starship Athena, and others have come into the healing chambers of Helio-ah. I see that some of you have come to my home planet, Alano, and others have come to Tomar's temple on Arcturus.

Please bring yourself back now to the Arcturian crystal lake and to your fifth-dimensional body here at the lake, where we all began. Just command yourself to return. Now you have expanded consciousness. You have all your chakras open. You are truly in the fifth-dimensional state.

Cohabit in the Fifth Dimension

I want to talk about cohabitation. Positive cohabitation, from Earth's perspective, is when a higher being, such as Sananda or an archangel, come into your aura and resides with you. There are several advantages to this experience. Higher beings can raise your thought vibration, which enables you to do things that maybe you could not do in a normal state of consciousness.

There is a concept in cohabitation where you, as a third-dimensional being, can cohabit with a higher being from the fifth dimension. Remember, in the conventional, positive cohabitational state, we think of the higher beings coming down and living with you in the third dimension. In this state of consciousness I now describe, you can bilocate, astral travel, and cohabit with higher beings on their dimension.

There is a great example of this from the teachings of Jesus/Sananda. One of the great teachings he offers humanity is that you can cohabit with him on the fifth dimension. His energy is big enough, and his heart is open enough that he can accept all people who want to be in the higher dimension with him. He can accommodate your energy. Maybe we could call this experience reverse cohabitation.

You can cohabit with me, Juliano. You can also cohabit with Helio-Ah, as well as other higher beings. It is a two-way street, and in some ways, it may be easier and more desirable for you to go into the higher realms. You have both options available. When you thought-project or bilocate to the fifth dimension as you are now, you can also cohabit with any fifth-dimensional being who is willing to be with you. That could be Sananda, P'taah, or other fifth-dimensional ascended masters. There are great advantages to reverse cohabitation.

Send an Invitation

In this part of the exercise, while already in the fifth-dimensional state at the crystal lake, choose an ascended master you want to cohabit with now. Send out the request, and see whether they accept it. After receiving a positive invitation, astral project your fifth-dimensional body to their presence. We will go into silence while you do this.

Enjoy the reverse positive cohabitation. When you return

to your Earth body, you can ask the ascended master also to cohabit with you when you return to the third dimension.

Now to return to your fifth-dimensional body at the crystal lake. You are leaving the positive cohabitation experience you have had with your ascended master of your choice, and you are back at the Arcturian crystal lake. It is time to leave the lake and your fifth-dimensional body and return to your Earth body.

Follow my lead. Go through the corridor above me, follow the corridor, and travel at the speed of light back to your third-dimensional body. Move to 6 feet above your Earth body. Command your astral body to be in perfect alignment with your physical body. At the count of three, reenter your physical body in perfect alignment — one, two, three.

You are now in your third-dimensional body, but you have brought back with you a much higher light. Let all the light, healing, knowledge, techniques, and practices of multidimensionality integrate into your mental, physical, emotional, and spiritual bodies. You can now practice lucid, multidimensional travel. And so it shall be.

I am Juliano. Good day.

Chapter 18

Epigenetics and the Human Race

Juliano and the Arcturians

Perhaps you are familiar with the study of epigenetics. Basically, it refers to the idea that you can control genetic factors with your environment — genes are not rigid finalities, and you can change outcomes. You have probably heard reports from doctors and medical communities that genetics plays a big role in many illnesses, such as heart disease and cancer. Some say the genes you inherit are like time bombs in your body. If you have certain genes, they will give you certain illnesses.

Epigenetics says your environment and mental processes can influence and even change the outcomes of such genetic time bombs. This has led to many brilliant programs focused on environmental factors, diet, and changing ways of thinking. From our perspective, this is fifth-dimensional, higher-level thinking, because it demonstrates that the mind has control over the physical body, even when the physical body is threatened by inherited genes.

We Arcturians have developed healing technologies that can help you activate new reactions and programs in the physical structure of your body. These programs and structures can even help you overcome what might seem to be incurable illnesses.

Helio-ah's Healing Chamber

One of our favorite healing interventions is Helio-ah's healing chamber in which two very prominent exercises take place. In one, you focus on visualizations and computer-like images from your memories. In this technique, Helio-ah helps you retrieve images that go back to the original programs downloaded in your mind in childhood. Helio-ah has used these childhood images to help people reprogram and heal from traumatic events.

The healing chamber, where the computer is located, has access to the images of trauma from the mental body. These stored images in the mental body can become the foundation for future activities and future unfolding of psychological constellations. If the image can be altered or even removed, that leaves room for replacing it with a more positive image. A new story can be downloaded into the unconscious and subconscious. Changing early traumatic images leads to tremendous healing.

The key from the computer healing visualization is that a new and positive image can cause a dramatic shift in your psychological functioning, even if the trauma occurred forty or fifty years ago. Downloading and recreating a new image has a powerful healing effect. This has great significance for epigenetics, because sometimes a genetic program for a certain illness was given to you by your parents when you were a child. These programs were downloaded and gave the body instructions to formulate and activate certain body rhythms or body blockages. I have seen this in many cases where people seem to have difficulty surviving past the age of their father or mother. They seem to repeat a parent's illness.

In this concept of the healing chamber, we correlate visual images with altering genetic programming. Instead of visualizing yourself reacting to an illness, such as a heart ailment, as your parent did, you visualize a new image in which you do not have your parent's circulatory illness or heart ailment. This method unites the concept of epigenetics with visualization and, in particular, retrieves and heals the visualizations from earlier childhood programs. The technique is relatively easy to perform and is certainly less intrusive than chemotherapy or dramatic surgeries.

Revolving-Chair Healing Technique

The second aspect of epigenetics and Helio-ah's work arises in the revolving-chair technique. I will briefly describe this technique, as it offers some important insights for the deeper theme we will review of epigenetics and the human race, or how the genetic programming of the human race as an entirety can be modified. In the revolving-chair technique, you thought-project your astral body to a special chamber on our starship where you enter a room with a chair that revolves and reclines. Helio-ah compares this revolving chair to the type of reclining seat used to train astronauts for zero gravity. The astronauts lie flat on a reclining chair that rotates them in a circle at high speed. This high-speed rotation simulates the effects of being without gravity. Naturally, you would experience dizziness, but you can train the body to overcome this effect.

During this healing work, we bring your astral body to the revolving chair in Helio-ah's healing chamber, and you start revolving. We state that lower densities and lower thought forms, are hereby removed from the astral body. This gives you several interesting insights into how the human mind and genetic structure function, because all illnesses lie in the programs and thought forms that operate in the mental body. These thought forms operate subconsciously, and, for the most part, you're not aware of the programs.

The subconscious (or unconscious) has tremendous abilities. Sigmund Freud associated the mind with an iceberg. Only 10 percent of the full iceberg is visible above the water, while 90 percent is unseen below the surface. In other words, you might be aware of 10 percent of your waking consciousness but unaware of 90 percent that goes on in your conscious and subconscious.

You can retrieve subconscious programs using powerful techniques such as hypnosis, but to activate and pull out those subconscious or unconscious thoughts and programs, you must overcome resistance in the psyche. Even when they are brought out, that does not mean they can be changed. Special skill and training are required to help you overcome these resistances, and sometimes we refer to this procedure as thought surgery. In thought surgery, older programs are brought up from the subconscious so they can be analyzed and changed.

Many of these programs come from early childhood, and some are passed from generation to generation. This means you could be operating on programs in the unconscious that are part of your soul group, racial group, or country group. I often speak of karma and about cosmic karma and Earth karma. There are also family karma, racial karma, and national karma. All of these, for the most part, fall below your conscious awareness.

In the revolving-chair technique, as your astral form begins to revolve, lower thought forms are removed. There are three speeds involved in this technique: low, medium, and high. The highest level releases deeply attached thought forms from the unconscious. This gives you an idea that many of these deep thought forms are intergenerational. Karmic thought forms attach deeply to your unconscious and require systematic and very powerful interventions to loosen and remove.

Another aspect of this method is the reset technique that "reboots" the mind. In many respects, your mind is like a computer. It stores memories and runs programs. Older programs of lower density can be removed, and your mind and brain can be reset. After old programs are removed, it is important to download new instructions and new programs.

These interventions — the revolving-chair technique and computer-retrieval technique — can be used for dealing with what I call epigenetic modifications. Other techniques also deal with these matters, but these two are the most prominent and offer the greatest potential to help us understand how we can use these techniques to change humanity.

Epigenetics and Humanity

We are ready now to look at the theme of epigenetics and humanity. Many of you see the inevitability of current Earth traumas leading to end-time catastrophes. Certainly, recent events demonstrate that the dramas unfolding on Earth seem to have an inevitable negative outcome. This can be linked to the sixth mass extinction and the destruction of the biosphere, which is also related to significant climate changes and other Earth changes, including earthquakes and volcanic eruptions. Ultimately, the most destructive Earth change would be an asteroid striking Earth, because such an event could lead to the death of the biosphere and the removal of 99 percent of the planet's life forms.

There could be an interaction between the mental processes of a species and an asteroid coming to Earth. Jupiter serves as the guardian of the solar system, because it can capture comets coming from outside the solar system and change their directions. In your solar system, as in many others, a large planet such as Jupiter is critical for the protection of a planet like Earth. Were it not for Jupiter, Earth's biosphere would have been decimated many times, and the chance of life surviving would be greatly diminished. So you can thank Jupiter.

There is a mental aspect to asteroids striking Earth. The laws of entanglement and quantum physics operate with asteroids. Attractive forces can help bring asteroids to this planet, and some have to do with darker energies. Other asteroids coming to Earth have a reset purpose, which was demonstrated with the dinosaurs. The creatures were so successful in their evolution that they became resistant to viruses and bacteria. Their populations grew out of control. Earth was programmed for humanity and higher life forms, but humans could not exist side-by-side with dinosaurs.

Humanity has a complex genetic structure, which has been tampered with by extraterrestrials. Multiple genetic programs are incorporated into humanity. The basic programs of competition, dominance, and war-like tendencies come from the Lyrans. About 500 million years ago, Lyran wars within their culture ended in the destruction of entire planetary systems. You are not the first, nor will you be the last, humanoid species sprung from the Lyrans. The Lyrans are the forefathers of Earth humans, the Pleiadians, and many of the human-like life forms in this galaxy. Negative and positive traits in their genetic structure have passed into your DNA. On the positive side, the Lyrans were extremely advanced scientifically and traveled interdimensionally. They originated many of the higher spiritual exercises we are now teaching you, such as thought projection. On the negative side, they went far beyond nuclear weapons and used interdimensional explosions.

An example of a recent interdimensional explosion occurred in Russia in 1908.[1] This explosion near the Tunguska River in Siberia

1. This event was deemed to have been caused by an asteroid, but no remains of an asteroid or a crater were ever found. It is considered the largest impact event on Earth in recorded history. Its force was 1,000 times stronger than the atomic bomb dropped on Hiroshima, Japan.

flattened forests. [**Author's note:** over 80 million trees were flattened.] The explosion was so loud and bright that people as far away as London, England, saw bright lights in the sky. It was comparable to a major asteroid hitting the planet or the explosion of a nuclear bomb, which did not exist in 1908. Scientists looked very hard to find a crater, but the land was swampy and no obvious hole or crater was ever found. The point is that it was not an asteroid; it was an interdimensional explosion from an extraplanetary source based on technology developed by the Lyrans.

Think about this event. On Earth, one country can send a missile to another country, and that missile might carry a nuclear bomb, but the missile can be intercepted by another missile. What type of technology can defend against an interdimensional blast? This blast at Tunguska came from another planetary system in another dimension. Why did they choose that area of Russia at that time? They were experimenting, and they thought such practice would not be detected or do much harm. In one sense, they were correct, because it did occur in a very isolated place on the planet. This is the type of technology that the Lyrans developed, and that knowledge was also passed on to the Atlanteans.

You have heard stories about Atlantis and how Atlanteans destroyed their civilization. Various mysteries and theories about how their continent was destroyed abound. Some say they experimented with the Sun and giant solar panels. Some say they had nuclear bombs. But our perception is that the Atlanteans used forces they did not know how to control. These forces had safeguards, but the safeguards weren't followed. The Atlanteans also experienced an interdimensional explosion similar to the one at Tunguska, but the Atlantean explosion was more damaging because it caused their entire continent and civilization to sink.

Seeking scientific advancement and technology is also programmed into humans. Humans have programming from the Lyrans and from higher beings. There also exists what I call the core Adamic genetic programming. This programming developed over several million years and is demonstrated in the various subspecies of human, such as Neanderthal, Cro-Magnon, and Australopithecus.

A core genetic development is unique to Earth humans. You might have heard stories of the Annunaki in the area of Mesopotamia.[2] These civilizations were visited by beings from the twelfth planet, located in an interdimensional area that cannot be seen by Earth's astronomers. The theory of the twelfth planet says this species came to Mesopotamia and trained humans to be their servants to mine gold and other materials they needed for their planet. They interbred with Earth humans, intermixing their genetic material. These beings from the twelfth planet have been described as the Nephilim, a word used in biblical Hebrew to describe those who come down from the sky. In Hebrew, it literally means "the fallen ones." It can refer to those coming from the sky in reference to the Annunaki, or it could refer to other beings coming from different extraterrestrial sources that also came down and intermixed with humans. Despite all this intermixing with other beings, Earth humans still have a core genetic strand that is unique to them.

The Human Program Needs to Shift

Let us bring all this together into the concept of epigenetics. I said that on a personal basis, you can go beyond your inherited genetics. You can use your mind and environment to override what might be a core program that is physically and genetically programmed so you can modify or even override that program. I have used the term "reset." When you access core programing, you can reset the whole program. One method of getting to the core is to remove lower thought forms.

Epigenetics also applies to the entire human situation and the human race. One of our missions, and one of your missions as a starseed, is to help shift the genetic programs now operating for humanity. These genetic programs are leading to the destruction of Earth and the biosphere. Only a small percentage of people, namely starseeds, have enough higher consciousness to understand and grasp this situation. They understand that the currently operating genetic program is "dark" and will lead to the destruction of the planet.

2. The Annunaki are a group of deities that appears in the mythological traditions of the Sumerians, Akkadians, Assyrians, and Babylonians. In his book *The 12th Planet*, author Zecharia Sitchin claims the Annunaki were actually a race of extraterrestrial beings from an undiscovered planet in our solar system called Nibiru.

These dark forces are like cancers that proliferate uncontrollably; left unchecked, they will cause this planet to go into a deep spiral. You are just now seeing some of the severe outcomes of this deep and dark spiral. The concept of epigenetics can be applied to the human race, and the destruction of the planet or biosphere is not inevitable. In order to stop this downward spiral, humans must be genetically modified.

In my classes on galactic anthropology, I talk about the study of planets and species in the galaxy and how a species on a planet can change during a crisis. In some cases, a species does not change, and the inevitable destruction of that planet occurs. In other cases, destruction occurs from external sources, such as from nuclear bombs and wars. What epigenetic ingredients are needed for changing the whole species? One obvious ingredient is a planetary crisis. In order for humanity as a species to change genetically, a crisis must occur.

For example, imagine you have a blood test and an MRI. You receive news that your arteries are blocked. It is only at that point that you marshal your efforts and begin to change. You might study nutrition and change your diet. You might say, "Okay, I am open now to epigenetics. I am open now to changing my thinking. How can I reprogram my genetic structure? It is not inevitable that I will suffer from these problems." The motivation to change usually only comes during a crisis; that is just the way humans work.

Unfortunately, the majority of people, especially those in power, do not agree that a crisis for survival is occurring, and the result is resistance. If everyone accepted that a crisis were at hand, you would see change. People would marshal their efforts, study, and take immediate action. Some of the resistance comes from the greed, ego, and lower energies of the animal self, which is very narcissistic. The possibility for financial gain, control, and so on, overrides what I call the "middle self," which is more focused on ethical behavior and social justice, two necessities for saving the planet.

The Omega Man/Woman

How can we apply the principles of epigenetics to a species? Starseeds can program and visualize the evolved man/woman genetically. I have called the new man/woman the omega man/woman. Its significance was described by famous French philosopher Pierre de Chardin, when he described the higher evolutionary possibilities of humanity that could be compared to the Christ figure, Moses, or Buddha. The omega man/woman could be compared to the higher beings that have been on this planet and had extraordinary mental powers.

Equally important, these higher beings had broad vision and tried to set new directions of evolution for humanity. We can argue about whether or not they were successful, but we can accept without argument that Jesus did represent a higher form of humanity, a form that was not engaged in violence, and that went into the fifth dimension. Other higher beings have been on this planet since then.

An extremely small percentage of higher, enlightened beings represent what I call the omega man/woman. The key ingredient in the omega man/woman is fifth-dimensional consciousness and higher consciousness. We want to accelerate the visualization and imagery of the omega man/woman so a new, expanded group of higher consciousness beings emerge on Earth. In the time between Neanderthals and Cro-Magnons, they both lived together and were very strong beings, but only one survived. Something about the Cro-Magnon resulted in greater survivability; they eventually evolved into the *Homo sapiens* of today.

A new form of *Homo sapiens* is on the horizon, which I call the omega man/woman. There are small pockets, small groups, who are forerunners of this new omega man/woman, which we want to encourage. You shape and shift yourself into the omega man/woman at certain times when you experience higher consciousness. This can happen through trance work, group activities, and meditations that help you move closer to this next evolutionary stage.

We want to expand and accelerate this evolutionary shift. At some point, two species of humans will exist: omega man/woman and normal *Homo sapiens*. The omega man/woman will have higher consciousness as their main ingredient, but they must also have survivability and be able to protect themselves. People with higher consciousnesses also need protection. For example, people in South America seek to protect the environment, but their lives are threatened. In some cases, they have been assassinated. To be an omega man/woman, you have to manifest ways to protect yourself and survive.

Download the Omega Man/Woman Prototype

You can visualize and download the omega man/woman prototype or blueprint into the collective unconscious and into the noosphere. Remember, I said that 90 percent of the iceberg — your conscious/subconscious — is below water. A substantial part of your consciousness is connected to universal consciousness, or what Carl Jung called the collective unconscious. The collective unconscious is an interconnection of all conscious beings. Downloading the image of the omega man/woman into the collective unconscious will help it manifest.

The power of this visualization can be accelerated through the use of the twelve Arcturian etheric crystals and the use of group consciousness and group meditations. These are very similar to biorelativity exercises in which you use group consciousness and meditations to telepathically communicate with Earth. In some biorelativity exercises, we download special affirmations to Earth.

We can accelerate omega man/woman thought forms through the twelve etheric crystals we have downloaded on Earth. In one exercise, we raise an etheric crystal, such as the etheric crystal in Mt. Shasta, and visualize a white screen on top of that crystal along with the image of the omega man/woman. What does the omega man look like? You can use the image of Jesus, but the traditional Western image of Jesus might not have been his real appearance. Jesus lived in a Middle Eastern community. He had black, curly hair, and looked more Mediterranean or Middle Eastern than Western images portray. What is important is coming up with an image that is fifth dimensional.

I would recommend the image include a halo around the shoulders and head. We also have the issue of man versus woman. I call it the omega man/woman, which means this perfected image should be androgynous; that is, the image should have both male and female characteristics. Look for a universal image that would represent the new aspect of the species that is going to evolve. I challenge you, as a group, to come up with this image.

To complete this exercise, I am going to use the image of Jesus Christ. Project this image onto the screen in front of the etheric crystal at Mt. Shasta, California. Add arcan power, our term for increased thought energy, and send that power to the screen. We can increase the arcan power of that image as high as possible, until we reach 50,000 arcans, which is an extremely high thought power. With a large group meditating together, we can reach 50,000 arcans of thought power for the omega man/woman image.

Download that image into the collective unconscious and project it into the noosphere and the ring of ascension, the fifth-dimensional halo around Earth. In some cases, we might use the Iskalia mirror — an etheric mirror over the North Pole we use to bring down higher light from the Central Sun to Earth. This will help increase the arcan power of the image.

We bring up the arcan power of this image, which becomes brighter and brighter on the etheric screen. Visualize this image as also containing the first Adam, the highest prototype form. The chakras of the omega man/woman light up. There is a strong halo around the head and shoulders, representing expanded consciousness. Keep this figure in your mind. At the count of three, download this image into the collective unconscious of Earth. One, two, three.

We will work with this figure in future chapters when we begin the process of bringing our thought power to 50,000 arcans, which is a level that will bring meaningful power to manifest that image. This is our mission and yours: Bring this higher, evolutionary being into manifestation on Earth — the only way this planet can be saved.

Chapter 19

Spiritual Symmetry and Starseed Activation

Juliano and the Arcturians

Throughout the entire universe, all physical and spiritual laws work the same — in symmetry. Physics and the laws of gravity are operational no matter where you are, including the planet you are on and the galaxy you inhabit. For example, an apple falling from a tree conforms to the laws of gravity known as Newton's laws. This is true on Earth as well as on all Earth-like planets in the Andromeda galaxy, or any other galaxy in the universe. Symmetry means that there is sameness throughout the universe.

Symmetry also exists spiritually and in different dimensions. You might think of each dimension as separate, having its own rules and regulations. This is partially true. To access the fifth dimension, you have to attain a higher level of vibration and a higher level of consciousness; you cannot enter when dominated by lower feelings such as jealousy, hatred, or competition. Nonetheless, there are complementary and symmetrical characteristics across dimensions.

The laws of spiritual attraction work on both the third and fifth dimensions: Your thoughts and the energy you emanate attract energies in alignment with you. There is, however, one significant difference: On the fifth dimension, the law of attraction is immediate. On the third, the law of attraction is slower, due to the density of the third dimension. This delay is for your own protection. The third dimension is geared toward your learning experience.

At time, you have dense thoughts that are of a lower vibration.

This is a normal part of being on the third dimension. Fortunately, not all of what you think of on the third dimension comes to be, and what you are attracted to does not always come to you. Things may come to you in a delayed fashion, giving you time to ponder and meditate on whether you really want them. The third dimension is like a school, preparing you to enter the fifth dimension.

Once you are on the fifth dimension, you can immediately interact with those you want to attract, hence the importance of prior training. This includes refining your thinking through meditation and experiencing denser energies so as to learn to make decisions not to attract them.

Symmetry throughout the dimensions means that the laws of attraction on the third dimension exist on the fifth dimension. There are other interesting symmetrical relationships shared by all dimensions. Your experience on the third dimension will be of great assistance when you enter the fifth dimension. You will be thankful to have gone through various trials and tribulations in attracting and rejecting energies.

The Symmetry of Manifestation

One of the symmetrical aspects of both the third and fifth dimensions concerns higher consciousness. Higher (or expanded) consciousness includes the ability to see and experience the unity of all things, and the true nature of all reality (including holographic interactions). The work in all dimensions focuses on how consciousness manifests reality.

On the fifth dimension, what and how you think are manifested immediately. If you wanted to manifest an Arcturian temple or a special spiritual group focusing on temple work, then you would immediately have that experience and be with those like-minded starseeds. Like all committed and concerned starseeds, you are interested and involved in planetary healing and planetary balancing.

You engage in exercises, and you are working to manifest a higher consciousness and higher movement toward rebalancing Earth and bringing fifth-dimensional light to this planet. It is not manifesting as quickly as you want. I am sure you are all aware of resistances to consciousness change and of consciousness's role in manifestation.

Currently (as well as historically), there is an effort to control your consciousness. This has been seen in the twentieth century through the mass movements called Fascism and Nazism. The idea was to manipulate people through controlling their consciousnesses. There are many significant examples in history of controlling consciousness, including government use of communication tools such as mass media. This occurs through news outlets and advertising.

Some of you may say this sounds like a conspiracy, that there's a group of people behind the scenes trying to control what you think and what you do. How do you make the distinction between reality/factual occurrence and fantasy? This issue is part of mass consciousness, as seen in the concept of fake news. This implies that the people who are trying to control your consciousness can make you doubt the reality of a thought you perceive as true. This is evident in controversies regarding climate change and environmental pollution.

Denying climate change is one of the most significant examples of consciousness control. One group says there is nothing to worry about, it is not real, and everything is normal. Another side says we are in a crisis and humankind is destroying the biosphere.

Mass Extinction Events

Earth is experiencing mass extinction. There have been five mass extinctions, some of them well known. The most famous occurred approximately 65 million years ago when an asteroid hit what is now the Yucatán Peninsula, which caused the end of the dinosaurs. That mass extinction led to the elevation of mammals, which were then able to control the planet, and to human domination. The destruction of hundreds of species made room for the emergence of higher beings, who now control the environment. If it had not been for the asteroid hitting the planet, mammals, particularly humans, would not have been able to emerge and successfully propagate.

Each mass extinction had different characteristics. Approximately 250 million years ago, it was weather-induced, by ice. There are climate cycles that lead to extreme conditions and thus mass extinctions. There are similarities, perhaps even symmetry, between each mass extinction. They usually involve harsh environments in which living species can no longer survive. The harshness could be due to ice resulting from freezing temperatures or chemicals from volcanic ash, destroying all living plants and animals.

Nowadays, there is great resistance to awareness of the sixth mass extinction. There are many reasons for this, including greed and desire to maintain control of resources for personal gain. In our planetary work, there is a great need to change consciousness to a more realistic perception of the danger of this mass extinction. This is different from other mass extinctions, because it is being caused by one species: humans. The dinosaurs did not cause their own demise. An external force caused it, and the others were due to Earth events and changes. Humans are causing this mass extinction, and they are capable of killing the entire biosphere. This means there would be no life for millions of years or even longer.

Following the mass extinction of the dinosaurs, 10 percent of the life forms survived. In the mass extinction caused by humanity, there could be less than 10 percent. There might be only 1 percent, which means a slower recovery. You, as starseeds, want to prevent this, and you are doing your best to preserve the planet and the biosphere. How can a small group of starseeds change the consciousness of the planet, encouraging people to act differently and respond in an appropriate way to this crisis?

Unity Consciousness through First Contact

Everyone knows that consciousness exists and that you have consciousness, yet it is extremely difficult to define. It is not a measurable phenomenon. There is no weight to consciousness; there is no tangible force that you can measure. Consciousness is the one factor that distinguishes humans from other animals. Other animals have a small degree of consciousness but not the heightened consciousness of humanity.

There are momentary events that bring the world together in consciousness. For example, 9/11 was a terrible tragedy, yet it brought a unique, very powerful unity consciousness for a short time. Unfortunately, that consciousness was not used correctly, and it led to further war and destruction instead of a unity of brotherhood and sisterhood.

One of the goals of planetary healers is to bring forth a unity of consciousness that would also manifest planetary balance and healing. Mass sports events, such as the Super Bowl or the World Soccer Cup, bring forth a unity consciousness, everyone focusing on a single event. This is not, however, being used for planetary benefit.

Finally, and most interestingly, there are charismatic leaders who seem to be able to bring forth a focus of consciousness, often described as messianic. There have been claims of a false prophet arising on Earth who will attract and unite many people. Fascism also relies on a charismatic figure able to mold the consciousness of people and then use this charisma for personal evil.

As starseeds, we hope that a mystical or charismatic event or person can arise who will unify humanity's consciousness for good. One possible event has been described as first contact with a higher dimensional being. First contact with a higher dimensional being may be used for healing Earth. Arcturian, Pleiadian, or other higher beings would make themselves known on Earth, which would immediately unify the consciousness of the world.

Several movies explore this theme. Among the most notable is *The Day the Earth Stood Still* [1951]. In this movie, a higher being comes to Earth and tries to get humans to change their ways. As a warning sign, he stops Earth's rotation, immobilizing everything for a short period of time. Interference in Earth's rotation causes a unified consciousness. This movie does not, however, suggest how this could change humanity.

Resistance to Change

There is a resistance to changing consciousness. You, as starseeds and planetary healers, have encountered this. The attempt to change consciousness is comparable to religious conversion. Some religious people proselytize, attempting to change peoples' religious beliefs. Many of you have had the experience of someone knocking on your door and trying to persuade you to change your religious consciousness and join their religious group, stating that they hold the truth. This is problematic, but it also demonstrates some important points: Firstly, there are people who are working to change your consciousness. Secondly, you can resist them. This is wise, since their beliefs are quite likely more rigid and more dense than would be appropriate for you. This suggests that you resist changing to a lower level of consciousness. Surprisingly, people throughout the planet also resist changing to a higher level of consciousness.

The resistance to going to a lower level is beneficial. You may have personally experienced entering a room where people of lower consciousness are, and you might decide to leave the room because you do not want to be around them. People of lower consciousness experience a similar resistance to higher consciousness. One of the spiritual laws regarding balance of consciousness is this: If you have a higher consciousness and a lower consciousness enters, it will either rise to you, or you will descend to its level.

You most likely have experienced this balance of consciousness in your personal relationships. Of course, one option is to disengage or not be involved in this type of interaction. However, disengagement may not work in favor of changing planetary consciousness. One of the keys to planetary change is working with peoples' resistance to change.

Unfortunately, we are now seeing a historical polarization on this planet. Each side becomes more encamped and more resistant to the other side. This is not good news, since polarizations can lead to wars and other external conflicts. There is a prediction that the polarizing events coming in 2020 will lead to more dissent and more conflict.

My proposal for changing planetary consciousness more effectively is this: We need to work together to activate starseeds. The goal of changing consciousness may not work if we try to change those who are already polarized and who already deny the gravity of the situation. How many times have you confronted people who are "climate deniers" or who deny the sixth mass extinction and planetary crisis? How many times have you met people who say, "Oh, you are right, the Arcturians are right, this planet is in danger. I am ready to accept unity consciousness and holographic energy, and I am ready to become a planetary healer"? I would guess it rarely or never occurs, especially when you consider that the resistance to changing planetary consciousness is becoming stronger among those who are already polarized.

Remember, there is resistance to higher consciousness, just like you have resistance to lower consciousness. You want to use your energy in a way that will have the most positive effect on planetary healing. I suggest the way to manifest the planetary healing experience on a mass level is through working to activate unawakened starseeds and, in particular, young unawakened starseeds.

Starseed Activation on Earth

What does the activation of starseeds involve? There are many starseeds on this planet, but many of them are sleeping. Many of them have not come into their awareness. Some are on drugs; some are living in repressed societies in the Middle East, Africa, Russia, the United States, Australia, or New Zealand. To activate them would require awakening and nurturing what is already in them: the seed of higher consciousness.

What is a starseed? What does it mean to be a starseed? The traditional definition of a starseed is a man or woman who has had a lifetime on another planet. Traditionally, starseeds have been on higher planets such as the Pleiades or Arcturus, or perhaps they came from one of the higher Sirian planets, the Andromeda galaxy or Antares. Some starseeds incarnated on Earth. Some of these starseeds have also seen this planetary drama now occurring on Earth in other parts of the galaxy. There have been planets destroyed within our galaxy because they could not resolve this polarization and ended in self-destruction. Now there is a danger of self-destruction on Earth.

I expand the concept of starseeds to include people who have had higher consciousness in their lifetimes on Earth and who have interacted (on Earth) with higher beings, such as those from other planetary systems. There are starseeds of higher consciousness who have stayed on Earth and reincarnated on Earth. Fortunately, they have had extradimensional experiences on Earth in previous lifetimes.

In some cases, these starseeds were instructed by higher dimensional or extraterrestrial beings. They have traveled on the ships of these starbeings, and in some cases, they were even transported to the planets where the visitors came from. They had extensive instructions and education in the nature of the galaxy and the nature of galactic anthropology and the history of planetary development. Therefore, they have a significant connection to these higher beings. Many sleeping starseeds also fall into this category. We want to activate them. We want to awaken them and have them use their experiences and thought power to contribute to the new planetary consciousness.

You may recall a theoretical experiment in which an anthropologist taught one monkey how to wash his food, and after 100 monkeys learned the same technique, all the monkeys exhibited the same behavior without being instructed. In this experiment, there was a manifest shift (the monkeys washing their food). The success of the experiment is apparent. Consciousness, however, is not as easily measurable.

Applying this experiment to consciousness: if there are 1,600 powerful Arcturian starseeds meditating and doing specific exercises, those 1,600 could activate a similar effect. This would activate thousands, if not more, starseeds to an awakening and movement for planetary change. Measuring the effect of 1,600 Arcturian starseeds meditations is difficult, because there is not an observable event. The only measurement might be an increase in the number of planetary healers, with more people participating in our exercises with you. There would be more people addressing climate problems, writing about it in newspapers and the media. There would be more protests and more signs, as well as the traditional means of controlling consciousness. There would be more successful efforts by those who are awakening.

Starseed Activation Meditation

> Let us begin the mediation to activate unawakened starseeds. We are gathered today to bring our consciousness together to focus our energy on activating those starseeds who are sleeping or repressed.
>
> Take three deep breaths. Feel the unity with the Arcturians and the Arcturian brotherhood and sisterhood energy. This healing energy gives you greater thought power and an ability to activate change throughout the planet. Feel and allow your spirit body to rise out of your physical body, allow it to drift upward to the top of the room, and then watch it travel further upward to the great halo around Earth known as the ring of ascension.

You are now in this wonderful, physical ring of ascension. Remember that the ascension is also considered a planetary event that will create an awakening of consciousness. You are now sitting in a huge circle in the ring of ascension around Earth. This ring of ascension has the energy of ascension in it, and you are feeling the wonderful light of ascension. [Tones.]

Let the light of ascension fill your spirit body, bringing you heightened, expanded consciousness and a great feeling of healing and well-being of connecting to all of the Arcturian starseeds in our group. As you look around, you notice that this ring of ascension is huge, and you and I and the other starseeds meditating with us only make up a small proportion of the available space within the ring. There is room for many more starseeds from Earth.

I, Juliano, send out the call from the ring of ascension to all starseeds who need to be awakened to join us in the ring of ascension. This is the affirmation: "Unawakened starseeds, join us now in the ring of ascension." Please meditate on that powerful affirmation. We will go into silence. [Silence.]

"Unawakened starseeds, please join us now in the ring of ascension." This powerful ring of ascension is emitting an activation energy. Remember that the ascended masters are with us in the ring of ascension. There is a symmetry between the ascended masters and the Earth beings, and the ascended masters want to activate the unawakened starseeds. [Tones.] The call is going out; the energy is being sent to awaken and activate all unawakened starseeds. "You are needed now, unawakened starseeds. Come together and join this movement for bringing higher consciousness to planet Earth." We will go into silence. [Silence.]

As you meditate, feel the healing light coming from this ring of ascension. It purifies your body on all levels. It increases the arcan power of your thoughts, their effectiveness and power to manifest in the third dimension. You are unique in your abilities because you are living in the third dimension, and you are open to your multidimensional light.

[Tones.] So this activation shall be. The power of the call has been sent out.

Now slowly begin the descent back into your physical body, leaving the ring of ascension, knowing you can return anytime you need to. Return to the room at 6 feet above your physical body and enter your physical body in perfect alignment, bringing the light of the ring of ascension into your physical body. [Tones.]

It is a great service you are doing to help in the awakening of the unawakened starseeds. I am Juliano. Good day.

Chapter 20

Raise Your Frequency to Connect with Other Starseeds

Juliano and the Arcturians

"Resonant response frequency" is a term used in vibrational energy work, spiritual meditations, and ascension work. Learning about this term can help you integrate concepts in the new physics with your spiritual development. Resonant response frequency refers to the particular vibration that resonates with your core self.

Each person has a core frequency. You have probably noticed that some of you have a lower core frequency while others have one that is higher. There are also hidden frequencies you respond to that are not in your normal consciousness.

If you are in the presence of an ascended master and they begin to emit a frequency of light that you resonate with, you will manifest a resonant response frequency. This frequency, this vibration, is part of your whole soul makeup. The higher frequency from an ascended master activates within you.

"Resonation" or "resonate" means that two frequencies align or are close to each other. They can be close in terms of quarters, halves, or full waves, as opposed to unequal or odd waves, such as five-eighths, three-fifths, or one-fifths. In the terminology of the new physics and radio and electronic magnetic propagation, frequencies in tune with each other usually have symmetrical numerical values, such as twos, fours, sixes, and eights. Therefore, it is easier for someone to resonate with a frequency that is in its numerical categorization and divisible in a similar numerical order.

What I call the "hidden resonant response frequency" is important in your work to activate other starseeds. Many people have resonant frequencies of higher energy, but they are still asleep and unawakened. They will respond to activation energy if you activate their hidden response frequency. Once they hear, and are influenced by, someone emitting this higher vibration, they can awaken and be activated.

I am sure that, at this time on the planet, we all agree it is time for all starseeds to awaken. The most effective response frequency that all starseeds resonate with could come from a first contact — an extraterrestrial or higher-dimensional being who has the knowledge and ability to issue a frequency that can awaken everyone.

Your Global Resonance Determines Where You Incarnate

Global resonance response frequency is the energy contained in the concept of the messiah and messianic light. Part of the idea of the messiah is that this beautiful, energetic person will know how to immediately fix the unsolvable problems confronting humanity. The messianic person will also know how to emit a frequency that the entire global community can respond to, meaning that even those who are polarized and of lower consciousness will be raised to a higher frequency. Those of lower consciousness would require a special activation energy.

This leads me to the vibrational characteristics of humanity and Earth. Each planet in this galaxy has a vibrational resonant frequency, which means, according to the laws of spiritual energy, that you are attracted to and incarnate on a planet that is in alignment with your resonant frequency. Earth, then, is in alignment with you and your frequency; you were attracted to and chose to come to this planet.

You are working to shift or raise your resonant response frequency so that you can enter the fifth dimension. You chose Earth because the necessary experiences are available here to prepare and train you for your fifth-dimensional entry into higher realms.

This idea is shocking to many. "Why do I have to be here?" you might ask. "I am ready to leave this planet immediately. I do not want to go through these Earth experiences." My response is that you worked hard in your soul journey and soul review to come to Earth. On a soul level, you knew you would find the experiences necessary to raise your soul frequency. You knew vibrations would be available on Earth that you would resonate with and be able to use to elevate your core soul frequency.

The concept of the resonant response frequency ties in beautifully with ascension, because ascension represents a new frequency and vibration. You do not have to be at the fifth-dimensional level to resonate and respond to that ascension frequency. Remember, I explained that your frequency might be a half or a fourth of the total response of the primary frequency. As long as you are in a vibrational and numerical harmonic balance with ascension energy, then you can resonate with it.

It is easiest to resonate with ascension when you are around an ascended master who issues the frequency so that you can respond and feel that energy. But when you are activated for ascension, you can easily respond. There are four primary core personal and planetary frequencies. First is the core frequency of Earth. Second is the core frequency of Arcturus. Third is the core frequency of ascension. Fourth is the core frequency of the ascended masters. Other planets in this galaxy and planets in other galaxies have different resonant frequencies. That means planets in the Andromeda galaxy have different core frequencies than might be available on Earth.

You Are Like a Radio Receiver

Everything — all planets, plants, and animals — vibrate at specific frequencies. Your soul group vibrates at a particular frequency. When you meet people who are in, or close to, your soul group, you resonate with them. Naturally, you want to seek out people who are at your same core frequency. These observations relate to the new physics, because the principles of vibration, frequency, resonating, and being in harmonic balance with others of similar frequencies, are explained similarly in the subatomic or quantum world.

Frequency waves are explained in the theory of electromagnetic radiation and radio waves. The analogy of radio waves can help explain how to improve your ability to resonate with higher frequencies and to protect yourself. When you are in a higher frequency and the experience is new for you, you want to protect yourself so that you are not "brought down" by lower frequencies. A person who is trained and has higher mastery can maintain their higher frequency even in the face of lower energy.

People sensitive to energies are called empaths. They feel other people's energies and are dramatically affected by them. Empaths might not have the proper shielding to protect themselves from low-level energy. Lower beings — especially in the lower fourth dimension — are intruding on Earth now. These are sometimes called ghosts or lower spirits, and many want to attach to you and bring you down to a lower level. There are various ways of dealing with this and of protecting yourself, including using crystals, special stones, and guardian angels for protection. Low spirits cannot tolerate high energy, so it is important to know how to hold a higher energy.

Radio technology has advanced dramatically over the past 100 years, including the development of more sensitive receivers and better signal-to-noise ratios. It is also better at isolating different frequencies on a crowded radio spectrum. Even with the most sophisticated receiver, you still have to know how to tune to the frequency you want, and that requires training, knowledge, and special skills in receiving operations. You need the skill to hold a frequency and weed out or block interfering frequencies.

With personal frequencies, lower spirits might interfere. People you live with or your neighbors could interfere with your frequencies. These interfering energies or frequencies can block your receptivity and sensitivity, which mean you might not be able to focus and receive the higher energies you wish.

I want to make something very clear: You really have to be very sensitive to receive higher light and higher energy. The most obvious reason is the way Western (modern) society has trained you to use your brain and receptivity.

The reticular activating system is a neurological system in the base of the brain. It controls what you are attentive to, and it can be programmed. For example, a new mother wants to be attentive to her baby. If she is in a deep sleep and the baby suddenly cries, the reticular activating system helps her immediately wake up and attend to the baby. Another noise, such as a television, does not wake her up. This is a good example, because it shows that you can train your brain which frequency you want to attune to.

In your case as a starseed and an ascension student, you want to sensitize yourself as much as possible to the new light and frequencies coming in from the fifth dimension. This requires some programming in your brain's reticular activating system, so that you can filter out signals and noises that are not relevant.

Returning to the example of the mother and child, you might think for the mother to hear her child, it has to cry loudly. But even a small cry is enough for her wakeful filtering system to pick up the information and distress from the child.

In other examples of empathic reception, we find that, telepathically, you can receive signals from people at great distances from you. This is truly amazing. Think about the sensitivity of radio receivers. One was built in 1950 and another was built in 2019. The one from 2019 has all the latest computer software, and it can pick up signals with greater clarity than the 1950 receiver built without advanced computer technology.

Like today's radios, there is specific "software" that you can download into your brain to increase your sensitivity. You also have ways to become more attuned with the resonant frequencies of people close to you and to ascended masters. You can strengthen your resonant response frequency to other higher spiritual masters.

Strengthen Your Sensitivity to Response Frequencies

The mother and child is an example of instinctual response programming. The mother does not have to train herself to hear her child, because it is part of the DNA programming in her reticular activating system. The mother is automatically, intuitively, and empathically connected to her child, and this occurs in part because she carried the child for nine months. We are talking now about establishing a sensitivity to ascension frequencies, to higher spiritual frequencies, and even to the frequencies of telepathic communication with ascended masters throughout the galaxy.

There are a number of ways you can strengthen your sensitivity to the response frequencies. The first is to be around people who share your interests and abilities to connect with higher frequencies. The second method is to read books about masters and study higher frequencies or higher masters' writings. Some of you might find the motivation to raise your frequency response by reading the Bible, the Bhagavad Gita, the Book of Tao, or other channeled material. Studying the lives of Jesus or the Buddha are other examples.

We support spiritual studies; we support reading books about spirituality and meditating on spiritual matters. We also support programming crystals with spiritual light and going to power spots or sacred spots around the planet. These sacred spots hold the frequency vibrations of higher energy. An example is the Dome of the Rock in Jerusalem. This is the place where the Israelites built the first temple on the rock, which was eventually destroyed. It is the place where it is believed that Abraham was to sacrifice Isaac, and in the Muslim religion where Abraham was to sacrifice his son Ishmael.

Other sacred places include Stonehenge in England, the Black Hills of North Dakota, and power spots in the area of Sedona, Arizona, such as Bell Rock. We could continue to name places throughout the world that hold spiritual light. The point is that when you visit these places, you train yourself to become more receptive to receiving higher spiritual vibrations.

Overcome Societal Blocks to Resonance

Think about telepathic energy and telepathic communication, and think about remote viewing or remote energy work. The idea is that you must have intense concentration to receive this energy, and you must open up a part of your brain that you don't normally use. This leads me to the concept of shamanistic training, because shamanistic training often begins at a very young age.

The person who is to become a shaman must have the telepathic ability to communicate with spirits and other worlds. The neural pathways of very young people are more open for developing the sensitivity necessary for telepathy. It is still possible to become a shaman at an older age, but certain neurological blocks have to be overcome.

Remember that Western society and cultural training do not encourage extradimensional or higher-dimensional connections. You are trained for computer connections and smartphone connections. You have to overcome a number of blocks to be sensitive to your resonant response frequencies. I think it is amazing that many of you have attuned to these higher spiritual frequencies because the Western world contains a great deal of density and blockages toward higher-dimensional energy.

I am frequently asked: "What about the 5G electromagnetic radiation coming from fifth-generation smartphones?" There is a lot of discussion about how 5G energies might harm your aura. It does have that potential, but there are ways you can integrate those energies using special techniques. Because 5G is at a higher frequency than 4G (going from 800 gigahertz to 1,200 or 1,500 gigahertz), it comes closer to the frequencies on the telepathic energy wavelength. My concern is that being around 5G without protection can influence and block some of your sensitive telepathic abilities and your abilities to receive higher energy from the fifth dimension.

Spiritual frequencies are at a high frequency level. The speed of thought is faster than the speed of light. At the speed of thought, you can go to places around this galaxy instantaneously. You cannot travel instantaneously to other parts of the galaxy at the speed of light — that would take hundreds or thousands of years.

In summary, you can do certain exercises — including being around higher spiritually minded people, reading spiritual books, using crystals, and going to sacred places — to enhance your ability to receive the highest-level spiritual energies. You can program yourself to receive spiritual signals in the midst of all the noise around you. But before we get into that exercise, I want to talk more about protecting yourself.

Protect Yourself from Low Energy

One of the ways you can protect yourself is by withdrawing from negative energy. You might have reached the conclusion that, as hard as you try, you cannot seem to protect yourself from low-energy vibrations. One of the main defenses you can use is to withdraw from that energy, if possible. This was practiced in ancient times. People in training to become ascended masters would go into caves where they had control over what frequencies they were exposed to, and this made it easier to only focus on higher light.

This is a good technique, but withdrawing into a cave does not work in this modern age. There are probably not that many caves available, and we need you lightworkers interacting with society. One interesting ascension practice is being involved in the world in some way, which is different than in ancient times. You could be so enlightened that you could be in the middle of New York's Times Square and still hold higher energy and light. That is not a goal for your work, but a metaphor of being able to be in this world and hold fifth-dimensional energy. In this ascension work, we encourage you to be part of this world, so no withdrawing into a cave. Sorry!

Be as sensitive as possible to ascension energies. Look at all the different energies around you, such as many different spiritual groups. Focus on a specific, ascending, higher frequency. Train yourself for that. The ascension experience is a frequency or energy vibration. Train yourself to be on the resonant frequency of ascension.

When somebody gives you information or ideas about ascension or they lead discussions about it, be receptive. Ultimately, we are talking about a sound emission that sets up the resonant frequency vibration for ascension. Sometimes the sound has been referred to as Gabriel's horn or trumpet. Hearing this sound is so intense that it is enough to send you into the vibrational ascension state.

You do not have to be at the higher state of that original frequency, but you do have to be in harmonic balance or a complementary state. So when you hear that frequency, you will be immediately elevated.

Some people might doubt whether or not they can ascend. I am sure you have heard these arguments: "I am not good enough." "I have not reached the spiritual level where I need to be." "I have not completed all my karma, therefore I cannot ascend." People offer many excuses about why they cannot ascend or why they are not ready to ascend. My point is that you can ascend as long as you are in the resonant frequency range of the vibrational energy of ascension.

It is interesting that the ascension sound has never been reproduced and will not be reproduced until actual ascension. At the same time, when you hear that ascension vibration, you will immediately know what it is. The Arcturians have also offered many exercises to sensitize you to vibrations and frequency responses, including the shimmering and cosmic-egg exercises [provided in David's books (see LightTechnology.com) and his many articles (see SedonaJournal.com)].

Shimmering Exercise

1. Visualize your aura in the shape of a cosmic egg.
2. See a blue line around your aura, which is also egg-shaped.
3. See the blue line vibrate rapidly.
4. Once the vibration, or pulsing, of the line of the aura reaches a certain speed, your aura starts to shimmer.

If you reach a high enough speed, onlookers would see your physical body flicker in and out of this reality, because you are vibrating so rapidly.

The shimmering exercise accomplishes many things, including healing and helping you bilocate and thought-project. Did you know that shimmering can also help sensitize you more to higher frequencies? By shimmering, you are improving your sensitivity to fifth-dimensional frequencies. You want you to be as receptive and sensitive as possible.

Reticular Activating System Meditation

The following meditation is intended to reprogram or deepen the program in your reticular activating system so that you can become more sensitive to higher spiritual vibrations, especially the spiritual vibrations of ascension.

Take three deep breaths. Become aware of your brain and your brain stem, which extends down from the back of your brain. You are now in your mind, which is an energy field that interacts energetically above the brain. The mind transcends the brain. You can look at your mind as the operator and the brain as the computer.

Visualize and go to the area in the brain stem called the reticular activating system, which is a group of neurons. This system can be imagined as computer chips inside a computer. There is no on-off switch that you can see, and like with higher computer boards, everything is molded together and streamlined. The mind can go anywhere, so direct it to go to the reticular activating system.

When you are there, say a friendly "Hello," the same as if you were visiting your heart, kidneys, or lungs. Just say, "Hello, I am here today to interact with you. I am here to download a new program and to expand an existing program in your realm." Ask for permission from your higher self and brain to strengthen that program.

Now repeat this download: "I am opening my reticular activating system to become more sensitive to fifth-dimensional energies on all levels. I am downloading instructions to my reticular activating system to be open to fifth-dimensional energies on all levels." You can reformulate the affirmation however it suits you.

Let the words of this affirmation transfer into your reticular activating system as special instructions. You only need to say: "I am now downloading these new instructions into my reticular activating system." At the count of three, it is being downloaded. You are now more deeply and strongly sensitized to all fifth-dimensional energies coming into the planet.

Let this new affirmation be firmly downloaded into your reticular activating system, making you more sensitive to your empathic abilities. You will become receptive and more sensitive on all levels; this includes the ability to communicate with other starseeds.

Spiritual Energy Is Available to You

I know that many of you feel alone and disconnected from other starseeds. By doing this activation, you are going to communicate more with those who might be in your area. You are going to find greater ways to connect to existing people in a group, and to spiritual energies around the planet. Many spiritual lightworkers and spiritual forces are transmitting to Earth.

Despite all the polarization and destruction you see, please remember that tremendous spiritual energy is being downloaded now to Earth. By doing this activation and downloading today, you will be more receptive and better able to integrate and receive all spiritual energies coming from the fifth dimension. And so it shall be.

I am Juliano. Good day.

Chapter 21

Explore the Arcturian Stargate

Juliano and the Arcturians

We will now explore the stargate in more depth and explain how maintaining and overseeing it relates to our roles as helpers of Earth. This is a time of great change, evolution, and possibilities for soul advancement on Earth. We Arcturians have come here to work with you on many levels, including through dreams, channelings, and, when possible, helping accelerate your karmic lessons and karmic problems. We cannot assume or take away your karma, but we can assist you in many ways.

The stargate is located in the fifth-dimensional Arcturian star system, and it is one of two or three stargates in this galaxy. Each stargate serves a particular sector of the galaxy. Because of our spiritual advancement, dedication, and desire to serve, we Arcturians have been chosen by the Galactic Council to be the overseers and guardians of this stargate. This has some important ramifications. Other third-dimensional planets are advancing like yours and have starseeds who will also use the stargate. These planets are in proximity to the stargate and to Earth, although I realize "proximity" is a relative term due of the great distances involved. Just remember there are more advanced ways of traveling through the galaxy than traditional propulsion systems.

We are happy to be the guardians and maintainers of this stargate. It is like a transport switching or sending system and can be compared to a large railroad station. When you walk through a station, signs direct you to tracks that lead to different cities. When you come to the stargate, you have a choice where you are going, but it is not like hopping on a train and going to another dimension or planet. The stargate requires many intermediate steps. Guides and teachers offer training, practice sessions, and education classes. You can review your life on Earth and meet and talk with your guides and teachers. With their input, you can make decisions about your future and the best place for you to go.

The Learning and Processing Center

From this perspective, the stargate is more than just a transfer station. It is a learning and processing center. You can spend a great deal of time at the stargate, and that is perfectly acceptable. In fact, coming to the stargate is such a high and wonderful experience that many want to stay and take advantage of the learning opportunities. You might also enjoy meeting and learning from the many beings who come to the stargate from other third-dimensional star systems in this sector of the galaxy. Some deal with planetary issues similar to those on Earth. Representatives from well-known planetary systems on the fifth dimension, including Pleiadians, Arcturians, and beings from Alano, also come to the stargate. You have the opportunity to interact with and learn from these higher and more-advanced beings.

This explains, in part, why we Arcturians are involved with Earth and reaching out to Earth beings. Part of our mission is to help prepare the way for starseeds to take full advantage of the stargate. It is important that we introduce the concept of the stargate before you come to the stargate system, because you have preparation and work to accomplish. Even for a starseed, it is too much to expect that you would immediately come to this stargate upon ascension or transition.

I often use the terms conscious transformation or conscious ascension. When you are in such a dramatic and highly charged situation as a transformation, which might be the death state, you want to remain as conscious as possible for as long as possible before your actual moment of transition. It is probably more critical for the ascension transition that you maintain the highest possible state of awareness. When you are in actual transitioning energy, you can consciously direct yourself to the fifth-dimensional stargate or to any higher realm or higher place you choose.

As a potential participant in the stargate, it is important that you choose to graduate and leave Earth's orbit or energy field so you do not go to a fourth-dimensional realm, even a higher fourth-dimensional realm. You want to direct yourself beyond the karmic field of Earth. Once you go through the stargate, you are free of all karmic attachments to Earth. This is why you want previous knowledge of the stargate and to prepare for that journey. You must acknowledge that you are prepared to graduate from Earth, you do not want to return to Earth, and you want to connect with your starseed abilities and heritage. You also want to be in a position to enter higher realms, namely fifth-dimensional realms.

This is a spiritual accomplishment; it is a spiritual advancement and a sign of spiritual evolution. Not everyone is capable or eligible to come to the stargate. As part of your training as an Earth being, I introduce the concept of the stargate, which is overwhelming without previous knowledge and discussion; you might not understand or cope with the demands of the stargate without preparation.

Advanced Spiritual Vibration

One issue that always comes up is the advanced energy, the advanced spiritual vibration, necessary to enter the stargate. I have introduced the concept of the spiritual light quotient (SLQ), which relates to your spiritual vibration and your ability to understand spiritual concepts. In addition, your spiritual light quotient vibrational frequency (SLQVF) has to be at a certain heightened, vibrational speed. You cannot pass through the stargate unless you vibrate at this higher frequency.

We often do preparation journeys to the stargate with our third-dimensional trainees, such as yourselves. When we bring you to the stargate, we caution that you cannot go through it while you are in an Earth incarnational body. One reason is that when you pass through the stargate, all karmic ties with Earth are terminated. We do not take on your karma, and therefore we cannot allow you to go through the stargate while you are in this incarnation unless you are ascending or transitioning in another way to our system.

But it is still beneficial to practice going to the entrance of the stargate and feeling its vibrational frequency. Also, I am allowed to open the doorway of the stargate a small amount, allowing you to experience the heightened light frequency and attraction; you are naturally attracted to the higher stargate energy and being in this great experience. You are preparing and working toward this transition in a most positive way. I am happy for you to receive this higher information and higher knowledge. You need mental information about what a stargate is, why you want to go to the stargate, and what you can expect to experience once you're there.

You have choices to make once you are at the stargate. One choice is which fifth-dimensional planet you want to go to. You might say, "Well, I want to go back to my home planet." Some have even told me they want to be an ascended master on Earth. Maybe you want to work as a prophet or a high ascended being on another third-dimensional planet in this sector of the galaxy. The best advice I can give you is to not make any decisions about where you are going until you arrive at the stargate. Perspective and information are everything in spiritual practice. You do not yet have all the information you need to make that decision now.

There are many unknowns and things happening on Earth that seem unexplainable. Many of these things are a direct result of the sixth mass extinction. Remember that the mass extinction affects everything. It affects weather patterns, ocean currents, and even your mood. It affects the energy field of the entire planet. Attempts are being made to understand why this is happening, including why certain groups control parts of the planet and why people behave badly and destroy the environment.

Someone coined the word "ecocide," which is similar to suicide or genocide. Ecocide refers to the activities of people who are purposely destroying the environment and making a terrible planetary situation even worse. The point is that you do not have all the information to understand the complexity of what is occurring, and that includes karmic complexity. I have often referred to the situation on Earth as a cosmic drama. A multitude of different energies, sources, and groups have come to Earth and are contributing to this cosmic drama. When you come to the stargate, you will have all the information, which is important and relative to your soul journey.

Your Soul Journey

This is a good time to introduce the important concept of your soul journey. Being on Earth, you are part of a greater soul journey that has lasted for eons, and you are now in a wonderful position to graduate/ascend and go into the stargate. Not everyone is able to go to the stargate. You must be able to graduate from the third dimension, which requires mental, emotional, and spiritual advancement.

Some of you have doubts and believe you are not good enough to ascend. You might think you have not resolved all of your karmic problems or that the stargate is for other people. You might feel a sense of despair and disappointment, or that you want to give up because you have not accomplished enough spiritually. I assure you this is not true. If you understand the concept of the stargate — how it is a transformational center and how you can go to other realms from there — then you are capable of going there. You have the spiritual light-quotient-frequency vibration ability to enter the stargate.

We are fulfilling our mission when we explain the stargate to you. We have come here to bring you knowledge and to introduce you to the stargate. If you understand what I am talking about, then you can go there — it is that simple. If people who are not starseeds start reading this information, they will not understand it and stop reading. They will not want to pursue the concepts of the stargate, because they cannot grasp the idea of what a stargate is and how you can go there.

Remember, the stargate is in the area of the Arcturus star system. The stargate is fifth-dimensional and has multiple functions. First, it serves as a transformational center that directs people to different portals that lead to planetary systems or dimensions. It also serves as an education and healing center, especially for those who don't feel advanced enough.

We are allowed to bring you through the stargate even if you believe you are not spiritually perfect enough. You might think this is taking on your karma, but it is not. As overseers of the stargate, we identify and work with many different starseeds. Some starseeds receive direct channelings while others receive visions and dream images. Some starseeds do not have any direct psychic or prophetic interactions with us or other higher beings. But if we believe you are moving in the right direction, have the right mindset, and have the spiritual light quotient to understand the concepts we are teaching, then we have the authority to bring you into the stargate. That would explain why those of you who do not feel advanced enough can still participate and enter the stargate. Once we bring you through the gate and we meet you there, we can direct you to the correct and necessary healing and educational training sessions. These sessions bring you up to the spiritual level you need.

The stargate is an accelerated experience and an accelerated chamber. While on Earth, you might need three or four lifetimes and many years of education and training to make spiritual advancements. It is not like that at the stargate. The stargate is accelerated and time is fifth dimensional. We work with you and help you make miraculous advancements in your spiritual and vibrational work that would probably not be possible on Earth. In comparison to the stargate, Earth is in slow motion, even though Earth is accelerating now. On Earth you would look at yourself and think, "Do I have to become like a Buddha or a Christ to ascend? I only have ten, fifteen, or twenty years left. How am I going to accomplish this?"

Advancement is slow on Earth, especially when you consider the stress of living on a planet going through dramatic changes. A polarized planet experiencing so much destruction to its biosphere is not the ideal place for spiritual advancement. If I were to say which planet is best for spiritual advancement, I would not choose one going through a mass extinction. I doubt you would choose that, either. You would want a planet ruled or directed by spiritual masters and teachers. You would want to live on a planet that does not have polarization and is free of disease and planetary catastrophes.

You are karmically involved with this planet and have been so for many lifetimes. Also, despite all the polarization and catastrophes, great opportunities for soul advancement exist on Earth. Here, you have free will. You can choose to start wars and other violent actions or follow a spiritual path. When you live on a free-will planet with such choices and you choose the spiritual path, you earn higher points for your ascension and spiritual advancement. This is a simple explanation for why many people still want to come to Earth.

Actually, souls line up to come here. You might think it would be exactly the opposite, but they seek free will and the opportunities for spiritual advancement. It is a paradox, because so many seeming barriers to spiritual advancement exist here, including fear for your safety, becoming involved in polarization and losing objectivity, and losing your spiritual perspective. I said in the beginning of this chapter that perspective is everything, especially in spiritual advancement and spiritual work. It is easy to lose your perspective in a dense, polarized planet.

Earth's Graduation

At some point in the future, planet Earth will be in a position to graduate. It is well known through the galaxy that service is the best way to overcome karma. Service can include helping other planets, such as serving as an ascended master or teacher. Some of you on Earth are in training — and will continue your training in the stargate — to become spiritual masters and teachers to other planets. Some of you have said you want to come back to Earth and serve as spiritual masters and teachers here. This type of service is wonderful, and we encourage you to continue your service after leaving Earth, but you are not required to come back to Earth.

Other planets are in need of ascended masters to provide spiritual assistance. We Arcturians teach others planetary healing technologies. As planets experience different stages of development, they often need assistance in planetary spiritual growth. We have described these stages as planetary stage one, planetary stage two, and planetary stage three. Each has unique conflicts to overcome and wonderful opportunities to be of service.

Contemplate your soul journey and path. Do you feel worthy enough, and do you have the right spiritual vibration to travel through the stargate? Please remember: If you are dedicated to service, then your service carries an extremely high weight and raises your vibrational energy tremendously. Just having psychic energy and psychic powers are not enough for your ascension and do not mean you can enter these higher realms. If you are dedicated to helping this planet and other starseeds, you will receive a great spiritual boost to your vibrational energy.

The following exercise sends you to the doorway at the stargate. We have done this exercise before, but I think it is important that we continue to practice it. In the face of a dramatic energy shift, such as during ascension, you want to have the right response and be able to direct yourself to the stargate. Having knowledge of the stargate is such an advantage. Our service is accomplished when we bring you and as many other starseeds as possible into the stargate. Bringing you directly to the stargate is one of our missions and explains why we teach and reach out to you.

Stargate Exercise

Take three deep breaths. Feel my presence, Juliano, to the best of your ability. I have established and created a corridor over you that is connected to my starship, Athena, which serves as a transitional step to the stargate. Allow your spirit to come out of your body and into the corridor that is around you, then travel interdimensionally at the speed of thought to my starship. [Tones]: "Ta, ta, ta."

You have arrived. We all come together in the welcoming center in Athena. Enjoy being with me and many of my other students who greet you. I have set up another corridor. As a group, we are going to participate in this new corridor that is around the welcoming center on Athena. On the count of three, we will be at the stargate's vestibule, or the fore room, which is right in front of the stargate. One, two, three.

You are with me in front of the stargate. You notice a few things. First, your connection to Earth is lightened; the feeling of denseness that comes with your connection to Earth is gone. Second, you are closer to your light body. In the transition from your room to my starship, and then to the center of the foreroom of the stargate, you have transitioned into your light body. Your etheric body is filled with light. It is also lighter in terms of weight.

I have set up what I describe as a garden, and we all sit comfortably in the garden at the entranceway of the stargate. Angelic beings guard the entranceway. Some of them are singing the famous hymn "Kadosh, kadosh, kadosh, adonai tzevaoth." (Holy, holy, holy is the Lord of Hosts.) You see angelic presences like Archangel Metatron and other ascended masters at the doorway, and perhaps some of your guides and teachers.

Take another three breaths, and let us go into meditation as you sit in the garden in front of the stargate. Absorb the wonderful energy. We will go into silence. [Silence.]

Let yourself be carried into a higher state of lightness in your light body. Just being this close to the stargate raises your spiritual light quotient frequency vibration. [Silence.] I have permission to open the doorway of the stargate three or four inches. The rush of light, energy, and spiritual upliftment will overwhelm you. At the count of three, I have permission to open the door six inches. One, two, three.

Experience this wonderful rush of higher light that nurtures your spirit. The light and spiritual energy flows out the door, and you absorb it just being in the same proximity. [Tones.] Your spiritual light quotient frequency vibration goes up fast. You have a feeling of great joy and a great sense of peace and harmony. Know that you will soon be able to pass through this doorway. Your work here now is part of your preparation for this wonderful transition. [Silence.]

Take three more deep breaths. Now I must close the door. One last surge of light comes through, and then I close the door. You have gathered and absorbed as much light as you can in this exercise. The door is closed, and you have been replenished, nurtured, and are ready to return joyfully back to your Earth body. Now follow me back to the starship where we gather in a huge circle of light.

You have an individual corridor assigned to your physical body and home back on Earth. At the count of three, go back to a position six feet above your body. One, two, three. You have traveled through the corridor at the speed of thought and now float six feet above your body. On the count of three, re-enter your body in perfect alignment. You will bring this great feeling of lightness, joy, awareness, and experience of the stargate into your higher consciousness, into your Earth body. You will have a higher perspective on everything. One, two, three.

Blessings to you.

Chapter 22

Great Spiritual Energy Is Available to You

Juliano and the Arcturians

Planet Earth is in a major crisis. The changes happening, even those in the past four weeks, are dramatic. We know that each of you is affected on many different levels by the rapidly occurring events on planet Earth. How are you to understand these events, and what is the best method for coping with them?

The dramatic events in the United States involving the school shooting in Florida were heartbreaking, and it has touched many people on the planet. This type of event is relevant to the entire planetary crisis and to the relationship between technology and heart energy.

We, the Arcturians, have continued to study planetary development in this galaxy. Earth is at the end of the first stage. Each stage deals with a specific crisis with a problem or task to resolve. This time on Earth is focused on technology versus wisdom and heart energy. Which is stronger? Can you have unbridled technology without heart energy? If there is unbridled progress in technology, there is an increased danger that the planet and the biosphere (the life form and the energy field around Earth) will be destroyed. This is one negative consequence of technology being out of control.

The opposite of that is having an open heart — being compassionate, understanding, open to pain, and able to respond appropriately. When you just allow the technology to develop without feeling or heart, more destruction will occur. You are seeing this type of heartless destruction on the planet. You see it in the oceans and the forests, as well as the plants and animals that are becoming extinct. Now it is becoming apparent even in your daily lives in such tragic events as what happened in Florida.

Humans Have Developed Self-Destructive Technology

Arcturians have developed a technology to resolve this issue. I will describe it using a well-known and perhaps surprising (to you) example of the Native Americans in North America and their relationship to the buffalo. You might ask: "Juliano what do the buffalo have to do with modern technology and heart energy?" You might know that the Native Americans had a particular ceremony for hunting the buffalo. They honored the buffalo as a sacred animal, but they also needed it for survival — the buffalo skins for their tepees and their clothing and the buffalo meat for food. They took only the buffalo they needed. They did not kill randomly or for pleasure. They had specific goals.

Before a hunt, the Native Americans prayed to the spirit of the buffalo and its herd to ask permission to take one buffalo during the hunt. Permission was granted, and they had a successful hunt. With this practice, they were in harmony with the buffalo. When the Europeans came to North America, they behaved greedily. The Europeans had rifles and guns — the technology to kill great numbers. They killed without any interaction with the buffalo herd's heart energy and without requesting permission.

You might have seen movies about the destruction of the buffalo and how difficult it was to stop the killing, which was out of control. This example can be related to modern humans, who have developed technologies of mass destruction — nuclear bombs, missiles, and lasers. In fact, modern humans have the technology to leave Earth, and they also have the technology to destroy themselves.

Destructive technology has been developed to destroy the environment. People are able to harvest rain forests with bulldozers and other elaborate equipment. It is no longer necessary to use their hands to harvest the forest. Of course, even during the times when people used only their hands, they still destroyed vast amounts of the forest, but they did not do it with the ease or at the level happening now.

Destruction is also happening in fishing. Fishing technology has advanced so much that people are able to catch many fish, and there are fish in danger of becoming extinct. This is true in hunting as well. I can go on, but I think you get the idea.

What is the relevance of the school shootings, and how is this related to modern technology? It's very simple: With the use of guns for killing buffalo, people lost their heart connections because they did it without ceremony. In school shootings, you see mentally disturbed people using technologically advanced weapons. It is not a laser or a death ray gun or anything like that, but it is a technologically advanced weapon, and the killers perform the massacres without being connected with their heart energy.

In the case of the Florida school shooting, the killer was totally shut off from his heart energy. If he were to engage in a fight with each person individually only using his hands, he could not do it. But with that weapon, he was able to commit mass murder without any heart connection. I realize that this person might be emotionally damaged, and maybe he did not have the ability to connect with his heart. However, this demonstrates that such technology can be used without heart energy, leading to tragedies.

Heal Humanity with the Sacred Triangle

What perspective can the Arcturians offer you, as it seems this problem has increased? You are seeing destruction happen because of a lack of connection with heart energy now all over the planet. I am sure your hearts are saddened by the killings and the destruction of the environment, and you might even feel confused and wonder how to solve these problems. From our perspective, the main conflict is an expression of technology versus wisdom. This must be resolved for the planet to survive and go on to stage two.

Planetary stage two involves the fifth dimension, unity consciousness, and universal brotherhood and sisterhood. We have offered a new paradigm — a healing paradigm — for planet Earth that I have called the sacred triangle. I have worked through this channel to teach the integration of the three spiritual perspectives that will solve the problem of technology versus wisdom and heart energy. It involves working with the Native American perspective, such as the buffalo hunting example.

When dealing with hunting food and the environment, it is

necessary that you connect with feelings. You need to connect with the heart energies, because without them, human technology will destroy the planet. The healing part of this paradigm is returning open human hearts to Mother Earth (Gaia) to feel her and all beings on her as part of this living planet.

It has been proven in some interesting experiments that plants respond to you — your heart energy and your thoughts. The downside of technology is that it has caused human hearts to close to the environment, animals, and fellow humans. We see the highly evolved Native American approach of opening your hearts to Earth as a planetary healing model.

The second part of the paradigm is galactic spirituality. In past times, galactic civilizations struggled with similar technology problems. We have come up with solutions that integrate the heart and the emotional body with the technology. I think the most important thing is that we, the Arcturians, have a galactic perspective. We have seen planets evolve, and we know that Earth is evolving. So we have some ideas about how to continue this evolution in a positive way.

One technique is called biorelativity, which is a method of telepathically communicating with Earth's spirit. Another method is communicating with the noosphere, the collective thought field of the planet. Right now, the planet's thought field is being dominated by the media (television, internet, radio). There are ways for starseeds like you to download new and powerful thought fields into the planet's collective unconscious. You can use your skills, thoughts, and powers as planetary healers.

The third aspect of the sacred triangle is the White Brotherhood-White Sisterhood energy. These involve the ascended masters that you all love, including in the angelic world with the great spiritual teachers Sananda/Jesus, Mary Magdalene, Buddha, Quan Yin, and Archangel Michael. These great teachers are part of the mystical tradition, and they are opening their energy to you now. Never before on this planet has there been such easy access to the White Brotherhood-White Sisterhood.

You might think this is a contradiction: "Well, you just said the planet is in danger of being destroyed, but now you are saying there are ascended masters available." This is an interesting paradox. Never before has there been such a great spiritual energy and such great spiritual possibilities on Earth with substantial access to ascended masters.

The age of prophecy did not end in 400 BC or with the destruction of the Jewish temples in Rome. Prophetic thinking and prophetic energy are still available, and they are even greater now than in other times. Still, it is a paradox that this openness to the higher dimensions with unity consciousness and unity thinking has occurred at a time of such great polarization. I am Juliano.

Conclusion

The Next Evolved Human

David K. Miller

We Arcturian starseeds hope a shift in humanity's consciousness will lead Earth to the fifth dimension. Juliano has talked about the hundredth-monkey effect, the idea that consciousness can spread to large groups after a core group reaches a state of awareness. Once a certain number of starseeds reach a high level of consciousness, we hope the ideals of higher unified consciousness will spread through all humanity.

There have been instances already where events have focused humanity's consciousness in amazing ways. For example, the world's consciousness unified and focused on supporting the United States after 9/11, creating a unified feeling of brotherhood-sisterhood in repairing the damage done by terrorists.

Young starseeds across the globe need to be activated. They have the energy, sensitivity, and higher perception to work together toward an expanded and unified consciousness that will eventually lead to healing and rebalancing the planet. The Arcturians' perspective on human evolution is optimistic. We, as conscious beings, have the ability to direct our evolution toward a higher level the Arcturians describe as the omega man/woman. *Homo sapiens* is not the last model or species in the evolution of humanity. The omega man/woman represents a species that is focused on fifth-dimensional consciousness and unification of the planet.

It can be helpful to see the planet's current crisis as a stage of planetary development. The Arcturians say that of the five stages of planetary development, Earth is only at the end of stage one. Planets exhibit higher stages of development when they control wars and keep their environments clean and balanced. What can help Earth resolve these conflicts? The Arcturians say spiritual intervention and spiritual upliftment of consciousness are necessary.

The Arcturians explain that during ascension, an opening will occur where the third and fifth dimensions intersect. At that intersection point, new spiritual light and information will download to Earth. Greater receptivity to spiritual light and information have occurred at different times in our planet's history, and the Arcturians say more spiritual people exist on this planet than at any other time. This can be hard to believe, with so many wars and conflicts, but with over 8 billion people on the planet, the number of spiritually minded starseeds could be two to three million. This is a high number of spiritual beings of expanded consciousness. The question is: How can those who are spiritually minded manifest higher light and bring a shift in consciousness so that change occurs rapidly?

Ascension sets the stage for bringing higher consciousness to this planet. How can we starseeds prepare for and attract the intersection of the dimensions? The Arcturians say part of the intersection can only occur with preparation and when a certain number of righteous starseeds set the stage and help attract the third dimension to the fifth dimension. At that point, more spiritual light and energy will attract greater spiritual intervention on Earth.

Simultaneous Existence

In studying the Arcturians, we learn that other dimensions exist simultaneously with ours. We can communicate with other beings, and higher beings such as the Arcturians want to communicate with us and help guide us toward personal and planetary healing. Their message is optimistic, because they say that we, as higher beings, have the ability to consciously shift our evolution toward higher light.

This is a time of great polarization, conflict, and danger on Earth. We starseeds are very sensitive and feel the challenges of being on a planet so out of balance. The good news is that many starseeds are awakening, opening up, and looking for ways to help repair this planetary crisis. The Arcturians offer us new spiritual tools and technologies to provide the foundation for needed planetary healing.

Questions and Answers

Queries from around the Globe

David K. Miller, Juliano and the Arcturians, and Vywamus

David: This section contains questions asked by members of the Arcturian meditation group known as the Group of Forty, led by me, David K. Miller, and my wife, Gudrun Miller. Answers were provided by the Arcturians Juliano and Vywamus. These question-and-answer sessions took place monthly over international phone lines, and they cover a variety of subjects. Some subjects relate to topics addressed in this book, while others relate to other material channeled by the Arcturians. Special thanks to Jane Scarratt, coordinator of the Group of Forty in Australia, for her work in organizing these sessions.

Alternative Universes

In a recent question, someone asked if they could venture outside the universe in a meditation. Juliano replied that this would be dangerous, because your astral cord would detach and you couldn't return to your body. My question is: Can you enter a parallel universe and return safely, or, more generally, do the Arcturians believe in parallel universes that we can access?

— Henry, New York

Juliano and the Arcturians: To answer your question about parallel universes, let me give you our observations. Every point or place in the galaxy and in the universe has a slightly different perspective on existence and what goes on in the universe. This is similar to how you see the stars. For example, if you are in Australia, the night sky is different from the night sky you see in Arizona. Both perspectives are interesting and valuable.

Regarding parallel universes, we use the terms dimensions and multiple dimensions, but we do not describe or use the concept of parallel universes. Multi-universes do exist, but there are separations. It can be difficult to wrap your mind around this idea, but not all universes are equal. Some are smaller than others, and some are in different stages of development — they could be dying out or being born. Some universes do not have any life, especially those in the end stages of development.

Our universe is young — probably in its adolescence. Remember that the universe is approximately 13.7 billion years old. That might sound like a long time, but the average universe lives about 100 billion years.

The idea of parallel universes has been an ideal of science-fiction and fantasy. For example, you are safe if you cross the street on the right-hand side in this universe, but that same action in another universe can injure or kill you. So we set up a whole different scenario that has different consequences.

The concept of parallel universes contains the idea that everything is exactly the same up to this moment you now experience. Then a deviation occurs that changes everything. To make this theory work, you would need to have an infinite number of universes and an infinite number of events. This leads to illogical and absurd conclusions. In one universe, you might have the faucet on your bathtub on the ceiling. Anything you think of would have an alternative existence in another universe.

We look at the concept of different universes and dimensions through the lens of thought forms. You can have the thought of another action, and that thought creates a new thought field for an alternate event, but that thought form might not have enough energy to create a different reality.

There Is Always Hope

You try to reassure us that starseeds are contributing to helping the planet, but then you speak of the impending sixth mass extinction, an increase in polarization of dark and light forces, and the possibility of our planet self-destructing. It's hard at times to remain optimistic. What are the positive signs that the work we're doing is really helping? Are there any ways we can avert self-destruction?

— Carel, Sydney

Juliano and the Arcturians: That is a very good question about the sixth mass extinction and what looks like the dire straits the world is in. Each planetary system has stages of development, and what you see and experience now on Earth is a crisis stage. In evolutionary theory, change can only happen because of or during a crisis. You are in this crisis, and even though you starseeds are making great contributions, there is still the view that things are going to turn worse and the planet might self-destruct. This possible outcome falls into another scientific theory called entropy, where everything appears to wear down and eventually run out.

Understand that this Earth is not going to catastrophically end. Part of what the starseeds are doing is preparing for the next evolution, which is already in process. During this evolutionary crisis, intervention by higher dimensional beings cannot occur without you and the systematic and great networking of starseeds across the planet. There has to be a base, a foundation, upon which change and the evolutionary leap can occur. You are setting the foundation and the stage for the coming evolutionary leap.

If the global crisis gets totally out of hand, and if the planet hangs in the balance between life or death, a dimensional shift will take place and higher dimensions will intervene. In fact, intervention by higher dimensions has already begun. The energy between what you normally perceive as a starseed and the higher light shines through the veil. I agree that it looks, from your perspective, as if darker forces are unfolding more and leading the planet to destruction, but from my higher-dimensional perspective, I see many shining lights. I see the creation of foundational energy that will allow higher beings and higher dimensions to sustain the intervention necessary to set this planet back on track.

Random Weather Events

My suburb of Berowra Heights in Australia was recently hit with a severe hail storm. The hailstones were very large and caused a lot of damage to houses and cars. If we look for the good in this mayhem, were there any codes or a message to Gaia?

— Yvonne, Sydney

Juliano and the Arcturians: This was an unfortunate weather event that caused destruction. Some of these events are random and unpredictable. Higher-developed planets and civilizations have more control over the weather, so random weather events, like you now see on Earth, do not take place. This was a truly random event, even though this goes against much spiritual thinking that says there are no random events. You might think this suburb was being punished for some reason, but I try to have the perspective and teach that the large imbalances now occurring on this planet can, in random ways, create problems anywhere on the planet.

People often ask me: "Where can I move to be safe?" The planet has no perfect place now that is safe; there is no utopia. I cannot tell you to go to the Solomon Islands or Costa Rica or any other place you think has perfect weather, because every place on the planet is susceptible now to unexpected events that can cause disruption.

I can say that this event in your suburb was somewhat modified so it was not as bad as it could have been. My only interpretation that would be helpful to you is that this is the unbalanced and unexpected state we are now in on the planet. The best way to protect yourself is to create planetary cities of light and domes of protection around those cities, and work with that energy so the place where you live has more protection. Every place has its own vulnerabilities, and you, as a starseed, lightworker, and planetary healer, can work to protect your place with spiritual light. Doing that will have positive effects.

Tips for Working with the Retinas

I have a question about some material in your first book, Connecting with Arcturians. *The Arcturians talk about the retina and how important it is to develop our abilities as starseeds. Where can I find more information about how to work with retinas?*

— Alex, California

Juliano and the Arcturians: There is probably no material outside of what I've given you about the retina. Some of the channeling we bring through is new information that has not been discussed before. The retina is related to what we call the reticular activating system, a term from neurobiology. The reticular activating system is part of the perceptual neurobiological system that allows you to have wider perceptions of different realities.

True reality is a vibrational world. You are trained to use your normal perception that enables you to see things as solid and fixed objects, which helps you function in this reality. If you saw true reality, you might become so dizzy that you'd faint. You need training to deal with the vibrational waves that are the true reality of everything.

For example, a table is not actually hard but composed of wavy lines. Everything in its essence is a wavy line or a wavy energy, but you are culturally trained to see objects only as solid. When I talk about training the retina, you connect the retina with the reticular activating system that controls how you perceive the world. The retina is part of your perceptual system. The perceptual system is within your opening mind, but the retina is part of your mind system.

Perception is part of the function of the brain. You can train the retina to see patterns so you can see the vibrational reality of this existence. To do this, the retina has to be made more flexible. How do you train the retina? Some interesting trainings have to do with looking at auras. Perceiving energy fields around people helps the retina become more flexible. If you want to see somebody's aura, do not look directly at them but off to the side. Then your retina reacts in a different perceptual way.

Another method to make your retina more flexible is to put an object in a semi-dark room and, again, look at it from the side. You can also meditate on the flame of a candle and visualize or see its light reach your retina. Then see the light waves shift as they reach your eyes. See the colors in the candle flame go from blue to red. This is a powerful retina training method.

Other Life Forms in the Universe

You've mentioned there are other 3D planets in our universe. Do they have human, animal, and plant forms similar to ours? How spiritually advanced are they compared to us?

— Paula, Sydney

Juliano and the Arcturians: Yes, there are other human life forms in the galaxy. We call the human species the Adam species. For example, humans on the Pleiades are more spiritually advanced than the humans on Earth. There are certain small differences in Pleiadian humans compared to Earth humans. For example, Pleiadian ears and eyebrows have different characteristics. Their third eyes are more open than those of Earth humans. Pleiadians do not have the physical illnesses you now have on Earth, as they have overcome many diseases, including those related to stress and pollution.

Humans on some other planets are developmentally lower than Earth humans. The basic human form is similar to your earth body. We use a human-like form for our Arcturian bodies. We appear somewhat humanoid, in that we have two arms and two legs. But we have a different digestive system, and we do not have your muscular structure, in part because we use our minds to lift objects. You might think we look like ballet dancers.

In our estimation, 5,000 planets in the galaxy have higher life forms. Some of them are not advanced. Some civilizations do not make it through the technology stage of development; they destroy themselves. This estimation of life forms is just in this galaxy. Some galaxies are larger than the Milky Way, which means there could statistically be even more planets with life on them. Using the figure of 5,000 planets with advanced life in our galaxy, if there are 100 billion galaxies in our universe, you can multiply 5,000 x 100 billion to get the possible number of planets with higher life forms in the universe. You can see why there is a possibility of an extraordinary number of higher life forms throughout the universe. The problem is that planets with life forms are so far away that connecting with them presents major problems.

The Starship Athena

Why did the Arcturians name their starship Athena?

— Birgit, Oklahoma

Juliano and the Arcturians: Athena is the name of a goddess from Greek mythology whose main characteristic is wisdom. Wisdom is one of the main spheres in the Tree of Life. We felt that because we were interacting with Earth, we should call our starship Wisdom. But that word does not have the flavor or characteristic of Athena. Athena is an archetypal energy on this planet and an archetypal energy in the galaxy. We want people who relate to us and visit us on our starship to understand that they are interacting with and coming through a galactic starship focused on wisdom.

What is wisdom? It is divine, higher energy that transcends logic. Wisdom transcends even your Earth experiences, and thus brings you insight and energy from higher light.

Light Language

I have a few of questions about the universal language of light: How do we go about learning this language? Is it downloaded through geometric symbols or dreams? Can we make a conscious decision to learn light language, or must we have a higher vibration to understand it?

— Micki, Victoria

Juliano and the Arcturians: The language of light, or galactic language, is basically a tonal language in which you emit sounds that send special energy waves to the listener's brain and create altered states of consciousness. It is not a language like English where you use words to represent thoughts and feelings. Regular language can have logical sentences and grammar, but the language of light is a vibrational language and approaches the status of sacred language. Earth has at least two sacred languages, Sanskrit and Hebrew. They share aspects with this galactic language vibration.

You might hear certain sounds in Hebrew or in Sanskrit that activate your vibrational frequency. For example, the sound of Om, when chanted, creates a spiritual vibrational energy. When you hear the word Om, it communicates a vibrational state that the higher-developed parts of your brain react to. This is similar to the results of galactic language.

In terms of learning the galactic language, it is all intuitive; the language comes to you intuitively. Think of the psychic phenomena known as speaking in tongues. People who do this go into an altered state of consciousness. To speak in the galactic language, you must also go into an altered state of consciousness.

Work with any existing words you resonate with, whether Sanskrit or Hebrew. By toning words in these languages, you can activate expanded consciousness. Opening yourself to sacred words in these languages can help you prepare to intuitively connect with galactic sounds.

Activate Your Spiritual Abilities

How do we activate advanced abilities, such as telepathy, levitation, remote viewing, healing powers, and bilocation? How long does it take to develop them?

— Christopher, Mullumbimby, Australia

Juliano and the Arcturians: First, let me say that spiritual advancement is not always measured in these advanced powers. Some people have great spiritual or psychic powers, but they are not advanced spiritually. We all have heard stories of people who are successful healers and can levitate or do psychic surgery, but this does not mean they are spiritually advanced. A famous healer in Brazil had great powers, but he also had some personality problems.

Therefore, I don't think it is a good idea to measure or focus your development on psychic abilities. Psychic abilities are often a side development of your spirituality. My suggestion is to do your spiritual work, study, and meditations, and maybe these other psychic powers will come to you. Maybe they won't. Do not do spiritual work in order to get spiritual powers. That is going backward. Such an approach is also ego-driven, because it indicates you want to gain something. One of the pitfalls of spiritual development is wanting to gather or gain fame or power. It is better to just open up to your higher purpose, and if the spiritual powers that you mention come to you, that is fine.

There are techniques for developing the spiritual power of telepathy, but developing telepathy by itself does ensure higher spiritual power.

Encouragement for New Group Members

As a facilitator of a fledgling planetary healing group, I wish to convey to members their importance as starseeds and how they might best serve the planet, others, and themselves. Can you please offer some words of encouragement we can use when talking to these new group members?

— Hannah, United Kingdom

Juliano and the Arcturians: You starseeds have the huge mission to be planetary healers and to assist in the evolution of this planet. As Group of Forty members, we try to awaken others, and we provide linkages so you can use your planetary healing abilities and powers to fulfill your mission, which includes raising the consciousness of the planet and providing the foundation for planetary change and evolution.

This is an overwhelming challenge. I would say to each member: "You are part of the foundation providing the base for this planetary shift. Many souls who are not incarnated would love to have this opportunity that you now have to use your planetary-healing abilities. So come together and do not waste your starseed heritage. Let us work at fulfilling the great mission of activating the planetary evolution that is before us."

I would also say to awakening starseeds: "You are special as a starseed, because you have the awareness of your galactic heritage. You have been on other planets in our galaxy before. You have a higher level of understanding of planetary evolution."

We all agree that we need higher levels of understanding and wisdom to help manifest this evolutionary change. Do not worry about your small numbers, because the power of your thinking, ideas, and spiritual energy are most effective for planetary work.

Juliano's Background

I am curious about you. You mention you are an Arcturian ascended master. Have you always lived on Arcturus and on the starship Athena, or have you had lives on other planets, perhaps Earth? Also, who were you before you ascended?

— Carel, Sydney

Juliano and the Arcturians: I have had lifetimes on other planetary systems, but not on Earth. I do not spend all my time on the starship Athena. I do multidimensional work and multidimensional traveling. For example, I have experiences on the seventh dimension. I spend some of my time on Alano, an Arcturian moon-planet closer to the Central Sun, and I have recently been working in other galactic systems.

No, I was not always an ascended master. I use that term to mean I am in the fifth dimension and that being in the fifth dimension I can raise energy and higher light in that dimension. I have had lifetimes on other Earth-like planetary systems where I struggled. Even our planetary system of Arcturus was third dimensional eons ago. Some of the planets in our system engaged in self-destructive behaviors. I was not on the planet that was destroyed, but I did experience the trauma of that catastrophe. Because of that tragic event, I have been assigned by our higher council to reach out to Earth. We work in service to help prevent your planet from such a fate. Also, we reach out to you to explain the stargate. I have taken on this mission of great service, and I am honored to work with you.

My special interest is working with Helio-ah and Tomar. We work together to develop special healing chambers for Earthlings. No matter how much spiritual work you do, you are still plagued by your Earth body. This is a difficult time to be in an Earth body for many reasons, including food and environmental contamination. Also, you experience a tremendous amount of stress trying to maintain your health. Overall, this is a difficult time to be healthy. We are in the developmental stages of transmitting more exercises for the personal healing of our dear, beloved Earth beings.

I feel a special closeness to Earth, because Earth has multitudes of different energies. We call Earth the Blue Jewel and believe this is a wonderful description. I am proud to be on the starship Athena, whose primary mission is to assist in Earth's development. Thank you for the interest in me and our work.

Results of Biorelativity Exercises

What are the effects of all the biorelativity exercises we are doing? I am especially interested in the meridian exercise to heal the rift in the space-time continuum.

— Corae, Nebraska

Juliano and the Arcturians: The biorelativity exercises you are doing are ground-breaking. They are setting up patterns of repair in the biosphere and in the meridian system. Earth's auras has fantastic leakages, but you are creating fantastic bridges to help close them. These holes have been created through radiation, nuclear bombs, and other shocking and reckless military experiments. These military activities have been done unconsciously and without awareness of how harmful they are to the planet.

Biorelativity helps to create a bridge of repair around the meridians. These repairs are still fragile. The repairs you have been doing are revitalizing the life-force energies of this planet. One of the greatest threats to the biosphere is closed and blocked life-force energy. Some of the blockages come from dams built over sacred power spots, the destruction of sacred power spots, and dumping contaminants in these sacred areas.

There is a lot of work to do, because part of the meridian system needs more connections to the cosmic field. Blocked meridians block out cosmic light and cosmic energy. I help you connect with Arcturus as a way to download higher light and energy into your system. In meridian work, planet Earth needs to connect to Arcturus. Let us do meridian work in which we bring down the cosmic light from Arcturus into Earth's meridian system. This is a higher level of biorelativity. We are not saying that you should only connect to Arcturus, and we acknowledge your connections to other star systems, such as the Pleiades and Antares.

It is important to connect the meridian system to the Earth's crown, which is at the North Pole. Connecting the North Pole energy system to Arcturus strengthens these alignments.

Your biorelativity work is ground-breaking. Never before has there been this global effort where starseeds work continuously around the planet for planetary healing. This creates a great shield and spiritual openings. You cannot do more advanced work until you have set the foundation, and we are still working with you on this great foundational structure for the meridian system that you are helping to repair with your biorelativity work.

Use of the *Merkabah*

Can we use the Merkabah *as protection? I was taught the Melchizedek sacred geometry method of placing myself in a 3D* Merkabah *and spinning it in opposite directions simultaneously as protection and a tool for ascension. I use this technique to feel safe when I am in a large crowd of people.*

— Carel, Sydney

Juliano and the Arcturians: Using the *Merkabah* for protection is a fabulous idea. I only caution that *Merkabah* technology was primarily developed for ascension and for leaving the planet or this dimension and traveling to other dimensions. So if you use the *Merkabah* for protection and spin it, just be careful that you do not leave your body when you are in those situations. If you are in a dangerous situation, you might have to make a protective move. For example, you might have to quickly cross the street, leave a place, or avoid somebody. In these situations, I would moderate the *Merkabah* spinning and not spin it too fast. Make sure you are still in your body. The Melchizedek method and *Merkabah* came from the Egyptians and were passed down to the Hebrews. They originally developed so practitioners could leave their bodies.

Having an inquisitive mind is good, and I want you to know how grateful and loving I feel toward you and how I receive your love too. This is a good opportunity for both of us to be of service and to assist in your evolution as well as the evolution of the planet. I make a promise to each of you that we will be more attentive to your personal healing, because we need and want you to be healthy so you can feel the benefits of this work and fulfill your planetary missions. It is much more difficult to accomplish this kind of work when you are not healthy.

Receive my blessings and the beautiful blue Arcturian light into your crown chakra for personal light healing.

Release Karmic Baggage

How can we heal or transform karmic baggage from our ancestral tree, particularly when we incarnate in an ancestral tree that has accumulated karma?

— Elena, Romania

Juliano and the Arcturians: In our definition, the ancestral tree is your soul group or soul family. What you are referring to, I believe, is your soul group as opposed to your entire ancestral tree. Your primary responsibility is to complete and work out your karma, and only when you have learned your soul lessons and completed your karmic work can you consider working in service to the soul group.

Transforming baggage from a soul group is not for everyone. I want to be clear on this, because some people's missions are specifically to work on energy from the soul group or what you refer to as the ancestral tree, while others do not have this type of mission. When you talk about ancestral work, you are really talking about releasing group karmic ties. Souls are stuck in the inter-dimensions and some are stuck particularly in the fourth dimension.

Let us use the example of people who have died traumatically through a fire or through war. These souls can get stuck in the lower fourth dimension, and to release them often requires going to the place on the third dimension where they were stuck.

Let us imagine that your ancestral group includes a person who died in World War I, say on the battle line between Germany and France. Helping to release this person's karma might require you to travel there and sense and feel their lost soul. You might need to connect with the lost soul and work with it to release from that situation. You would tell the soul you are there as a healer, to release the connection and "stuckness" they are experiencing. This intervention requires skill. Lost souls do not easily say, "Oh, thank you, I am ready to be released." You might have to do some convincing. They might need you to coax and educate them.

Another level of collective karma exists with a country like Germany, which has the collective karma from WWII and the Holocaust. Cultures and groups can accumulate karmic debts due to war and genocide. Terrible genocides committed by the Europeans against the native peoples in Central America and South America resulted in the deaths of over 20 million people and created ancestral karmic debts.

New Vibrational Technology

We have been told through channeled information that a sound can extinguish fire. About a year ago I saw on TV some young inventors trying to create this technology. Does this mean we are now ready for such discoveries? What are the important aspects of this regarding climate change?

— *Jo, Queensland, Australia*

Juliano and the Arcturians: The idea of a sound being used to affect climate conditions such as fire relates to the subject of vibrational planetary healing. Vibrational planetary healing has similarities to personal vibrational healing that uses sounds and vibrational tones. Tones from the human voice or crystals and crystal bowls can change the vibrational frequency of the physical body.

I am glad you asked this question, because it allows me to report that vibrational healing for the planet requires a certain knowledge of toning and sounds. It also requires more of a group energy and the arcan power of people working together from around the planet.

The obvious or primary vibrational tone to call forth harmonious energy is the Sanskrit sound "Om." You can also use more complex tones and sounds. It is true that specific tones or sounds with the right frequency can extinguish fire. They can also change ocean currents and weather patterns. But using such interventions requires an extremely high level of spiritual technology. Such spiritual technology is possible but will not be revealed for one simple reason: It would be misused. A tone that can change the climate can also be used for military purposes.

Such things as HAARP — High Frequency Active Auroral Research Program — can also produce and affect climatic events. You might say, "High-frequency radio propagation is not really a tone or sound." But it gives you an idea of the magnitude of the power that is needed to change a climatic event. These radio frequencies from HAARP can produce millions of volts and millions of watts. The sound needed to put out a fire would have to have the vibrational power of that kind of enormous high frequency, aurora-radio-wave propagation voltage. HAARP is on the edge of modern research. Using sounds to put out fires is not like personal toning or using a crystal bowl.

Pets and Ascension

Are there dogs on Arcturus? You have said we will be able to ascend with our pets. Can you please elaborate on this?

— Diana

Juliano and the Arcturians: Regarding the ascension of pets, I would like to talk about power animals. In the shamanistic world, power animals visit and work with you. They can bring you messages, healing, and even personal power. Your pets can elevate through ascension and become power animals for you.

You elevate the spirits of your pets tremendously, and they are closely bonded to you. They provide a great service to you and you provide a great service to them, because you elevate their spirits. You can look at pets from this perspective: They will become power animals for you in the fifth dimension and you will be able to elevate them to the higher dimension when you ascend.

Pets also have soul families, so do not be greedy or selfish if they do ascend with you. Yes, you can bring them to the higher realm, but they still need the freedom to visit and communicate with their soul group, with whom they can provide information and higher energy. They help elevate their soul group, just like you elevate your soul group, so let them have this opportunity.

The Importance of Silence

Science is starting to tell us that silence and quiet are important for the brain and for developing creative ideas. Can you explain the importance of silence and quiet for us?

— Jane, Australia

Juliano and the Arcturians: The best way I can talk about silence and quiet is to talk about electromagnetic energy. Your entire body, including your brain, is electromagnetic. Your brain has either a positive or a negative charge. Your life even has an overall charge. When you meditate, you neutralize the charge: You are neither positive nor negative. That is referred to in the spiritual world as equanimity, which is one of the higher states of consciousness in meditation. Equanimity means you do not go into any charge, positive or negative, when somebody compliments you or is negative toward you. In meditation, you transcend negative and positive. You neutralize the charge and can transcend and go into higher state of consciousness.

Dementia

According to statistics on Google, close to 50 million people worldwide lived with dementia in 2017. This number will double every 20 years, reaching 75 million in 2030 and 131.5 million in 2050. What is causing this phenomenon? Why are some people affected and not others?

— Carel, Sydney

Juliano and the Arcturians: The idea of dementia is directly related to the environment. Dementia is caused by contamination that occurs through mold, weed killers, and chemicals in the food and air (including microscopic metals). Modern society lives in a very toxic environment on all levels. No place on this planet is pure, and you ingest a higher rate of contaminants than at any other time.

Earlier causes of dementia were also related to diet and chemical contamination. Ash from volcanic eruptions, for example, spread around the planet. So contamination of the air is not a new phenomenon.

Dementia is also caused by circulatory problems, such as strokes and clogged arteries and veins, but this current epidemic of dementia is directly related to contamination, including environmental molds that are becoming more prevalent as the planet warms. Dementia is not a normal part of aging. The nervous system contains neural fibers that defend themselves from contaminants and the resulting inflammation by building plaque in neural cells. Inflammation tries to keep invasive particles from spreading to other parts of the brain. Eventually, the plaque itself becomes a hazard and leads to further death of brain cells, which can then lead to dementia.

Why some people get dementia and some do not is very complex. How your body reacts to contaminants is related to your immune system. How easily does your immune system fight off contaminants? Your immune system has a light quotient. If your immune system is not struggling with other issues, it can hopefully fight off some of the effects of high contaminant levels. For example, many believe that exposure to agent orange in the Vietnam War caused the neurological condition called amyotrophic lateral sclerosis. Some U.S. soldiers exposed to agent orange got this condition, but others did not. Some people have immune systems that can better handle pesticide exposure.

A concept in the study of dementia is called brain reserve. Brain reserve refers to how much your brain can tolerate before it falls below a certain threshold and enters the clinical diagnosis of dementia. Issues of karma are also related to dementia. For example, a person might have spread deadly contaminants in a war. To pay off this karmic debt, he or she might come back in another lifetime and have to deal with the effects of dementia caused by contamination. So you can see, this is a very complex subject.

Jupiter

I saw on a TV program that a probe sent to Jupiter discovered it is a water planet, contrary to the belief that it is devoid of water. Also, a large area appeared to have been displaced, possibly by a huge meteor. One scientist suggested this large displacement might have eventually become Earth. Is this true?

— Paula, Sydney

Juliano and the Arcturians: To say that Jupiter is a water planet is a bit misleading, because it might have been a sun at one time, due to its gaseous state. Jupiter does not have the temperatures now to be a star, but it has certain similar features. Do not be fooled. Water exists in many parts of the solar system, including on some of Jupiter's moons, on Mars, and on Earth's Moon. Water is common throughout the galaxy and the universe.

I am not of the belief that a comet struck Jupiter and created Earth. If anything, the comet displaced Jupiter's gases. The galaxy is a violent place. Collisions from comets and asteroids are common. Life is very fragile.

Earth is over 4.5 billion years old. There is evidence that another planet collided into Earth 500 million years ago, and that collision possibly created the moon. Why is this important? The Moon is extremely important to life on Earth and relates to Earth's tides and seasons. The Moon relates to a whole series of functions on Earth that allow life to exist.

Resistance to Higher Evolution

I understand that four negative energies are part of our challenge toward higher evolution and ascension. Can you please identify these four negative energies? I also understand that a large number of positive energies are assisting us. Can you identify them as well?

— Jane, Perth

Juliano and the Arcturians: Are you sure there are only four negative energies? I can think of twenty that are part of the resistance to higher evolution. Basically, the resistance to higher consciousness is the main factor in preventing the evolution to ascension.

What are some of the other negative factors? There exists within humans the animal self, the dominant feature on this planet. The animal self is based on domination, control, and other lower energies. The lower animal self has a certain frequency characterized by egoism and egotism. Focusing only on the animal self in your development prevents evolution in the human species. The animal self blocks unity thinking, the most important emotion and thought field for ascension.

How Arcturus Changed

Juliano, you have said that Arcturus was a 3D planet at one point. Did your planet experience the chaos we have on Earth, and what was the catalyst that changed people's thinking?

— Micki, Melbourne

Juliano and the Arcturians: Our third-dimensional planet was in chaos at one time in the distant past. We come from a multi-planetary system, like Earth's, but two or three different planets had life at the same time. The catalyst for our shift was a conflict that broke out on one of our planets, and it self-destructed with a nuclear-type explosion. Everyone on the planet died. It was a traumatic event that left a very serious impression on us; it shook us to the core.

Can you imagine (and I hope this never happens here) a nuclear explosion wiping out every country on Earth? A nuclear war would be a traumatizing event for the whole planet. In our case, we had a traumatizing event on one planet in our solar system, and that event convinced us to immediately promote higher evolution within our system.

Modalities for Intuition

Why can some people allow their inner voices and creativity to flow and others cannot? What can people who are blocked do to allow their psychic abilities to flow?

— Paula, Sydney

Juliano and the Arcturians: Some people connect with higher realms through intuition and others connect with visions or words. Some connect through sound and music. What is your primary modality for receiving from the higher realms?

You might receive visions but look for words as your primary modality for reception. You might receive music but look for visions. Your gifts are not all the same. My advice is to connect with the modality that suits you. If visioning is not your modality, it does not benefit you to say, "How come I am not receiving visions?" You have a unique perspective and receive intuition using your own modality.

The Androgynous Self

Scientists have shown that brains are male or female. In the case of a transgender person, the brain is one gender and the body is another. If we imagine a society that draws no conclusions whether someone is female, male, or somewhere in between, would transgender people be free of their suffering?

— Isobel, United Kingdom

Juliano and the Arcturians: Sexuality is such an important aspect on this planet. Some people who are female feel they are male, and some who are male feel they are female. Some people change their sex physically so the brain and body match. People suffer over these issues. Perhaps the most important thing to understand is that the soul is not male or female. In its ultimate state, the soul does not have a sex-based identity.

All of you have been male or female in different lifetimes. You might identify with being male from another lifetime and want to come into this lifetime as male. You might have had problems being female in an earlier lifetime, and you want to incarnate as male.

Understand that you are evolving into what is known as an androgynous being. Androgyny means having the features of both male and female. My concern is that when people who are female want to become male, they give up their female part. Or people who are male and want to become female give up their male part. Both parts of the self — male and female — are important. In the evolution of the androgynous self, you accept both sides.

Those who are transgender might think that if they just become the one side, such as the female side, that will solve all their problems. But it does not solve the issue of androgyny, which refers to the integration of both male and female. Androgyny and transgender issues need to be looked at on a soul level. My recommendation is to look again at what it means to be androgynous and how to embrace both sides.

This can also be looked at in terms of politics. Some people think having female politicians will improve the world. But some females who become leaders act the same as men. So just because they are in a female body does not mean that they are going to have female compassion or intuition. We need world leaders who are truly feminine and exhibit feminine traits when they lead their countries.

The answer to the transgender issue lies in embracing the androgynous evolutionary self.

The Importance of Dreaming

I'd like to know more about my dreams. I'm told that dreams are other realities we live in while we also live our 3D lives. If that's the case, why do dreams feel different from third-dimensional reality? Does dreaming actually help us, and in what ways?

— Christopher, Mullumbimby, Australia

Vywamus: I am Vywamus, a soul psychologist. Dreaming fulfills many different purposes. It is specifically related to your soul development, the level of spiritual light quotient you are on, and your personal and planetary work or mission. Not everyone is advanced on a spiritual basis. Those who are advanced might have dreams from higher realms, dreams with high psychic importance, dreams with spiritual messages, and dreams with masters.

The dream world is related and calibrated to your level of spiritual development. Sigmund Freud defined the purpose of dreams as wish fulfillment; they reflect hidden desires that you might not be able to express. Freud believed the dream world is related to sexual repression, which reflected the Victorian morals and repressiveness of his culture. So we might say that people in Freud's culture had repressed wishes they expressed in their dreams. The dreams of Aboriginals and other shamanic people of Earth are likely totally different and reflect their cultures.

The dream world provides a balance that allows you to stay mentally stable. Dreaming occurs during what is called REM (rapid eye movement) sleep. During REM sleep, you experience the deepest dreams. The highest spiritual dreams occur during this period, and they require stages of relaxation and consciousness that only exist in REM sleep.

It has been suggested that people deprived of REM sleep, and therefore unable to dream, become emotionally unstable. One important function of dreaming is to maintain mental stability. The mind and brain need contact with the interdimensional world. The interdimensional world has a different time frame, logic, and mental abilities. In the dream world, you can bilocate, compress time, and experience the space-time continuum in a totally different way. It is important for your transition from this planet into other dimensions that you experience and be reminded of the interdimensional world.

Again, the level of dreaming is calibrated to your spiritual development and your psychological development.

Protecting Your Aura

How is the aura protected under anesthesia, particularly if you're suddenly put under an anesthetic?

— Micki, Melbourne

Juliano and the Arcturians: For the most part, the aura is not protected during anesthesia and is susceptible to outside entities and attachments. There are many cases of people who have had surgeries with anesthesia and unknowingly obtained attached entities. Entities can attach when you are vulnerable, which is the case during anesthesia.

One way to provide protection to your aura in these cases is to use the exercise I call "future time protection." In this exercise, you send a protective energy field to yourself in the future time of the surgery. Say your surgery is in ten days. In meditation, picture a calendar and go ten days from now. See yourself in the surgery room and send a protective energy field around your aura.

We can offer you protection and even remove vulnerabilities from past experiences. This is called time travel using bilocation in the past and the future. You would think, for the most part, that high spiritually minded people would want to protect themselves during anesthesia. But vulnerability in energy fields and auras is still a new field of study and the answers and solutions to these vulnerabilities is only now coming to the forefront of discussion.

Problems can occur when you suddenly and jarringly leave your body. This can happen during a car accident or sudden catastrophe. As a solution, you can call for protection during your regular meditations. Call on your guides to protect you now and in the future to make sure your aura is protected.

On a related topic, I have received questions about pulsing electromagnetic energy work, an electromagnetic healing technique done with special devices that mimic Earth's electromagnetic energy field. Protecting yourself and bringing yourself into a healing vibration is related to the health of your aura. If your aura is already weak, has holes in it, or is misshapen from drug use, you are even more vulnerable. The best defense is to maintain a healthy aura. The exercise of shimmering is a powerful way to maintain proper electromagnetic, geomagnetic balance.

Your aura responds to electromagnetic energy, and your energy field is compromised by the internet, smartphones, computers, the electrical lines near your home, and so on; the list is long. When your environment is surrounded by electromagnetic energy, it can be very difficult to consistently bring your energy field into optimal balance.

This is why I am developing many different ways to use the aura shimmering exercise to help you maintain electromagnetic harmony balance.

How to Calm Severe Storms

Can you give us an exercise to calm erratic and severe weather patterns?

— Corae, Nebraska

Juliano and the Arcturians: Visualize a ring of golden light around the area of concern. See this golden light filled with harmony and balance so a calming energy begins to permeate the area and bring it more into alignment with calmness. *El na refa na la* is Hebrew for "please heal now." Let healing and harmony light surround and permeate the entire area. Let this golden harmony, the golden aura of light, surround and stay around this area so it calms on all levels for the greatest good. So it shall be.

Feng Shui

Feng Shui seems to have a complex set of rules. How important is it to follow these rules? For example, is it bad luck to sleep with your head facing southwest and to have mirrors in your bedroom?

— Carel, Sydney

Juliano and the Arcturians: Feng Shui is based on Chinese philosophy, Chinese medicine, and Taoism. The idea of sleeping in a certain direction and using mirrors is based on the energy from those cultures. There is a high degree of reliability as to how Feng Shui was originally discussed and brought to the planet, but its roots are still based in Chinese culture and reflective of what the energy was like during the ancient times when these ideas were developed.

Regarding mirrors and sleep positions, it is important to calibrate where you are on the planet. You might find that being in Australia can have a slight variation in calibration as opposed to being in Beijing, China. You might find that having a mirror in one direction in your house is useful. But please understand that you do not need to be overly rigid about this approach. Let me make a comparison: Penicillin in Western medicine was a great discovery. A doctor believes it will cure everything, and he gives it to everyone who comes to his office. But penicillin does not work for some people; they are allergic to the drug and it can even kill them. So one method of healing does not work for everyone, and Feng Shui does not work for everyone.

It is important to be flexible and take into consideration the energy fields of the planet and the energy fields around you. Use Feng Shui as a tool, but don't use it as a rigid answer to all problems. Use your intuition.

The Illusion of Reality

If we create our own realities and everything is an illusion, what is the purpose of being involved in anything at all?

— Renata, New Zealand

Juliano and the Arcturians: Is it true that you create your own reality and everything is an illusion? You do not have all the information in your mind and consciousness about this reality. In the same way we don't give penicillin to everyone and don't use all the rules of feng shui for every house, look at this belief as a perspective and not in a rigid way.

For example, you say, "Oh, we create our own reality." Well, yes, you do create a lot of your reality, but a lot of this reality is created by the collective unconscious, collective energy fields, guides, and teachers. A lot of this reality is created beyond you. You incarnated here, but you did not create the whole Earth reality. Yes, you can change parts of your reality as higher consciousness teaches. But I am not going to say you create everything, because group consciousness and collective consciousness began the third dimension. Some of this reality is beyond the individual person.

This same perspective might not be so useful if you look at this reality as an illusion. Then there is no meaning to it and this reality is all just a game. This is a perspective too. You can view this reality as a play. You can suffer and feel pain in this illusionary theater of life, because even in a theater, suffering feels real. The illusion of life that the Hindus call maya is a perspective. It is dangerous to just throw everything off and say this is an illusion, therefore what happens in life does not matter. The truth is that what happens in this lifetime does matter. It matters because what you do here affects your soul development. What you learn here affects where your soul journeys in your next life.

Here is another perspective: In the Kabbalah, it is said that this reality is a dream in God's mind. God is dreaming this reality and dreaming you. This is another mystical perspective on this reality. You do not have all of the information about all this third-dimensional reality. You can say, "This is all an illusion," or, "This reality is a dream," but that does not answer everything. There are levels of perception and understanding of this reality. The mystery and meaning of this reality are not explained by saying this world is an illusion.

Yoga, Tai Chi, and Qi Gong

Apart from the cosmic egg, shimmering, and white and gold light, does Yoga, Tai Chi, or Qi Gong help with physical/spiritual protection as well as raising our vibrations?

— Micki, Melbourne

Juliano and the Arcturians: One major benefit of Yoga, Tai Chi, and Qi Gong is helping the aura and energy field of the practitioner. Many people benefit from these exercises; however, others are not in alignment with them. Tai Chi and Qi Gong exercises were introduced to Bodhi dharma and brought to India and China to provide harmonic balance using the physical body. When a person is able to do certain exercises, Bodhi dharma says they have healthy alignments and open meridians. These exercises can shift energy into more healthful patterns.

The traditions of Yoga, Tai Chi, and Qi Gong are beautiful and powerful and can help you balance. But not everyone needs to do them. People who follow shamanistic principles in the Native American tradition also achieve high levels of balance. If you feel attracted to these methods, use them. Walking is also wonderful. People who do Zen walking achieve similar results. My teaching to you today is to be flexible. If you are attracted to a particular practice, it has the potential to help you achieve balance and improve your protective energies.

Strange Sounds

I have read reports about very eerie moaning and cracking sounds, as if Earth is breaking apart. They have been recorded on tape and have occurred in Russia, Canada, and other places. Do you have an explanation?

— Birgit, Oklahoma

Juliano and the Arcturians: Let me go back to the Schumann frequency. This is a natural frequency emitted by Earth's magnetic field that some say resonates at 8Hz. For the purpose of this discussion, let us say that the Schuman frequency is a measurement of Earth's geo-magnetic wave, and this magnetic frequency helps keep Earth in balance.

Man-made electronic devices (such as electromagnetic radiation caused by nuclear energy and electronic warfare practices such as HAARP) imbalance Earth's energy field. The Schuman frequency has been altered, and it is not uniform across the planet. Also, dams and the waste and destruction of many sacred sites have caused blocks in Earth's meridians. Military experiments by Russia and the United States create high-frequency electromagnetic energy that further disrupt the electromagnetic energy field of Earth. North Korea has exploded nuclear bombs in the inner earth. These harmful activities create discordant frequencies throughout the planet that can put the Schumann frequency out of sync.

Sound waves come from disruptions in Earth's crust. You know these as Earthquakes, but plates rubbing against each other can cause moans and irregular sound patterns as they travel through Earth's crust. We have identified three or four possible sources for these sounds. Some are caused by military experiments using electromagnetic energies in the inner earth. This is unfortunate. Earth is able to absorb a lot of these energies, but think how many nuclear experiments were done in the early 1950s and 1960s and how they might have damaged Earth's crust.

The Purpose of Blessings

What does it mean when people bless everything? What does this actually do?

— Anonymous, Sydney

Juliano and the Arcturians: The idea of blessing is basically offering a vibration to an event, person, or animal. When you say "bless," you are asking for or sending a vibration of higher light, higher energy, and higher harmony. You are asking that the highest good, purification, and healing be directed toward whoever or whatever you send the blessing to. This is what is traditionally meant by "blessings." It is beautiful to say blessings, even when you eat. You are blessing the food and its source.

A blessings is an acknowledgement that all is connected. You want everything that you touch and look at to be in the highest harmony possible, and so it shall be. As a spiritual being on Mother Earth, you have the great power of consciousness to bless things and bring them into higher balance and higher frequency.

Leave Fifth-Dimensional Bodies Behind

When we are in our 5D bodies on the ring of ascension or on Arcturus during meditations, is the correct procedure to always transition out of our 5D bodies before returning to our 3D bodies? I ask this because this is not always stated in every exercise. Often, we are guided just to return to our 3D bodies with no mention of leaving our 5D bodies behind. What happens if we bring our 5D bodies with us?

— Carel, Sydney

Juliano and the Arcturians: It is an oversight on our part when we don't give you complete instructions. When you are done with any of our exercises or meditations, you have your spirit body or astral body leave your fifth-dimensional body in the ring of ascension. Then your spirit body or astral body returns to your third-dimensional body. So you do not bring your fifth-dimensional body back; you move your spirit body out of your fifth-dimensional body.

I will add that your spirit body receives the imprints and interactional energy of your fifth-dimensional body, so when you leave your fifth-dimensional body on the ring of ascension, your spirit body keeps all those vibrational energies and imprints. I hope this clarifies it.

For your second question, you cannot bring your fifth dimensional body with you; it cannot inhabit your third-dimensional body. All you can do is bring your spirit that was in your fifth-dimensional body back. Your spirit received the vibrations, input, and imprint from the fifth-dimensional body.

Extraterrestrial Interference and Free Will

I understand that galactic intermediaries who did not have our best interests in mind altered our DNA, reducing some of our divine faculties. How could the Creator allow that to happen, since it was not our free will to become lesser beings and forget who we were originally meant to be?

— Alessandra, Washington

Juliano and the Arcturians: The history of Earth is filled with master-slave relationships, and you do not have to look to extraterrestrials to find this type of domination. For example, Spaniards in the fifteenth and sixteenth centuries dominated native people in Central and South America. White people in Australia dominated the Aborigines. So when you describe domination or control by extraterrestrials, I want to be clear that this master/slave relationship has a history with your own population.

Why it is allowed has to do with free will and karma. If you allow free will, you cannot choose who can have it and where it can take place. For example, you can't say it's okay to have free will in the United States but not in Africa. Free will has to work for the whole planet, galaxy, and universe.

I agree that free will has led to some very cruel catastrophes, including extraterrestrials coming in and changing human DNA. The good news is that the clarity and purity of human DNA still exists, even after tampering. Human DNA is resilient and has overcome extraterrestrial intervention. It can be purified, rectified, and returned to its highest state.

So my short answer to your question is that this phenomenon of extraterrestrial intervention also exists as a paradigm in master-slave relationships on Earth. As the famous scientist Stephen Hawking said about extraterrestrials, how or why would you think they are going to be benevolent? Some lower extraterrestrial energies are not benevolent, and it is wise to be protective. Many cases of free will in the universe have led to unhappy consequences. This is part of the nature of this universe, which is based on free will.

The Significance of Uluru

I understand that Uluru, or Ayers Rock, in Australia is the heart chakra of Gaia. How did this enormous rock in Australia come to be? What lies beneath it? Is there extraterrestrial activity in the rock?

— Micki, Melbourne

Juliano and the Arcturians: Uluru is one of several places on Earth that connect to the heart of Gaia. There are others, but Uluru is one of the most powerful. Australia was visited by extraterrestrials millennia ago, going back into early aboriginal history. We are talking 40,000 to 100,000 years ago. This rock was raised and brought from a quarry in another part of the planet and levitated to the Australian land mass.

I would like to make a comparison. A black, onyx-type rock in Mecca called the Kaaba also has extraterrestrial origins and was placed there to represent heart energy to Gaia. Mohamed was there in approximately 636AD, but that rock was recorded historically long before the time of Mohamed. Millions of people come to Mecca to be around the Kaaba, and permission has never been given to geologists to evaluate or determine its origins. I would compare Uluru in sacredness to the Kaaba in Mecca.

Attenuation is a term used in radio theory. A radio signal can be so strong that it can blow out a receiver, so signals have to be attenuated or lessened in intensity so a radio can receive it without damage. Both Uluru and the Kaaba were put in place to attenuate extraterrestrial energy so people could receive it without harmful effects.

The only terrestrial or extraterrestrial activity underneath Uluru is from Inner earth. Uluru is connected to the energy in Mount Shasta and to the ascended masters, including Adama. Uluru does have wonderful, powerful connections, and it is good that so many people are attracted to it. Light workers are working with that energy and it is becoming more acknowledged and useful for communicating with Gaia.

The Big Dipper–North Star–Stonehenge Connection

What is the relationship between the Big Dipper, the North Star, and the sacred site of Stonehenge? Or is there no relationship?

— Corae, Nebraska

Juliano and the Arcturians: In order to understand this, I must first explain the concept in astronomy known as precession, which refers to the wobbling of the earth. One wobble makes a small circle, and it takes approximately of 26,000 years to complete that small circle, or wobble. The zodiac and the North Star were not in the same place 6,000 years ago; what is the North Star today was not the North Star 6,000 years ago. It wasn't due north because of the precession of Earth. The pyramids in Egypt are related to the three stars in Orion's Belt. When those pyramids were built, they were in better alignment with Orion's Belt than they are today. Certain calculations and computer models could show you where those stars were 6,000 years ago.

The same alignment issues are true for Stonehenge. Therefore, I cannot tell you that the current North Star and the Big Dipper had that same relationship and alignment when Stonehenge was built. The alignment of the North Star and the Big Dipper has powerful energy, and the Stonehenge area is in a special corridor that relates to and interacts with the heavens, but I cannot tell you with certainty that these are the same star alignments today that were in existence when Stonehenge was built.

Function of the Ego

Can you describe the function of the ego and why is it considered advantageous not to have one?

— Carol, Sydney

Juliano and the Arcturians: I do not want to say that it is better not to have an ego. You need the ego to live and interact on the third dimension. At this time, it would be impossible to gather food, make a living, and live on Earth in any meaningful way without an ego.

The problem is that the ego is part of the animal self, middle self, and lower self. If your ego is dominated by your animal self, then you have domination, jealousy, and other lower emotions. You have a choice where you focus your ego, and you have a choice whether to keep your ego in balance and in harmony with higher light. Many people on this planet are not interested in balancing their ego with higher light and are only interested in lower energies. This is also an evolutionary issue. Part of the evolution of the human race rests on the ability of the ego to focus on higher light.

The ascended masters offer guidelines for working with the ego, and perhaps the best example is humility. When they were incarnated on Earth, many ascended masters were very humble. They did not work for personal gain or for any kind of domination; they worked without ego. But that term "without ego" is a misnomer, because if you are humble, you still have to eat and look after your body. Doing those things requires an ego.

To evolve, you need to keep the ego in balance and turn its focus toward higher energy and higher light, not to lower energies. In your terminology, "ego" often applies to a sense of selfishness or self-centeredness. This is a confusion of your terminology. For example, you say somebody has a lot of ego, and that is not good, because that person is not humble.

Limiting Internal Polarization

How can we think about the following without creating polarization within ourselves?

- *higher and lower energy*
- *3D life and ascension*
- *planetary healers and users/abusers of Earth*
- *starseeds and those who are not starseeds*
- *genocide and peace*

— Kilian, London

Juliano and the Arcturians: You live in the third dimension, which has divisions. In Taoism, it is called yin and yang. We are very fond of Taoism, as it is based on galactic and universal energies and light. Yin and yang, higher and lower, are necessary aspects of the third dimension, so no matter how hard you try, you will experience lower energies at some point. The solution to this polarization is to work with balance.

Higher and lower energies are contained in the yin and yang symbol, which looks like intersecting fish. It is a great teaching tool. The lower fish contains an element of higher energy, and the higher fish has aspects of lower energy. Your soul mission on Earth is to learn to balance and work with both sides. Experiencing both is the unique opportunity for soul advancement on this planet. You need to have this experience for your soul evolution. This particular type of polarization experience is not available on the fifth or other higher dimensions.

Third-dimensional life and ascension can be considered higher and lower energies. The yin and yang symbol or metaphor is that the energy of ascension is in both the third dimension and the fifth dimension. These energies interact, so don't look at them so much as a polarization. You can't have yin without yang, and you can't ascend without a place to ascend from.

Planetary healers and the users and abusers of Earth can also be considered a dichotomy, especially since the users and the abusers don't often have a sense of balance for Earth. This is a new dichotomy and why this is called the New Age, because we are trying to bring in newer Earth consciousness that transcends polarities. Sometimes you have to go to a whole new paradigm, a transcended paradigm, that rises above both polarities and includes a newer balance.

Starseeds revolve around the concept of people having galactic awareness. Some people are not starseeds, but they are still very advanced. There are many examples on this planet of prophets who were not starseeds.

In regard to genocide and peace, that goes back to the master/slave paradigm, which is part of the evolutionary process and evolutionary crisis facing this planet. Astrology has the concept of ages or eras, such as the age of Pisces and the age of Aquarius. Periods of shifting and changing occur even beyond traditional astrology, because traditional astrology eras are around 2,000 years. The 26,000-year cycles I've mentioned relate to master/slave domination and contain karmic energies. For example, at one point in your incarnational history, you have been a victim of genocide, and at another point you have enacted genocide. Having peace without genocide would be considered a balance. Look at these issues with the broadest perspective possible.

Physical Bodies and Ascension

You have explained ascension many times, but I'm still not clear what happens to our physical bodies when we ascend. Do our 3D bodies stay behind, or do they transcend with the higher frequencies? How will friends and family react if we just disappear?

— Carel, Sydney

Juliano and the Arcturians: The physical body does not stay here when you ascend. I have used the term "alchemical" to describe the ascension process and what happens to the physical body. Alchemical is a mystical term that describes a transformation. The physical body vibrates so quickly during ascension that I have called it "shimmering." I have also compared it to the device used in the *Star Trek* TV series that transports physical bodies from the spaceship to someplace else.

In the ascension process, you vibrate/shimmer at such a high rate that you flicker out as you go into a higher dimension; you disappear from the third dimension. You are still in a vibrational state, but you're frequency is out of range of the rods and cones of third-dimensional eyes. To you friends and family, you would seem to have disappeared. Once in this shimmering state, you can use your mind and the help of ascended masters to direct your physical body to the fifth dimension or any new dimension.

DNA and Christ Consciousness

When we ignite our extra ten strands of DNA, will we discard our negative aspects (warrior nature, jealousy, addictions, etc.) and have twelve pure strands working with Christ consciousness?

— Wendy, Sydney

Juliano and the Arcturians: Yes, you will have higher consciousness and higher strands. I don't want to use the word "discard," because those aspects are still parts of you. An interesting comparison in psychology is integrating the old self, or the inner child. In healing the inner child, you don't discard it; you bring it into balance and raise the vibration of the inner child to work with it.

Some great work in modern psychology has been done with

integrating the disowned and negative parts of the self. True healing comes in owning, balancing, and healing those negative or wounded parts. This healing technique represents a true advancement in modern psychology. I would use this analogy when you talk about DNA and the parts or strands of the DNA that are related to the lower vibrations of jealousy, warrior nature, and so on. You don't discard those strands; you heal them and bring them into higher integration.

I mentioned earlier that if lower energy is entangled in human DNA, it still can be made pure. Interventions and intermixing with other beings have taken place; Earth-human DNA is very prized throughout this galaxy. As a species you have the ability to heal and recover your DNA. Let us use a different terminology and say that you can "heal and bring into unity" the lower parts of the self rather than "discard" them. This means your DNA is going to be stronger and more able to fight off any intrusions.

Types of Light Energy

What is the difference between the various types of light we invoke, such as Zohar, Adonai, soul, and etheric? When I stand in white light, I understand it as the light of Christ/manna (soul nourishment) from heaven.

— Angela, Perth

Juliano and the Arcturians: That's a beautiful description of manna, coming from Christ light. There are different light frequencies. Zohar light is a form of light from Adonai. It emanated as a higher light at the beginning of the universe, so it has the flavor of primordial light. There was a purity in the earlier history of the universe that might not be as accessible today.

The light of Adonai is a stepped-down version of the light of Yahweh. (I use that name hesitantly, because I know Kabbalists don't like to speak it. But for our purposes, I will use it.) The light of Yahweh is undifferentiated, and the light of Adonai is the side of Yahweh shown to Earth, so the light of Adonai is more accessible and easier to understand.

If you saw the light of Yahweh, you could not comprehend it. I'll use the example of electricity. Let's say your house can handle 110 volts or 220 volts depending on where you live. If I sent you 5,000 volts, it would blow all the circuits in your house. I might tell you that 5,000 volts is more efficient and you can do more things with it, but you would need a transformer to step down the voltage so your house can handle the higher bower. So it is with the energy of Yahweh; it is too high for you to directly receive it.

The light of Adonai is stepped down for Earth, and Christ light is stepped down from the light of Adonai. Christ is the intermediary between you and Adonai. Christ works with all these higher energies and puts them together so you can comprehend them and heal with them. That's the beautiful service of Christ energy.

Help from Hollow Earth

Will the people from hollow Earth help us move through ascension?

— Wendy, Sydney

Juliano and the Arcturians: Yes, the people of hollow Earth want to be of spiritual help, but they don't want to mix with the third dimension after working so hard to balance themselves. They have worked hard to keep their energy pure, and it has been a long process for them, but they are committed to the fifth dimension. They are committed to bringing Earth into higher light in the right places, at the right times, and with the right people. But they will not come out in the general world, and they will not intervene in a planetary intervention like some Arcturians and others are doing.

But they are accessible and willing to work toward higher ascension if and when you are able to visit them and work with them. They are very protective, and with good reason. They have isolated and insulated themselves from lower Earth energies and have created an etheric, energetic planetary city of light in Inner Earth.

Lord Arcturus

In David's lecture on how to channel, he mentioned Lord Arcturus. Can you give us some information about this being?

— Paula, Sydney

Juliano and the Arcturians: We are happy to talk about Lord Arcturus. I am looking for the right metaphor to describe him, because he is a very high-ranking Arcturian. Perhaps you can think of the Pope and his relationship to the church. Lord Arcturus oversees and coordinates our outreach through the galaxy. Because of his elevated position in this realm, he has certain privileges, rights, and knowledge that some other Arcturians do not have.

Several Arcturian starseeds have direct contact with Lord Arcturus, and he gladly works with those who seek him out. Lord Arcturus has overseen and worked with several planetary ascensions in the galaxy, and he has extreme knowledge of the ins and outs of the ascension process. He has intimate knowledge of the starseeds working with him on Earth, and he knows the problems of third-dimensional planets.

His experiences and successes as an overseer and coordinator of Arcturian outreach with other galactic systems has earned him the title of Lord. It is similar to a knight being given a certain title, such as Sir. He has higher respect and authority in dealing with planetary matters outside the Arcturian system.

The Arcturians have a higher role in galactic systems, and we are spiritually in charge of this part of the galaxy. The Arcturian Council has divided the galaxy into four realms, and it is our responsibility to work with souls who seek higher dimensions in your realm, which is one of the outer realms.

Loved Ones after Ascension

With our new understanding of what happens to our 3D bodies when we ascend, what happens to the loved ones we leave behind? Will they be part of our ascending soul group? Will they understand why we just disappeared? Should we give them some prior explanation?

— Carel, Sydney

Juliano and the Arcturians: When you ascend, your loved ones will be shocked and distraught, but they will also know of your spiritual practices. Your ascension will dramatically boost their spiritual progress. Your loved ones are not working on this like you are, because they doubt the truth of ascension. So when they see firsthand that ascension has occurred, they will overwhelmingly be transformed or, to put it another way, their spiritual light quotients and openness to spirituality will rise very quickly. But they cannot go yet, so they will still stay on Earth.

Your ascension is an individual matter. When that time comes, you are given the choice to ascend and must agree or decline. We recommend that you not use that nanosecond to review your life. Do not think, "What's going to happen to my dog?" or "What will happen to my loved ones?" If you hesitate, ascension can pass you by, because ascension is extremely high spiritual technology that allows an opening between dimensions that brings in higher energy. It takes the ascended masters great effort to open that interdimensional corridor. I jokingly use the example of a weight lifter wanting to lift 500 pounds. He can do that for a brief time if he is in really good shape, but he can't hold it forever. The opening for the ascension only opens briefly when the right time comes. So say yes, and go. The loved ones you leave behind will be transformed by your ascension.

Will your family be part of the soul group that ascends? Well, are they part of your soul group now? Family members will undergo a tremendous transformation, because anyone who is close to a person who ascends will be positively and spiritually affected. They can choose to be part of your soul group. You can invite them. You might have asked why you're with someone not as spiritual as you to begin with. One reason is because they know they will open up spiritually by being with you.

The short answer is that yes, they can join your soul group. After you've ascended you can, if you choose, be in a position to communicate with those loved ones. Spiritual communication, once you are deceased, is limited to certain people in certain situations for higher advancement. But those like you who have gone to the fifth dimension can be given certain privileges to communicate with them.

Let us compare death to ascension. You might know when someone is going to die. For example, they might be in a hospice program. Because they are deteriorating, you feel that you are prepared, but when you get a phone call in the middle of the night that so-and-so has died, you will still be shocked. When you ascend, your family will be shocked, but they will get over it and be happy for you. They will experience grief, because the separation is like a death in that they will not see you in this plane any more. But they will also experience a tremendous spiritual transformation. Think of the Apostles and Jesus's followers. How did they feel after he died? How did they feel after they discovered he had ascended? They were joyful, because it gave them hope and influenced them in positive ways. They believed that a spiritual transformation for the world was about to occur.

It is always good to explain what you are doing. Share your spiritual beliefs and spiritual practices. But you don't have to convert people; ascension is not about proselytizing. On the other hand, do not hide your beliefs. Discuss them and share them. Your discussions can cause an opening, although perhaps not for a few years. Later, they will say, "Oh, yes, I remember what you said."

The Fate of Narcissists

There are so many narcissists in this country and probably the world. They insist on stealing energy from everyone, and they refuse to see truth. I wonder how the world is going to move forward if the majority insist on belittling, abusing, and stealing from the rest of us. Does a narcissist have to wait for their next life to awaken, or is there a solution to flipping a narcissist into a self-empowered human being in this life time?

— Christopher, Mullumbimby

Juliano and the Arcturians: Most of humanity still operates from the animal self. What you call narcissism, I call the animal self, because the lower animal self is concerned only about itself and what it can accumulate and control. We need people to go into the middle self, which is the more ethical self. There is a greater need to correct, save, and work for all humanity and to save Earth. The main way Earth's situation will change is through some major intervention. That could be a first contact or a messianic intervention. A major change could also come from some overwhelmingly influential event on the planet that forces self-centered people to begin looking to the higher self.

One of Jesus's roles was to help humanity connect with the higher self. Higher ascended masters elevate people so that they can connect with the higher self. The narcissist can only be shaken by some overwhelming spiritual or messianic energy, and we believe such an event will happen that shakes them loose of their lower thinking.

Earth after Ascension

When our planet ascends, will there still be a 3D planet left as well as a 5D planet? If so, what life forms, if any, will be left? What will happen to humans of lower density? Will they remain or go to another planet that resonates with their lower vibration?

— Carel, Sydney

Juliano and the Arcturians: I am going to say jokingly that all of the above is true. When you ascend, you disappear and go into a higher realm. Planetary ascension is more complicated than personal ascension. Earth is a whole planet and cannot ascend as a unit, because it has so many lower energies. If some parts of a 3D planet elevate and others do not, it will be left behind.

Look at it this way: A fifth-dimensional Earth already exists; part of Earth is in the fifth dimension. Let us look at personal ascension. Your fifth dimensional body already exists and you will inhabit it when you ascend. This is part of the preparation we are doing with the Arcturian crystal lake exercises, for example. Planetary cities of light and certain areas of sacredness or holiness will go, but the rest of Earth will remain in the third dimension. I am also talking about the etheric energies of Earth. You have to conceive that Earth is a multidimensional planet.

The other part of your question has to do with those left behind after ascension. Will people of lower consciousness be allowed to stay, or will they go to another planet? That issue has yet to be decided. Some people might go to another planet. Usually mass migration and mass incarnation from one planet to another occurs for cosmic karmic reasons. For example, Saddam Hussein and his henchmen were sent to another planet that is now dominated by similar types of people. But these decisions are made by the masters and people overseeing individual soul groups. Some people may still stay on Earth.

How Auras Vibrate

Before our reactivation meditation at our planetary city of light, we cleanse and protect our auras. I would like a more precise description of how the aura vibrates. For example, do we visualize the aura pulsing in and out, like in an exercise class where we flex our muscles in and out, or does it shimmer like a glittering disco ball?

— Carel, Sydney

Juliano and the Arcturians: You have a great opportunity to creatively work with your aura, and I cannot give you hard and fast rules. I can give you outlines of what works and things you need to do, but you adapt them to your individual aura, your individual energy field. You can do what you just described or visualize the aura in the cosmic egg. You can visualize attachments discharging from the aura, and then close the holes left over from those attachments. Many exercises depend on your creativity and skills of visualization, focus, and concentration. You are all at different levels.

The most important thing is to cleanse and purify your energy field. The idea of purification goes back to the ancient religions on this planet and even to the ancient Israelites who were given instructions on how to purify themselves. Some purification exercises were accomplished symbolically through ritual bathing in what was considered pure water. Some Native Americans received information on purification from their star families and were instructed to use the sweat lodge. When you are in high heat, your pores open and you can release negative energy. You can also achieve purification through mantra meditation. The key to aura work is the cosmic-egg exercise. You can also use that exercise to open your crown chakra and receive Arcturian light and energy. Focus on downloading Arcturian light and energy through your crown chakra, and let that higher light download into your aura.

There might be 1,000 different aura exercises, and as we work together, I'm sure we will describe even more. The point is to expand your identity to include your aura.

Grace and Giving

Can you explain grace a bit more? Is it like a point system? For example, on Earth we have rewards cards that give us something extra when we reach so many points. Can we use our "grace points" to take away karma?

— *Anonymous, Sydney*

Juliano and the Arcturians: That is a wonderful analogy. I believe you are referring to rewards cards and credit cards that might give you a 1 percent rebate when you make a purchase. For example, you earn $100 when you spend $10,000 on purchases, and the rebate is then deposited into your account. Grace does accumulate into your account. Through grace, you are forgiven karma. I also use the analogy that with grace you can skip a grade, accelerate your growth, and move into the fifth dimension.

From our standpoint, you earn grace in service. If you are dedicated and sincere in your service toward others, you help your ascension. When it's time for ascension, you might not be at 100 percent. In that case, grace can help you skip a grade and accelerate your evolution. That is how grace can help you.

Grace really comes from commitment and doing things from your heart. Maybe you've heard of the different levels of charity. In the Kabbalah, one level of charity is signing your name on a check and everybody knows you gave $10,000 to a social service. In a higher level of charity, you remain anonymous. Nobody knows of your contribution, and you do not want them to know. In your analogy, it is like you get more points when you do that kind of anonymous giving. But the first kind is still good, because at least you are donating. My point is that when you donate at the highest level, you do not expect a reward. You just do it for the purity of service.

It is the greatest service to take care of someone's funeral, because you get no reward from the person who died. In a higher level of grace, you don't do things because you want to get the reward points; you do them just for the joy of service

The Upcoming Wave of Ascension

Is the fact that we seem to have less and less time an indication that the first wave of ascension is close?

— *Mikki, Melbourne*

Juliano and the Arcturians: The fact that it feels like you have less time means you're realizing the finiteness of this reality. An aspect of this reality is that everyone thinks they are going to live forever or that there is no such thing as death. Maybe that can be defined as an illusion, but this tells me you're more focused and aware of your limitations and the limitations of this reality and the third dimension; you want ascension to be here, now.

You need to finish your karma — your life lessons — as quickly as possible. Once you give permission for your soul to bring these lessons, they can seem overwhelming, and it might seem that you don't have enough time to finish them. Part of grace is that you work to the best of your ability to complete them.

Sun Cycles and Climate Change

Is all this climate change actually due to a cold Sun cycle and not because of humans?

— Marie, Gold Coast

Juliano and the Arcturians: The solar cycle was first observed in the 1700s, and the average solar cycle has been described as lasting from seven to eleven years. Unexplainable periods of lower solar activity last even longer. This phenomenon is called the Maunder Minimum; the last one lasted seventy years. The minimum is a lower point of solar activity that can last for decades. When they say lower solar activity, that means fewer sun spots, solar storms, and solar particles coming to Earth. Does lower solar activity mean cooler temperatures for Earth?

We're talking about a very fractional change. If the sun is 5,000,000 degrees, for example, it might experience a 1 percent decrease. One percent of 5,000,000 is miniscule, but it could be enough to lower the amount of energy and heat coming to Earth, and it could trigger changes. So you are correct that a relationship exists between the Sun and Earth's weather, but it's complex. On a very linear level, the Sun sends a lot of energy to Earth, but there's no feedback from Earth to the sun. Our observation is that interactions occur between the Sun and all the planets in the solar system, the Sun and the Central Sun, and the Sun and the rest of the galaxy.

We have talked about the amount of time it can take for the solar system and Sun to make one revolution around the galaxy. Estimates range from 400 million to 500 million years. These are tremendous cycles.

The Sun is affected by multiple issues, but let's just bring it back down to Earth and say that this lower solar activity produces less heat, even though by a small amount, and it could contribute to what some call colder energy. But the sun is interacting with an earth that's getting hotter and hotter due to human-made causes.

A feedback loop system exists between the Sun and Earth. Imagine this system as the Earth heats up. (Some people still don't believe this, but Earth is getting hotter because of human-made activities.) The Sun, as part of the feedback loop system, might try to counteract some of Earth's heating by cooling itself down so not as much energy hits Earth and the planet doesn't heat as fast. That would give Earth a little more wiggle room and make global warming less severe. The sun's feedback loop with Earth is complex, because the sun also interacts with other forces that I've described, including its position as it travels around the Galactic Sun.

The short answer is yes, the Sun is giving off slightly less energy, and this does have an effect on the planet's temperature. But at this point in the history of the planet, global warming is predominantly caused by human activities. Global climate change can be ameliorated somewhat by the Sun, but do not be fooled. Even now, a solar mass eruption could be catastrophic to Earth's electromagnetic energy field.

Ocean Pollution

Our planet is drowning in plastic. Plastic has recently been found at the very bottom of the Mariana Trench, the deepest part of the Pacific Ocean. How can we starseeds and biorelativity healers approach this problem? I have heard of a bacterium that can consume and dissolve oil. Can it also dissolve plastic? If it is so, can we activate this bacterium through meditation?

— *Yvonne, Sydney*

Juliano and the Arcturians: Yes, you are correct. A bacterium can be produced that eats plastic. The problem is that it would have to be done on a massive scale. This is a global problem with far-reaching consequences, and scientists and Earth's planetary healers have still not evaluated the dangers of widespread plastic distribution across the planet. I would compare this issue with radiation and groundwater contamination, because it is very difficult to separate contamination from the water and radiation from the soil.

My recommendation is this: The planet is in a time of great need for new scientific interventions to cleanse and rebalance. The bacterium is one answer, but it is not the total solution. Many new Arcturian starseeds and starseeds in general are awakening in consciousness. At the same time, others have not yet awakened and need to be awakened.

Think for a moment about the greatest scientist in the 20th century, Albert Einstein, who made his best discoveries when he was a young man. We need to awaken the higher consciousnesses and higher scientific minds of young starseeds so they can download and receive the correct scientific information to do this purification and cleansing of Earth. Cleansing the planet has to be a global movement. A global effort must be made to begin this, and we must work in biorelativity for quantum energy and quantum healing. The correct scientific and intuitive energy must come to the right starseed scientists who can make the correct discoveries that can be successful and accepted.

As you can see, it is not just one event but a series of events that will lead to the cleansing of the planet. I recommend that we look into the biorelativity and the chain of events I outlined. This can be downloaded and projected into the noosphere so that a series of investigations and cleansing activities with higher scientific reliability can be received, activated, distributed, and accepted around the planet on a quantum level.

Councils on Arcturus

Is there a hierarchy or council on Arcturus?

— Josh, United States

Juliano and the Arcturians: There is a hierarchy on Arcturus, but it is not linear like on Earth, where one person is better than another or has more power. Our hierarchy is more like a circle, where everyone sits around the table in equality. There is a distribution of roles and tasks are assigned, but no task is viewed as better or higher than another.

Specific people are assigned to hold the energy of the planet through meditation. People are assigned as healers. People are assigned for incarnational work from past lives and future lives. The list goes on. People do oversee the entire civilization, which might seem equivalent to your leaders, but from our perspective, these are just assigned roles. We have specific councils that meet. For example, a council oversees our interactions with Earth starseeds.

Negative ETs

Are negative extradimensional, extraterrestrial, or interterrestrial beings or organizations still operating on the planet, or are only negative humans left?

— *Christopher, New South Wales*

Juliano and the Arcturians: Many negative humans, ETs, and entities operate on Earth. The problem has gotten worse because of the holes in Earth's aura and the holes in the space-time continuum surrounding Earth, but these are not the only reasons for negative and lower energies.

Earth is now more vulnerable to negative energies. We look at negative energies and entities in the way you might look at your body's immune system. You live in a world with lots of pathogens. Your immune system might be weakened from exposure to radiation, contamination, past-life issues, unresolved issues, and so on. The population's immune system has weakened to certain diseases. We find this, for example, in the outbreak of Ebola.

This is one small but significant example of lower immune systems becoming more vulnerable. Vulnerability also comes from drug use, which includes pharmacological drugs as well as street drugs. Unfortunately, many people are also exposed to large amounts of pesticides in soils that wash away during flooding or rains and get into drinking water. So contamination is widespread. Due to this contamination, you have to work hard to keep your aura and energy intact.

Another problem is radiation. The damage done to Earth's aura by above-ground nuclear testing is phenomenal. Even though it was stopped forty to fifty years ago, the damage has not been repaired. This also lowers your immune system and ability to fight off lower energies. Using drugs lowers the immune system. Earth's weakened aura lowers its protective shielding. Lower energies and entities have greater opportunities to come into the Earth.

I think the correct medical term is opportunistic, which relates to the idea that a bacteria that enters a weakened body has a greater opportunity to take advantage of that weakness. Lower energies and lower entities are also opportunistic. This is an opportunistic time for lower energies and entities to continue to proliferate on Earth.

Ancient Humans and the Garden of Eden

You mentioned that over the past million or two million years, a number of human species have existed, including Neanderthal, Cro-Magnon, and now modern Homo sapiens. *As I understand it, we were in light bodies before we came to Earth. Once on Earth, we got caught up in the third-dimensional reincarnation cycle, took on karma, and began the descent into lower levels of consciousness. Where does this fit into the timeline of* Homo sapiens? *Did we arrive at the time of the Garden of Eden? When was the time of the Garden of Eden? How long did it last before we lost sight of our godliness?*

— Carel, Sydney

Juliano and the Arcturians: First, the time line is approximately 20,000 years ago, and this would be equal to the Atlantean civilization. This time line could go back 30,000 to 40,000 years, equal to the Lemurian civilization. When you describe descent and being stuck in karma, I want to clarify that beings voluntarily came to this situation for a variety of soul reasons.

The Creator requested that higher beings come down and elevate this third dimension, and beings like Cro-Magnon and Neanderthal did not have higher consciousness. Higher consciousness came into existence only recently, about 20,000 years ago, and that is even generous, because some people would argue it was 5,000 or 6,000 years ago. If we give the figure 20,000, that gives you at least a little leeway.

The prototype of this form that you now inhabit took several million years to develop, but the self-consciousness you now exhibit as a species only recently came to the planet. The Hebrew Bible has an interesting perspective: Adam was downloaded into the Garden of Eden, and special energies allowed him to adapt to this area. He was asked, not forced, to step into the third-dimensional world.

Garden of Eden events were used to download higher consciousness, and they occurred several times in the history of your species. If the original downloading was not successful, then it was tried again. The Atlanteans achieved higher consciousness and a return to the Garden of Eden, but we can agree that the Atlantean experience was not successful, because it ended in the destruction of their civilization. The concept of the Garden of Eden relates to my prediction of the omega man/woman, where a higher consciousness will again be introduced.

Celestial Equator

In our meditation on the equator, you mentioned that the plane of Earth's equator projecting outward to the celestial sphere defines the celestial equator. Can you explain this for us?

— *Anonymous, Sydney*

Juliano and the Arcturians: Keep in mind that the celestial equator is an imaginary equator projected onto a circular universe on the night sky. It is not an actual celestial equator, because the original astronomers from ancient Greece, Rome, and so on, believed the universe was a sphere and Earth was in the center of that sphere.

We now know there is no acceptable description of the shape of the universe. When you talk about the Big Bang, people imagine there was an explosion that went out equally in all directions, similar to a large sphere. But one of your scientists has described it as an explosion of dynamite that shoots off in many directions.

Nonetheless, this was the early accepted perception of the shape of the universe. Therefore, the celestial equator is projected onto this imaginary sphere outside Earth. This perception is useful for identifying objects and positions of stars, so the model has great acceptance. But it is an imaginary celestial equator projected onto a perceived shape of the universe.

Fifth-Dimensional Egos

Do fifth-dimensional beings have egos?

— Belinda, Sydney

Juliano and the Arcturians: Yes, they have a sense of self, but it is a higher ego, an expanded ego. The ego is not necessarily negative, but the ego on Earth is predominantly ruled by the animal self. In higher realms, the ego is strongly influenced by the higher self. The ego is of higher consciousness and connected to the soul.

Travel with a *Merkabah*

In a previous lecture, Archangel Metatron gave us a chant to raise the Merkabah. *How can I activate this* Merkabah *permanently to travel to the fifth dimension and to my home planet? Will I experience any imbalance if I do not activate it correctly? How will I know that my* Merkabah *is activated properly and permanently around my energy field?*

— Hong, Vietnam

Juliano and the Arcturians: *Merkabah* is a visionary Egyptian word meaning chariot or traveling etheric vehicle. *Merkabah* travel was used by ancient Israelites, mystics, and ancient Egyptians. Elaborate hymns and rituals were performed to do *Merkabah* travel to higher realms. Some of these rituals and hymns have been passed down while others have been lost.

The original concept of the *Merkabah* is correct. As I said, the rituals, hymns, and mantras used then are, for the most part, unknown today. Also, and I say this somewhat humorously, the original *Merkabah* vehicles were shaped like chariots to look like the traveling vehicles of that day. If they had known about smart cars, SUVs, or spaceships, they might have used one of those vehicles as the symbol for *Merkabah* travel.

We have set up the Arcturian crystal lake and Arcturian corridors to be of greater assistance to starseeds. These makes it safer and easier for you to practice your *Merkabah* travels. You can work with me and the Arcturians to use these corridors to travel to the Arcturian crystal lake. When you become comfortable with that, you can travel to your home planet or other places in the galaxy.

We set up these corridors and the crystal lake because we realized those ancient rituals and hymns would not be discovered, and we wanted something for you to use that was safe. Also, in today's world, it is difficult for you to meditate and practice six to eight hours a day as people did who traveled by *Merkabah* in Egyptian times. For them, this was a full-time job. They also had the benefit of using the pyramids' special energy centers to enhance their spiritual work.

You can create your own *Merkabah* vehicle. If you want to use the symbol of the chariot, that is fine, or you can use a magic carpet, bubble, sphere, or Toyota Camry. The Arcturian corridor and Arcturian crystal lake give you security. We set up the corridors because we wanted you to travel safely through the fourth dimension. If you study and read some ancient Jewish manuscripts, you will find they had problems with lower entities attaching themselves to people traveling through the fourth dimension. In our method, you go through the Arcturian corridor and do not have to worry about lower energies attacking you. You go to a safe place on the fifth dimension and travel to other fifth-dimensional places from there.

Healing Earth's Aura and the Space-Time Continuum

In a previous lecture, you mentioned holes and rifts in the aura of Earth and in the space-time continuum. Is there anything we can do individually to help close or heal these holes and rifts?

— Jan, New Hampshire

Juliano and the Arcturians: The holes and rifts in the space-time continuum and Earth's aura are major problems. Repair is the role of planetary healers. I have recommended that you approach the repair of Earth's aura the same way you approach healing your personal aura. You have certain tears, rips, and rifts in your aura, which are just part of the baggage of being on Earth. No matter how spiritually-minded you are or how much spiritual healing you have done, your aura still has some minor tears and rifts. You might have bigger rifts due, in part, to physical trauma, psychological trauma, or wars.

The job of repairing Earth's aura is done through planetary healing work. You need large planetary healing groups to do this. You can apply the exercises for personal aura work to healing Earth's aura, such as: shimmering, cosmic egg work (then go around the aura looking for holes and visualize them being repaired), and sending light to areas with dark spots. For example, a very dark hole over Iran and Iraq lets in much negative energy that could lead to another world war. This has to be repaired. The technology and knowledge are there; the problem is how to apply these healing techniques on a global basis. How can we get meditators together worldwide to do Earth balancing exercises? These exercises need to have strong arcan energy and enough power to repair Earth's aura and the space-time continuum.

The rift in the space-time continuum is even more complex. This rift allows future beings to come in as well as beings from other places you might not want. As a healing visualization, imagine a gigantic needle being directed by a healer and sewing up the rift.

Climate Change Is Real

You have told us that you perceive a mass ascension on Earth will happen soon. Can you please define "soon?" Also, I don't see signs of mass extinction taking place, and climate temperatures seem to remain bearable. Are we just adapting, or what is really happening here on Earth?

— Mary, Vancouver

Juliano and the Arcturians: What is bearable to you in Canada might not be bearable to people in Bangladesh or India where they experience temperatures of 130°F. Some pockets on Earth are still intact from climate change or catastrophic climate change, but other pockets suffer greatly.

There is a concerted effort to block the reporting of these catastrophic changes. How many people in the United States read about threatened islands in the South Pacific or heat waves in Bangladesh or India? People deny the crisis. Sigmund Freud described the defense mechanism called denial, and I understand why politicians and leaders deny this crisis, because the consequences of accepting it as truth means people in power must make radical changes they are not willing to make. Change primarily involves giving up oil and carbon.

So just because you do not see the collapse of the biosphere in your home country does not mean it is not happening in other parts of the world. It is all perspective. It is happening, but this is a huge, complex planet — huge in the sense of the amount of life. On some planets, only certain areas have a biosphere, but Earth has biospheres on the whole planet. This is unusual, but it means Earth has a great deal of flexibility. As ice melts, new areas for agriculture will appear that did not exist before. Continents and lost civilizations will be discovered under melted ice packs. But the mass extinction is still occurring.

"Soon" means two, three, or four years. The ascension date is being balanced by the ascended masters for maximum usage and to take into consideration the need for keeping starseeds here on the planet as long as possible to assist in the purification of the planet.

Details of Ascension

If we have no physical bodies after the moment of ascension, how will family members and those left behind deal with requirements like death certificates, wills, bank accounts, and so on? Will the phenomenon of instantaneous ascension become so publicly acknowledged that governments have to address it?

— Paula, Sydney

Juliano and the Arcturians: You are correct that mass ascension has no precedent, and it is difficult to predict how these details will be resolved. There was a somewhat humorous movie made by a Christian group called *Left Behind*. The movie attempted to document what would happen when ascension occurs. Some of these things were rather ridiculous. For example, in the movie a plane crashed after an airline pilot ascended, because the copilot was too shocked to fly.

These are difficult questions and not going to be easily resolved. Some laws say that if somebody has disappeared for two or three years and no news about them has come forward, they are considered dead. Then a death certificate can be issued. To the best of the ascended masters' abilities and people's abilities, attempts will be made to resolve these issues. There will be mass confusion for other reasons at the time of the ascension. Some catastrophic changes will occur right before ascension, including major disruptions in world economies and world communication systems. It will be like everything is nice and stable, and then suddenly that stability is broken.

Babaji and Cultural Change

There are many stories of great saints who lived and still live in the Himalayas. I am interested in Mahavatar Babaji, the ageless sage mentioned in Yogananda's book Autobiography of a Yogi. *According to legend, he was born in 203 AD, and his practice of intense devotion in Kriya Yoga helped him overcome the dying process. As a result, he is able to materialize and dematerialize at will.*

Is it true that Babaji is the ageless saint who overcame the dying process, and is this similar to ascending and being able to come back to the third dimension at will? Did Jesus go to India to study Kriya yoga with Babaji (as Jesus also ascended and came back to his disciples), and do they work together to help the planet and humankind? Why have the teachings of spirituality by so many holy men and women in India not changed attitudes about the caste system, the untouchables, and the appalling treatment of women?

— Carel, Sydney

Juliano and the Arcturians: Babaji is the real thing. He ascended and used his energies to come back, the same choice you can make when you ascend, although we have asked you not to make this decision until you are on the other side. Babaji has lots of support that enables him to do this. It is a true miracle, a true blessing, and it would be wonderful if more of his life were known, especially his accomplishments as a spiritual teacher. It is a great honor to be with him; he still does wonderful service.

Why have his work and spiritual interventions not changed the caste system and the treatment of women? Cultural and religious mores are so strong that even higher beings like Babaji have been unable to change them. In some cases, these higher beings (I am not saying that Babaji was like this) accepted the caste system as part of the normal way of the universe. That might sound strange, but the Hebrew Bible is another example. Many higher beings are depicted in the Hebrew Bible, which promotes slavery and says homosexuality is wrong and punishable by death.

This tells us that prejudices existed even among high masters, and cultural and religious convictions were very difficult to break. How could somebody become an ascended master and still experience these prejudices, or at least not try and stop them in their culture? You do not have to be 100 percent perfect to ascend. The help of your guides and teachers and your devotion to spirit all play important roles in ascension. Devotion and intention are very important for the success of your spiritual work.

Your devotion and intention are great assets. The great masters who ascended through their devotion were able to overcome their prejudices, but they were not able to change their cultures. It is a tragedy that the caste system continues and that women are brutalized and traumatized. Even countries with higher spirituality have lower cultural practices and prejudices. Higher guides and teachers also need to look at how they can contribute to cultural change and equality for all beings.

City of Light Guardian

You have suggested that each city of light choose an ascended master to be its guardian, overseer, and guide. For example, a city could choose Kuthumi to be its guardian and overseer. That city could then call on the energy of Kuthumi to be downloaded into their area. His energy would permeate many people's consciousnesses in the city, and hopefully people would even teach his name as the guardian of your city. Can you explain the difference between having an ascended master like Kuthumi as our guardian and having spirit guides from crystals as our guardians?

— Elizabeth, Sydney

Juliano and the Arcturians: I am happy to answer this question about the planetary cities of light and the ascended masters. First, the spirit guides on the Planetary Tree of Life are ascended masters, and these ascended masters have been assigned to each sphere, because they are able to represent and hold particular energies. When you seek a guide for a planetary city of light, you have many options. I said you could choose Kuthumi or others, because each planetary city of light has unique members. Some members might have relationships with Kuthumi or other spirit guides they feel strongly about. Kuthumi, for example, might resonate with their energy.

We embrace flexibility. We are not about having a rigid structure, although we certainly endorse structure when needed. If you, as the planetary city of light, want to use the ascended master that is closest on the Planetary Tree of Life to your city, then by all means use him or her. But if you feel an affinity for a particular ascended master, choose him or her to be your guide or patron. There is flexibility in the ascended masters and the Planetary Tree of Life, because the original Kabbalistic Tree of Life used the Hebrew patriarchs such as Abraham, Isaac, Jacob, Moses, and Joseph as their guides. Different guides and teachers resonate with different people, so flexibility is always important.

Effects of 5G

Some countries have banned 5G from use, but it looks like 5G has the green light in Australia. How will 5G affect our physical and spiritual bodies? Apart from the cosmic egg and Arcturian blue healing light, what else can we do to protect ourselves both spiritually and physically?

— Micki, Melbourne

Juliano and the Arcturians: With 5G and all electronic devices, the effect is based on the rule of the square of the distance. This means that the closer you are to the transmission, the more potentially damaging it can be to your body and energy field. The best example I can give is holding a cell phone right by your temple. Even though it emits low wattage, perhaps a quarter of a watt, it emits at a very high frequency. A cell phone close to you has a higher potential to create disruption in your energy field and affect your brain. Even moving the phone six to ten inches away dramatically decreases the harmful effects.

The term "5G" means the fifth generation of smartphones. This technology uses frequencies higher than 4G, therefore the potential for harmful interference to your brainwave activity increases. First, note the distance you will be from the 5G source. Secondly, how vulnerable are you? There is no way to be electromagnetic-radiation free, unless you live in a cave, surround your house in aluminum foil, or live in a lead-lined bedroom. Those who are younger, especially children under the age of sixteen, are more susceptible to the effects of damaging high-frequency waves, such as 5G. The brains of older people can tolerate and work with some disruptive frequencies.

There is also a cascading effect. Everyone is exposed to a lot of toxicity, including electromagnetic radiation. You can tolerate a certain amount of toxicity without harm. But you can reach a point where one more exposure is enough to set off a brain dysfunction. You can modify the harmful effects of 5G electromagnetic radiation by taking breaks, breathing fresh air, and going into open spaces or forests. You might have a spot in your home that is electromagnetically free, and I recommend having a meditation room that is electromagnetically free. The cosmic egg exercise can help you re-solidify your aura. Anything that helps you reorganize your energy field is always good.

The truth is that you are living in the twenty-first century, and there is literally no way to escape this problem. I do not see that 5G is much more harmful than 4G.

Inner Light and Kundalini Energy

How can we activate our inner light, and how can we raise our kundalini energy?

— Elena, Romania

Juliano and the Arcturians: You have your own path. To raise your vibration, you can follow our Arcturian spiritual teachings. You can follow the Kabbalah or Christian mysticism. You can use yoga, which has specific exercises for raising kundalini. Many roads lead to the top of the mountain. The basic advice for raising kundalini and finding inner light is to work with your chakra system, which you can open through specific exercises. Some of these exercises include pumping up the chakra, rotating the chakra, and linking the chakras as triads. One of the most exceptional chakra exercises is sitting at night under the star Arcturus and receiving cosmic energy. If Arcturus is not available in your region, there are other stars, such as the Pleiades, or you might have a favorite star. Sit outside and receive that cosmic energy.

The lack of accessibility to the night sky and to cosmic energy and light is a tragedy of the modern era. Ancient people at least had this nightly access. I recommend sitting outside at night, especially between 9:00 and 11:00, and opening your crown chakra and receiving the light from your favorite star.

Galactic Cycles of Light and Dark

I have heard that the planet cycles in waves of light and dark that last over 7,000 years. The period of light we are in right now will last 200 years, and this is the best opportunity to ascend. After that, the dark takes control for 500 years, and suppression of the mind will be total. An ascended master will then appear and bring back balance, but the suppression of the mind for so long will make it impossible for at least half the population to ascend. Is there anything we can do now to help this possible future situation?

— Christopher, New South Wales

Juliano and the Arcturians: People have different ideas about the coming and going of light and darkness. I do not totally agree with your time frame and will present another model I am more comfortable with that is based on an actual astronomical phenomenon. I am referring to the astronomical energies related to the positions of the stars, the galaxy, and the Central Sun. For example, we have talked about the Central Sun alignment in 2012 that created a great opening and opportunity for further mind expansion.

The model I offer is based on the precession of Earth, which has been defined as the wobble of Earth and is similar to a spinning top. When you spin a top, there is a point at which it slows and wobbles. One revolution of such a wobble is called a precession of Earth. The Earth has a wobble that takes about 26,000 years for one rotation. This wobble is extremely important astronomically, because even a part of one rotation relates to the position of the North Star. For example, 6,000 years ago, the North Star — now Polaris — was not the North Star due to the precession of Earth. Some pyramids in Egypt were built in alignment with the Belt of Orion, but the Belt of Orion no longer aligns with the pyramids.

The second aspect of the relationship to the position or the wobble is the zodiac, which is traditionally divided into 2,000 year periods. You have left one period and are now coming into another — the Age of Aquarius. The wobble of Earth has come into alignment with the constellation Aquarius which has certain significances. So the light and dark periods you refer to are actually more accurately described in the relationship between the zodiac and the positions of the stars.

There are theories of what the Age of Aquarius is like. There are discussions about openings, the Age of Pisces, and other cosmic alignments. Using these models brings different frequencies and opportunities. Earth is now in an ascension mode, and this period has ascension openings.

The stars themselves are not causing these openings — the constellation Aquarius is not causing the opening. The positions of the stars and their relationships to Earth's position represent an alignment of cosmic energies now coming to the planet. Another factor is the revolution of the solar system around the galaxy and the Central Sun. One estimate is 500 million years, which is an extraordinarily long time. The last time Earth had this same energy field was 500 million years ago.

What Happens after Death

What happens when we die? Where does the soul go? Is there anything we can do for a departed soul?

— Sia, Sydney

Juliano and the Arcturians: When you die, your soul goes to the fourth dimension; the key point is that you stay in Earth's incarnational cycle. When you go to the fifth dimension, you are freed from Earth's incarnational cycle. The fourth dimension has low, middle, and high layers. Some people get stuck and are not able to pass through to higher levels. Some people who go to the fourth dimension go into a deep sleep and do not wake up for centuries. Others awake immediately and go on to other lifetimes. There are many different factors.

Yes, there are things you can do to help people. If you sense that a person is stuck, you can send them light, love energy, and encouraging messages. People who die traumatically can have a particular problem. If they died in a war, for example, their soul energy can be stuck on the battlefield. You can go to the battlefield and send out energy to release this person. This was big problem in the American Civil War where many lost souls got stuck at the battle of Gettysburg.

But there are many other examples of large battles where souls got stuck after they died.

Try to open communication with the dead person. You can send them energy light from the third dimension. Occasionally, people on the fourth dimension can communicate with you and send you energy and information.

The Expanding Universe

Astrophysicists tell us that the universe is expanding and that the galaxies farthest away from us appear to be moving away at the fastest rates. At the same time, we are told that within about 4 billion years, our Milky Way galaxy will collide and merge with the Andromeda galaxy. How is this consistent with an expanding universe?

— Henry, New York

Juliano and the Arcturians: We need a way to conceptualize the universe. The simplest model is to picture the universe as a round balloon. Imagine one dot is in the center of the balloon and one dot is two or three inches below that. As you blow up the balloon, those two dots move farther and farther away. This is the traditional way of thinking of the expansion of the universe. As you point out, that means these two galaxies are moving away from each other. So how can it be that they will intersect and collide?

The answer is very mysterious. Even though humanity likes to represent the universe as a sphere or a big balloon, that is not accurate. The universe has no known shape. What would be the shape of an object that is infinitely long? You cannot imagine it.

The second part of this answer is that, being infinite, the universe is so enormous that the two galaxies that are now, say, millions of light-years apart, are really an insignificant distance apart. The laws of expansion of the universe do not exactly apply to these two dots or two galaxies that are on a path to collide with each other. I want to emphasize that in terms of infinity, the Milky Way galaxy and the Andromeda galaxy are like specks of sand.

The laws of how things intersect do not apply to something of infinite mass. The normal laws of space and motion, which include the phenomena of galaxies intersecting and coming toward each other, cannot explain the collision of galaxies. In summary, it is your perspective that is important. From Earth's perspective, there is no way that expanding galaxies would collide in an ever-expanding universe. But from the perspective of the infinite universe, such a phenomenon is totally logical and possible.

End-Time Events

I have learned from the Arcturians that we are ascending with Earth. I have also learned that if our mistreatment of her body reaches a certain point, she will shake us off like a dog shaking off fleas. Can you clarify for me please?

— Ulli, Sydney

Juliano and the Arcturians: A dog shaking off fleas is a very good metaphor. I think shaking is a fitting description of end-time events. In end-time events, Earth responds to blockages of her meridians, such as the removal of forests, pollution of oceans, and so on. But shaking off these things is more complicated, because we are talking about a spiritual intervention. We are talking about enlightened beings on the planet who want to communicate with Earth spiritually. They are trying to change the spiritual light quotient of the planet. But the truth is that you are in end-time events now. End-time events also refer to uprooting technology and civilizations. Different factors are destroying the biosphere. They have to be addressed, and that is what you are seeing now. That would be my comparison to the shaking dog.

Past-Life Memories

Why are we born with no memories of our past lives? We are told that the reason we reincarnate hundreds or thousands of times is so we can integrate our pasts with the present and evolve spiritually. Was this decided by God, or did a malevolent group of extraterrestrials trying to control humans make us reincarnate here through the astral plane? Could you please tell us the real reason?

— Carel, Sydney

Juliano and the Arcturians: The real reason is in your DNA and the codes placed into your pineal gland and third eye. In their early stages, civilizations block memories of past lives. There are also codes based on angelic DNA activations, which are part of the Adam species. You lose your initial memory of past lives because this is a freewill planet. If you remembered everything that happened to you before, you might act in a way that would not be in your highest interest.

For example, if your brother killed you in a past lifetime and you both incarnate again, you might decide to kill him in this lifetime to pay back the karma. Obviously, that would not be a good solution to the karma problem in this lifetime. This is a very simple example. Basically, the baby gets a kiss on its forehead before it enters and comes to Earth. That kiss causes a temporary forgetting so the individual has the opportunity to make freewill decisions.

Past-life memory is not totally erased. In fact, through hypnotic regressions and other methodologies, therapists can help you remember and recover past-life memories.

Male or Female in Fifth Density

I understand that male-dominated thinking created Eve as the "trouble maker," and if the world had been female-dominated, it would have been a male. When we enter the fifth dimension, will our 5D bodies be totally androgynous, or will we be male or female? Do we make that choice?

— Jane, Gold Coast

Juliano and the Arcturians: Your soul is androgynous, but even in the fifth dimension there are males and females. You can choose to be male and female, but these are not the male and female you experience on Earth. The male on the fifth dimension has integrated many female characteristics.

You have been male in many lifetimes and female in many others. Each experience has advantages. Now we are coming to a point where people want to be both male and female in the same lifetime or don't want to identify with either sex.

We come back again to flexibility. In the fifth dimension, you have many choices, and you can be any of these or all of them. That is part of the beauty of the fifth dimension.

Origins of the Kangaroo

It was nice to hear about animals and where they came from, such as the whale and the horse. Can you tell us about the kangaroo? Where is it from, and is there a sentient kangaroo species?

— Christopher, New South Wales

Juliano and the Arcturians: The kangaroo is a figure from the Andromedan galaxy, which has a multitude of planets similar to Earth. A lot of these animals are galactic and on an evolutionary reincarnational cycle, just like humans. Animals also have what I call cosmic reincarnation, in which there is a wider choice of situations or planets throughout the galaxy that offer specific opportunities. For example, if you only incarnate on Earth, certain experiences might not be available to you, or you might have to wait 100 to 200 years or longer for a specific experience. If you participate in cosmic reincarnation and you feel the need to reincarnate immediately after your lifetime, you can find an appropriate situation throughout the galaxies. Animals such as the kangaroo have evolved to the point that they have cosmic reincarnation.

Some higher beings brought the kangaroo to Australia, but this was all part of a grand plan in alignment with the kangaroo's evolutionary status.

Importance of Ceremonies

Can you explain the importance of ceremonies? We have ceremonies when we marry, are christened, or have birthdays. Why do we bother with these events?

— Anonymous, Gold Coast

Juliano and the Arcturians: A ceremony provides a sacred time and a sacred place. It takes you out of normal, logical, linear time to sacred, holy energy around the event. Ceremony also provides a stepping stone, because it is difficult in your linear life to transition from normal consciousness to expanded consciousness. A ceremony gives you a way to prepare and move into expanded consciousness. Ceremonies are very valuable, and we encourage them for this reason.

Create a Positive Reality

Some people and ETs say we create positive realities for ourselves and others by only focusing on good things. But the rubbish patch still exists in the Pacific Ocean, and other injustices and suffering go on whether we acknowledge them or not. How is this any different from being indifferent or in denial?

— Anne, Sydney

Juliano: Everyone has a sphere of influence. You can influence a certain number of people and a certain aspect of the planet. Part of your work is to expand this sphere of influence. It is true that many of these events, such as the rubbish in the ocean, continue. When people speak of creating a reality, they usually refer to their personal reality. You can help shift and change the planetary reality, but you need to gather more personal power, which is part of the idea of the Group of Forty. You want to increase your personal power and increase the energy for change. You have to accept limitations exist, even as you hope and work toward expanding your sphere of influence.

Past Lives in Helio-ah's Holographic Healing Chamber

In the meditation "Personal Holographic Healing of a Past Event and Healing Near-Future Events" by Helio-ah, the dials on clocks in the holographic chamber on Athena are set to 12:00. I can turn the dial of the first clock to a time in my life I would like to heal, and 6:00 represents when this lifetime started. Once this is healed, I can turn the dial on the second clock as far into the future as I wish. My question is, can I turn the dial back past 6:00 on the first clock if I want to heal an event in a past life?

— Carel, Sydney

Juliano: The holographic healing chamber has numerous buttons. When Helio-ah teaches you how to work with energy in this lifetime, she calibrates the setting on the clock or the screen to the energies of this current life. There are buttons to the right of this holographic computer. One button brings up the program for your present lifetime. In this present-lifetime program, 12:00 takes you back to your birth. Let us say you want to go to a past lifetime. Now the program and clock have to be recalibrated for different settings and different energy access. Helio-ah presses a button labeled "Past Lives," and the program then represents your past lifetime instead of your present lifetime. The program has the same basic structure, going from 12:00, which represents your birth in that past lifetime.

The computer setting in the holographic healing chamber needs to be changed from present life to past lives. After changing the setting, you work in the same structure that Helio-ah described for the present lifetime; the clock is calibrated so you can go backward or forward in time.

Appendix A

Advanced Biorelativity Exercises

Juliano and the Arcturians, Adama, David K. Miller, and Chief White Eagle

Planetary biorelativity healing is an important skill necessary for the survival of planet Earth. Planetary healing and biorelativity focus on connecting to the spirit of Earth: You, as a planetary healer, can form a relationship with Earth. The stronger the relationship, the more influence and affect you have on the planet. You have a network that increases your thought power. We call thought power arcan energy, which increases planetary healing when you meet the following two criteria: At least forty people must be connected, and they must be located in different areas of the planet.

This section focuses on exercises for Earth's aura that I divide four parts: emotional, mental, spiritual, and physical. Earth's aura has four bodies, just like the human aura. When we look at Earth's aura, we often want to work on the physical part in biorelativity. For example, we want to stop storms, earthquakes, and volcanoes. But how do we use biorelativity to work with the spiritual, emotional, and mental parts or Earth's aura?

Earth's Spiritual Layer

The spiritual part of Earth is the overseer of all purpose and directions for development. It is described, in part, by the Earth's spirit names: Gaia and Mother Earth. If you want to strengthen your bond with Earth's aura, then using the name Mother Earth is important. How do you relate to your mother? You show your mother respect;

you show her love. You strengthen the spirit of Earth's aura by showing respect through ceremonies. If fifty people around the planet want to relate to the spirit of Earth, you can do an exercise in biorelativity where you all come together in a ceremony. For example, each person could build a small medicine wheel on their property, and all could enter their medicine wheels at the same time in ceremony.

Another way to relate to the spiritual aura of Earth is to chant together and honor and respect Earth by spiritually chanting Earth's spiritual name: Gaia. Visualize Earth's blue aura above the emotional, mental, and physical layers. You want to strengthen your connection to the spirit of Earth and send her energy and light.

Another important way of connecting to the spirit of Earth is by working with the guardian of Inner Earth known as Adama. Adama is located at Mt. Shasta in California. You can go into Inner Earth and help strengthen the connection and healing of the spiritual aura of Earth. We will now lead you on a special exercise to connect with Inner Earth and Earth's spiritual aura.

Take three breaths. Feel yourself go into a deep state of relaxation and expanded consciousness. Your spirit body rises out of your physical body and goes to the top of the room where you join other exercise participants in a circle. I, Juliano, meet you, and as a group we travel at the speed of thought to Mt. Shasta, California. [Tones.]

We are now over the mountain in Mt. Shasta, California. An etheric crystal is in the mountain, which we begin to raise. As we raise the crystal, I call on the guardian of that crystal of the Inner Earth, Adama, to speak with you.

Explore Inner Earth

Adama: Greetings, I am Adama. I live in the Inner Earth, the spiritual home of Gaia. We will visit the spirit of Earth and help strengthen Earth's spiritual aura. One of the great openings to Inner Earth is here in Mt. Shasta. Inner Earth is an interdimensional corridor. Only those of higher consciousness like you can enter this corridor and go to the spirit of Earth. I open a doorway that is hidden in the mountain. Follow me and Juliano as we enter Inner Earth. [Tones].

We travel into Inner Earth on a mission to strengthen the spiritual aura of Earth. We come now to a great palace, a great center of light in

Inner Earth. We have prepared a special chair, a special room, for you to join me in meditation. Choose a seat in this room in my palace. Feel the great spiritual energy of this Earth. In Inner Earth, we are close to the spirit of Gaia. Take three deep breaths.

In the center of the room, in the center of the circle, is a holographic image of Earth and the four layers of Earth's aura. We will now work with the spiritual layer of the aura. Because we are in Inner Earth, we have great powers to communicate with her spirit. Connect your third eye to the holographic image of Earth and send spiritual energy to Earth's aura. Say these words: "I, (say your name), am aware of the spirit of Earth. I, (say your name), am aware of the spirit of Mother Earth. I am aware that Mother Earth is a spiritual energy." As you think and send that affirmation, see the spiritual aura of Earth become a deeper, brighter blue.

"I am aware that Earth is a spiritual energy. I am aware that Earth is a spiritual planet. I am aware of Gaia, a spiritual planet." Send these thoughts into Earth's holographic image here in my palace in Inner Earth. We will go into meditation now.

"I am aware of Earth's spiritual energy. I am aware of Earth's spiritual aura." Choose whatever sentence you feel is appropriate, and project that thought into the holographic image of Earth and Earth's spiritual aura. See it become brighter and brighter. We will go into silence now. [Silence.]

"I am aware of the spirit of Earth. I am aware of the spirit of Earth." The Earth's aura becomes a deeper blue. The Earth responds to your recognition and love.

Now let us look at the emotional energy of Earth, the emotional aura. The emotional aura of Earth is composed in part of all the reactions throughout the history of the planet. Remember that Earth is 4.7 billion years old and has experienced many changes, such as ice ages and asteroid strikes. Now Earth is going through rapid, dramatic change. Earth has emotions; she has outbursts of energy. Given today's abuse of the planet, Earth might respond or react with strong emotion. Together, let us send a golden, harmonic light — a light of balance — to Earth's emotional body. We are here in Inner Earth and in the center of a special healing room. Look at the holographic image of Earth, at the second layer, the emotional layer of Earth's aura. It is filled with multiple types of emotional energy, both light and dark. Send golden, harmonic healing light to the emotional body of Earth. We will go into silence now. [Tones.] Earth's emotional body has received the golden light you sent. Now send this affirmation: "Let Earth's emotional body be in golden, harmonic balance."

Next, we go the mental body of Earth. The mental body of Earth is composed of thoughts from the Creator and the historical record of all planetary thoughts from the beginning of Earth. Earth is a growing planet. You must think of her as a living being, but Earth is an adolescent and not a full adult. Earth has ideas and programs in her mental body, just like you have thoughts and programs in your mental body. We want to put a new program, a new thought pattern, into the mental body of Earth. The new thought is: "We, the planetary healers on Mother Earth, want to install a program in which we work together to rebalance this planet. We, the planetary healers, want to work with you, Gaia, to help rebalance this planet." Send that program, that thought message, into the mental energy field of Earth. Let us go into meditation while you focus on that program. [Silence.] Earth has received your new program. She is aware that you have worked with her before, but this new program will help strengthen her bond with you.

The final layer of Earth's aura is the physical layer. This is the layer we most often work with when we do the biorelativity. In biorelativity exercises, planetary healers want to change certain weather patterns, earthquakes patterns, and generally lessen the destructiveness of Earth's catastrophic events. On this layer of the aura, you see Earth physically as she is today. This includes all weather patterns, ocean currents, and earthquake patterns. As a living planet, Earth is always changing. Focusing on this layer of the aura, use this affirmation: "I admire the physical beauty of Earth. I admire the physical beauty of Gaia." Think about the holographic meaning of these statements. In holographic work, one part can represent the whole. In biorelativity, you often go to the area that needs work and is having problems. In this biorelativity exercise in Inner Earth, focus on the physical aura of Earth and strengthen it by going to a beautiful place and admiring and appreciating Earth's beauty. By holding and admiring the beauty of Earth, you strengthen her aura and her physical energy. In your meditation, go now to that beautiful place and admire it. Send it admiration and love, and Earth's physical aura will strengthen. Let us go into silence as you visit this beautiful place. [Silence.]

As you hold this holographic image, see Earth's physical aura grow stronger. See Earth's mental aura grow stronger. See Earth's emotional aura grow stronger. See Earth's spiritual aura grow stronger. Now I will strengthen the holographic image and strengthen Earth's energy field.

It is time for us to leave Inner Earth. Together, we leave my palace in Inner Earth and travel upward to the top of Mt. Shasta. I, Adama, welcome you any time to my chambers, to my palace in Inner Earth, where we can directly speak to and interact with the spirit of Inner Earth.

Meditations and Exercises

David: This section contains three examples of biorelativity meditations and exercises for planetary healing. Biorelativity is one of the main spiritual tools the Arcturians teach to help rebalance Earth. With these biorelativity exercises, starseeds can come together in meditation and telepathically communicate with the spirit of Earth to achieve balance and healing. These planetary healing meditations can also help unblock Earth's meridians. The exercises include spreading higher light and higher consciousness through the noosphere and through the general consciousness of humanity.

The Arcturians believe that by gathering together in meditation groups, our thought power — what they call arcan energy — can directly heal planetary imbalances and help move Earth toward a fifth-dimensional foundation. During these biorelativity exercises, usually fifteen to forty people participate. Those participating in the Group of Forty come from around the globe. We meditate together using international phone lines or internet webinar sites. Our Arcturian meditation groups hold over fifteen biorelativity sessions per month.

These three meditations represent different biorelativity techniques that I hope you find useful. They should give you an idea how Arcturians approach planetary healing. If you are interested in learning more about biorelativity, or want to participate in these exercises, please visit GroupofForty.com or contact the author at davidmiller@groupofforty.com.

List of Biorelativity Exercises

- Use etheric crystals to increase arcan power
- Visualize TV radar to find storms and visualize storms changing directions
- Merge future and present Earth and visualize the two worlds next to each other
- Send affirmations to Gaia
- Use a medicine wheel to talk to Earth
- Connect with Central Sun energy to increase thought power using the Iskalia light mirror
- Visit Inner Earth and work with Gaia
- Go to the moon and see Earth as a whole planet
- Go outside the solar system and work to harmonize Earth within the solar system
- Place the image of Earth in the Arcturian crystal lake
- Coordinate all twelve etheric crystals and see them interact, creating a new meridian system (a bypass system)
- Picture all the great Earth healers coming together to balance Earth
- Work with Native grandmother and grandfather spirits
- Do holographic work in which one part and the whole benefit
- Use an etheric screen and etheric crystal to create an affirmation for the omega/man woman image to help manifest it on Earth

Biorelativity Meditation — Technique 1

Juliano and the Arcturians: Let us start this biorelativity session by visualizing the ring of ascension. The ring of ascension is an interdimensional halo around the earth. It has the unique ability to interact and receive energy from the fifth and third dimensions. You and fifth-dimensional masters can bilocate to the ring of ascension where you can interact and receive messages. They can also download energy and information to you.

In this exercise, fifth-dimensional masters will download special light and special healing to weather patterns in the United States. Ascended masters have access to special healing energies that otherwise would not be available to third-dimensional planetary workers.

To begin our biorelativity exercise, take three deep breaths. Go deeper and deeper into a trance state and raise your access to higher dimensions. Your spirit body rises slowly but directly out of your body. Using thought projection and bilocation, you send your spirit to the ring of ascension. This huge ring circles the planet and in some places is miles wide. Go to that part of the ring of ascension that is over the United States. [Tones]: "Oh."

Feel the joy and expansion of consciousness in this part of the ring of ascension. I, Juliano, along with Sananda, P'taah, Lord Arcturus, and Helio-ah, reside with you in this section of the ring of ascension. I now download into the ring of ascension special planetary healing technology and tools that you can use to help with flooding and stabilize weather patterns over the United States. With the help of Lord Arcturus, I now download these patterns onto a big screen in front of you in the ring of ascension. [Tones.]

This is a multidimensional screen, similar to your computers that contain the computer inside the screen. Projected on the screen is the central part of the United States where flooding and unstable weather are occurring. Envision with me a golden dome of light placed over the ground in all areas of concern. This interdimensional planetary healing dome breaks up unstable weather and encourages it to pass over.

See this golden dome on the screen over this area as you sit in the ring of ascension. Now visualize the weather forecast radar that you see on TV showing green or red for unstable, strong storms. See those storms pass over these areas because of the golden dome of protection. Meditate on all unstable weather passing over as the weather comes in contact with the golden dome. As you meditate on this golden dome, project strength into levees that might be compromised or weakened. Visualize them as strong and sturdy. Visualize the earth absorbing more and more water and the flooding quickly receding.

Let these thoughts in your meditations be strong as you interact with this beautiful screen in the ring of ascension: "All levees are stable, the storm passes quickly, and the earth deeply absorbs all waters so floods can recede." With your assistance, I will download this energy and healing exercise into the noosphere of the Earth. One, two, three.

This golden dome, which is about 500 feet high, will now etherically transfer to the third-dimensional realm of Earth. Say to yourself: "With the help of this group, I hereby transfer this golden dome into the central part of the United States where there is weather instability." Meditate on that affirmation.

Before you return to your Earth body, know that this image of planetary healing we created together on the screen will stay in the ring of ascension so the masters, including Lord Arcturus, P'taah, and Helio-ah, can hold this image for you, for the middle parts of the United States, and for all parts that are unstable. We will continue working on this beautiful image of healing. Before you return to your Earth body at the count of three, take one last breath of the energy of the ring of ascension. Feel its beauty and higher light, for we work together with you for rebalancing this planet. Come back to your Earth body in perfect alignment, saying to yourself, "I re-enter in perfect alignment." One, two, three.

Hold this vision of light and planetary healing on a screen above and in front of your third eye. See the same image we worked with in the ring of ascension. Let the Midwest come into balance. Let U.S. weather patterns come into balance with our assistance and the assistance of the ring of ascension and the ascended masters. So it shall be.

Biorelativity Meditation — Technique 2

Chief White Eagle: Heya-ho. Greetings, I am Chief White Eagle. We are gathered today in this pow-wow of planetary healers to talk and show respect to Mother Earth and ask that she respond to our request. How often do we have the opportunity to speak directly to Mother Earth? How often does Mother Earth request us to do something for her? The time has come for humanity and Mother Earth to have a two-way relationship. While we ask for her support and to change certain patterns, we must listen and learn what Mother Earth wants from us. [Tones]: "Heya-ho."

Open up your inner ears, your inner hearing. Just like you have an inner third eye, you have inner hearing. Attune your inner hearing to Mother Earth, so before we ask for the balancing of weather patterns and stabilization, open your heart and inner ear to Mother Earth and see and feel what she wants to tell us. Let us go into silence and meditation while you attune to that inner hearing. [Silence.]

Heya Ho. I want to hear from you, so I ask the channel to tell us what you have heard from Mother Earth. What is the request? What message are you receiving from Mother Earth? I will have the channel read the names of the people. [Tones]: "Heya-Ho."

I, Chief White Eagle, say to Mother Earth that we are listening to you. We hear the need for a balanced vibration. We hear the need for protecting the forests, cleaning the oceans, and bringing balance in all ways. Please continue to speak to us and we will listen to you. I, Chief White Eagle, have received a message that Earth is trying to get our attention. She is trying to awaken those who are in control of this planet, to awaken them to the need for balance. Today, we ask Mother Earth to bring balance to the Midwest, but please understand this is just a bandage; it is a request to modify an imbalance that has multiple causes and needs to be addressed globally. [Tones]: "Heya-ho."

Oh, Mother Earth, I meet here with these wonderful starseeds around the globe. We request that you bring a balance of weather patterns back to the Midwest and to the Southeast United States. This includes a balance of calm and stable weather, a balance without storms and tornadoes, a balance of normal temperatures, and a balance that recognizes the need for the creation of light vibrational energy in alignment with a balanced and harmonious earth. We sit today in this circle of light in the etheric tepee and download this affirmation into the spirit of the Earth: "Mother Earth, bring harmony and balance to the weather patterns over the United States now. Mother Earth, bring balance and harmony to the weather patterns over the United States now." We see this affirmation over the blue sky, over the horizon of the United States.

In meditation, now see these words emblazoned in fiery-red energy like a marquee across the United States, perhaps fifty miles above the continent: "Mother Earth please bring balance and harmony to the weather patterns over the United States." We will go into meditation. [Tones]: "Heya-ho."

At the count of three, let us lower this beautiful affirmation into the noosphere and into the spiritual center of the feedback loop system of Mother Earth. One, two, three.

The affirmation has been downloaded into Mother Earth and into that area of the feedback loop system. She has received your request and knows our mission is to continue holding the sacred light and sacred energy of this planet and to hold our spiritual interaction with Mother Earth on the highest frequency.

All my words are sacred. We love and respect you, Mother Earth. Please respond to our request today.

Biorelativity Meditation — Technique 3

Juliano and the Arcturians: I bring my starship Athena over the United States, home to thousands, if not hundreds of thousands, of starseeds living on this North American continent. Some have compared the current U.S. population to Atlantis before its downfall and geographic upheaval. Perhaps what you are experiencing now is a similar warning, a similar situation. Perhaps you remember your lifetime in Atlantis and being as concerned then as you are now about the outcome of the planet. Just like in Atlantean time, many people in power are in denial about the seriousness of the situation.

Let us first, in our biorelativity, come together in a circle of light over the United States and meditate on raising the spiritual light quotient of this country and its leaders, the decision makers, so they are moved by spiritual insight; they will understand that technological advancements have overtaken spiritual wisdom. At this moment in our biorelativity meditations, we starseeds come together and seek spiritual energy to raise the spiritual vibration of this country. [Tones]: "Omega light."

Visualize a halo of light around the United States, including Alaska and Hawaii, the same way you visualize the ring of ascension around Earth. We understand that some natural disasters are obvious while others are slow-moving, such as bee deaths, soil contamination, and ocean dead zones. It all comes down to one core factor: the spiritual light quotient of this country. It will take spiritual upliftment and a move away from materialism, economics, and the stock market. It will take an understanding that Mother Earth is a living spirit with great powers of purification and cleansing, but do we really want the balance to tip so far that an end-time event must occur for final purification? We want to see this happen preemptively and preventatively.

So we visualize this halo of light around the United States into which we Arcturians download omega light. [Tones]: "Omega light." Omega light brings out the highest evolutionary energy and highest spiritual evolution. Now visualize this intense omega light as a halo around the United States. Let us meditate on that now in silence. [Silence.]

Omega light fills this halo of light around the United States and now permeates the noosphere, the country's whole etheric aura. This light goes into the subconscious of all peoples, for it will take a spiritual awakening to shift consciousness toward a new view of what is happening on this planet. To the best of your ability, see this halo as an endless source of spreading light, of higher light, throughout the noosphere of the United States and its etheric aura. We will go back into meditation. [Silence.]

See this light spread like a golden, thin layer of etheric light over the entire United States. This light will begin a spiritual awakening of interacting with Mother Earth and seeking a new spiritual balance in all aspects of American life, including how we treat nature. [Tones]: "Omega light."

As this omega light spreads, let it come into your aura, consciousness, and energy field so you can raise your vibration and be a more powerful planetary healer. Again, we will go back into meditation as you absorb and see that light spread throughout the country.

Let the omega light come into your crown chakra and let it go over the farmlands in the Midwest where the soil is contaminated. Let it go over the dead zones in the Gulf of Mexico. Let it go over the areas where bees are sparse, and let the proper conditions return so bee colonies can once again propagate to their fullest extent. [Tones]: "Omega light."

This country, the United States, has the highest potential for high consciousness and high spiritual light. Let that potential activate now to the fullest extent.

The light has spread throughout the country. The halo will remain in effect for the next twelve hours. May there be an upliftment of the spiritual light quotient so new solutions and cleansings can correct the imbalances in this country.

Advanced Biorelativity and the Omega Earth

Biorelativity helps create balance and harmony on Earth. Balance and harmony help maintain proper conditions in the biosphere, including the correct percentages of oxygen, nitrogen, and other chemicals necessary for all life.

Earth is a living spirit with a feedback loop system; it receives information from across the planet and makes necessary adjustments to maintain balance. Earth's balance has been stressed since at least the Industrial Revolution in the 19th century, when more pollution and contaminants went into the soil, air, and water systems. This has been going on now for over 150 years, but Earth's strong feedback loop system and has been able to maintain balance. Now Earth is stressed and struggling.

Besides the chemicals I just mentioned, the feedback loop system copes with factors such as ocean currents, the jet stream, earthquakes, and volcanic eruptions. A variety of different energies affect the biosphere. You have seen in the biorelativity exercises that we attempt to work with all of these sources, all of these energies, in order to maintain balance. But we are now in an era of the new physics, or perhaps it should be called the new astral physics. Earth's balance is affected by many different sources, including the Sun, galaxy, and Central Sun.

We also must talk about the future and the past, because time is relative in astral physics — how you experience time is based on where you are and how fast you travel. I will not get into a technical discussion of time here, I only want to explain that in advanced biorelativity, we work with Earth's balance in the solar system and with time.

In some biorelativity exercises, we look toward the future Earth, which we see differently than what you now experience. Earth also has to be in balance with the solar system and all its planets. For example, what happens on Jupiter needs to be in balance with what happens on Earth. So while we work with the protective energies and aura of Earth, we must also work with the protective energies and aura of Jupiter. Why do we use the example of Jupiter? Because it is the largest planet in your solar system and protects Earth and other planets from harmful cosmic forces. Jupiter captures comets coming from outside the solar system and can change their directions.

I want to discuss asteroids for a moment. They are mainly in the asteroid belt, which is the space between Jupiter and Mars. There are thousands, perhaps millions, of asteroids in this belt, and some have unpredictable or irregular paths. Sixty-five million years ago, an asteroid struck the Yucatan Peninsula area of present-day Mexico, which resulted in the fifth mass extinction the destruction of the dinosaurs. The asteroid was several miles in diameter and struck Earth at high speed. The resulting dust cloud blocked sunlight and destroyed vegetation. Dinosaurs died because there was not enough food. Ninety percent of all life forms died.

We do a protective-balance biorelativity exercise in which the energies of asteroids and comets are not allowed to enter Earth's aura. When we do biorelativity, we also telepathically and spiritually work with the energies of the solar system. Biorelativity can help keep objects, like asteroids from the asteroid belt, from striking Earth and protect Earth from other harmful cosmic energies.

Higher planets or advanced planets have completed stage one of development and have gone on to stages two and three. These planets work with their solar systems, protecting them from asteroids and comets. They also work to protect themselves from their sun, their star. Why is a sun dangerous? Earth's Sun, for example, has huge nuclear explosions and solar storms that create harmful, coronal mass ejections. There are several examples from the 1980s and early 1990s in which solar storms wiped out electricity and radio communications in Canada for short periods of time.

The Sun's radiation and storms could wipe out all satellites in Earth's orbit. The conditions would have to be just right for such an occurrence — Earth would have to be in the right position in its orbit around the Sun and the sun storm would have to directly face Earth — but such a storm could strike and wipe out all satellites. Such an event could damage computers, electronic devices, the internet, and telecommunications, causing catastrophic results for civilization.

In advanced biorelativity, we extend our work and energy fields to the Sun, planets, and other places around the solar system. We can do a biorelativity healing to project protection around the edge of the solar system or around the Sun. Again, higher planets have gone through stage one and are now in stage two of planetary development. They work with all energy in their solar systems, because they know that harmful cosmic energy comes from many different places.

You need an aura shield around the solar system, because you want to block any harmful rays or energies from reaching Earth. These are advanced levels of biorelativity that work with the solar system.

Now I will discuss biorelativity in terms of time. We work with the future of a planet as well as the present. Let me make a comparison between your future self and present self. Let us say that in the future you are an ascended master. You fulfilled your special mission and have attained higher consciousness. In the future, you are more in balance and alignment with the highest energy. In our work in planetary and personal healing, we say that looking at your future self is very important. Here is another example: Perhaps you are going to plant a tree. You know the tree is going to be 100 feet tall, so you give the tree enough room so it has the space to grow. You are interacting with the tree in the future.

In the future, you have higher enlightenment and can connect with and bring back to the present the energy of your future self. In advanced biorelativity, we want to know what is the future of the planet and how to connect with that energy now.

I am going to lead you in two exercises. The first works on the solar system and protecting Earth from asteroids, comets, and forces from the Sun. The second exercise works on the future Earth. Knowledge of the future can help you change your behavior in the present. If you know that putting contamination in the ocean will kill the ocean, and if you see that future, you will hopefully change your behavior so that negative future does not manifest. The future is not written in stone. In future work, we look at the highest level, the highest possibility of you and the planet.

We earlier discussed the omega man/woman, the highest evolutionary stage of humanity. We can also visualize the highest evolution of the planet — the omega Earth. What does omega Earth look like? It is in perfect balance with itself, the Sun, and the planets in the solar system. Higher life forms live in harmony with each other. The weather, volcanoes, and earth movements are balanced. Many different harmonies are represented by the omega Earth.

Solar System Meditation

Let us do the first biorelativity meditation with the solar system. Visualize the solar system to the best of your ability with the Sun in the center. See the planets Mercury, Venus, Earth, Mars, Jupiter, Saturn Uranus, Neptune and Pluto. If you can, visualize beyond Pluto and see the outer edge of the solar system. Place an etheric protective shield — seen as a white light — around the solar system. This huge shield protects from harmful cosmic energy that could come to Earth.

See the planets in balance with each other and with the Sun. See Jupiter, the largest planet, serving as the guardian of the solar system by deflecting comets that might hit Earth. No objects dangerous to Earth get past Jupiter. Visualize Jupiter as having a strong magnetic and protective force. See a great balance between Earth and the Sun. Any harmful energy or storms from the Sun do not harm Earth, Earth's aura, or Earth's electromagnetic field.

There are three levels of shielding: A protective level that wraps around the outside of the solar system, Jupiter's strong electromagnetic force, and the Sun in balance with no harmful solar storms striking Earth. Hold these three things in your imagination while we meditate in silence. [Silence.]

See all asteroids in the asteroid belt staying away from Earth. See a strong protective energy field around Earth that pushes away any asteroids that come close to Earth. Again, we will go into silence. [Silence.]

Visualize the Sun, and see all harmful storms that give off dangerous electromagnetic energy pushed away from Earth. All planets that have gone through stage one and have progressed to stages two and three of planetary development have used biorelativity effectively to balance their solar systems in this way. [Tones.]

Your work balancing these forces also goes into the noosphere so that new technologies, new warning systems, are created to protect Earth. New planetary technologies will be developed in the near future that ensure the survival of planet Earth, the Blue Jewel.

Future-Earth Meditation

Now let us go to our second exercise, which is to bring positive energy from future Earth to present Earth. For this exercise, thought-travel to the Arcturian starship Athena, which is over Earth's North Pole, approximately 100 miles above the planet in an interdimensional corridor.

Take three deep breaths. Feel and allow your spirit body to rise up from your physical body, out of your crown chakra, and up a corridor to the North Pole and to my starship Athena. [Tones.]

As you travel through the corridor, you enter my beautiful starship, Athena. I, Juliano, am there to greet you. I take you into a large auditorium where you see two large screens. The screen on the left shows an image of present Earth and the screen to the right shows future Earth. Sit down in a chair as we work with these two images. As you look at the image on the left, you see holes and distortions in Earth's aura. You see energy and meridian blockages, contaminations, and a great deal of stress in the oceans. The biosphere, including weather patterns and geological patterns, are out of balance. You see wars, conflicts, and energies of polarization.

Now look at the Earth on the right, which I call Omega Earth. Like all advanced planets, wars and polarizations are erased, weather patterns are controlled, storms are weakened, volcanic eruptions are non-existent, and there are no earthquakes. This image represents a future time when Earth is at its maximum balance and energy. Omega Earth has unity consciousness; spiritual light shines through everyone on the planet. The oceans are clean and Earth's aura has no holes. Disease is eradicated. All plants and animals thrive. Hold this image of future Earth and visualize it as omega Earth. We will go into meditation as you focus on that energy and anything else that comes to you that needs to be in omega Earth. We will go into silence. [Tones]: "Omega Earth."

See omega light from the fifth dimension fill the future Earth and bring new harmony and balance. [Tones]: "Omega Earth."

Look at the two screens in the auditorium. See a pipe or a cable connect future Earth, omega Earth, and present Earth. See the energy of future Earth pump into the energy of present Earth. Future Earth is filled with highest ideals and principles and the highest healing energy, including unity consciousness and omega light and balance. We will go into silence as you see this energy transfer from future omega Earth to present Earth. [Silence.]

A tremendous amount of higher energy transfers from future Earth to present Earth and is received on all levels. Let the energy of omega Earth be received into present Earth. Enough rain will fall across the planet and droughts will cease. All aspects of the biosphere will experience greater balance of weather. The oceans will thrive, and, best of all, mankind will have new respect for taking care of the environment. Continue to see the transfer of light from the higher future Earth to present Earth so that all things necessary to manifest and achieve this higher balance will happen.

Now it is time to leave the auditorium. Walk out of the auditorium on my starship Athena. We go to the corridor and travel at the speed of thought toward your home on Earth. [Tones.]

You arrive six feet above your body. At the count of three, re-enter in perfect alignment. One, two, three. You are back in your body. You still feel the power of this strong energy work with future Earth. You can easily, at any time, travel back to Athena and work with this transfer of energy from future Earth, omega Earth, to present Earth.

Thank you for your participation and willingness to work with these higher biorelativity forms and exercises.

Glossary

Adam species — A term used by the Arcturians to describe *Homo sapiens,* or Earth humans. Man (Adam) is formed from the earth.

Adam Kadmon — The Hebrew term for primordial, or first. It is the prototype for the first being to emerge after the beginning of creation.

Adonai — A word for God in the Hebrew Bible that means "My Lord." It is also the galactic word for God.

Adonai Tzevaoth — Hebrew for "lord of hosts." See *Kadosh, Kadosh, Kadosh.*

altered states of consciousness — A term in modern psychology used to describe different states of consciousness. This includes the dream state, trances, meditation, and heightened perceptions of reality. The latter state is usually described as being able to see ultimate truth and experience the present more fully. In the 1960s, the term was also used to describe drug-induced changes in consciousness.

Andromeda — A large spiral galaxy 2.2 million light-years from the Milky Way. The Andromeda galaxy is the largest member of our galactic cluster. It is commonly referred to as our sister galaxy.

Andromedans — An advanced, higher-dimensional race of beings from the Andromeda galaxy. A specific group of Andromedans is currently working with the Arcturians in their effort to facilitate Earth's ascension process.

arcan — An Arcturian term used to describe the energetic power of thought forms. It is compared to watts. The higher the wattage in a light bulb, the brighter the light. Likewise, the higher the arcan power of a thought, the greater effect it can have on this reality.

archangel — The highest rank of angels in the angelic hierarchy. The Kabbalah cites ten archangels. They are considered messengers bearing divine decrees.

Arcturians — An advanced race of beings living in the fifth dimension in the area of the star Arcturus.

Arcturian Planetary Tree of Life — The updated version of the Kabbalistic Tree of Life. The Arcturians have modified the ten-sphere Kabbalistic Tree of Life, expanding it to twelve spheres and assigning updated spirit guides (Sananda, Chief White Eagle, Quan Yin, etc.) to each sphere instead of using biblical matriarchs and patriarchs (e.g., Jacob, Moses, Aaron, King David, and so on). The Arcturians have described in more detail how the Arcturian Planetary Tree of Life can be interpreted and used for planetary healing. Therefore, twelve geographical locations around the planet have been assigned to hold the specific energy of the spheres.

Arcturus — The brightest star in the constellation Boötes, also known as the Herdsman. This is one of the oldest recorded constellations. Arcturus is the fourth brightest star seen from Earth. It is about twenty-five times the diameter of the Sun and a hundred times as luminous. It is a relatively close neighbor, approximately forty light-years from Earth. High up in the sky in the late spring and early summer, Arcturus is the first star you see after sunset. You can find Arcturus easily if you follow the Big Dipper's handle away from the bowl.

ascended masters — Teachers who have graduated from Earth or are on higher dimensions. An ascended master can be from any Earth religion, including the Native American traditions. Ascended masters can include archangels, higher beings from the galactic world, teachers, and prophets. They often come back to Earth to teach us from the higher realms.

ascension — A point of transformation reached through the integration of the physical, emotional, mental, and spiritual selves. Unifying the bodies allows you to transcend the limits of the third dimension and move into a higher realm. It has been compared to the rapture in Christian theology. It has also been defined as a spiritual acceleration of consciousness that allows the soul to return to the higher realms, freeing it from the cycle of karma and rebirth.

Ashtar — The commander of a group of spiritual beings who are dedicated to helping Earth ascend. The beings that Ashtar oversees exist primarily in the fifth dimension and come from many different extraterrestrial civilizations.

aura attachments — Connections that occur when people or entities etherically attach to your energy field to take your energy.

Baruch Hu — The Hebrew transliteration for "blessed are you," referring to the Creator.

bilocate — The ability to be in two places at the same time. One can be physically in a body and mentally or spiritually in another dimension simultaneously.

biorelativity — Encompasses the use of mental telepathy and thought processes to interact with Earth and the spirit of Earth. Downloading energy through corridors can be viewed as an acceleration of biorelativity. When you connect in a group consciousness in a biorelativity exercise, you created a powerful interactive force.

We can use biorelativity techniques to send healing energy to our planet. The practice is similar to group prayers in which people send positive thoughts to change the outcome of an illness. In biorelativity exercises, groups of starseeds around the planet send healing thoughts to specific areas in the world. Storms, hurricanes, and even earthquakes can be averted, deterred, or reduced so that minimal damage is inflicted. The Arcturians point out that on higher planetary systems, groups constantly interact telepathically with their planet to ensure maximum harmony between inhabitants and planetary forces.

biosphere — A term used to describe Earth's entire environment, including the oceans, atmosphere, and other necessary ingredients that keep and support all life.

B'nai Elohim — The children of light. Hebrew for "sons," or "brotherhood of the Elohim." A term used to describe advanced ascended beings who may go on to other planetary systems in the galaxy to become prophets and spiritual guides for these planets.

calibration, spiritual — Refers to the alignment of energies from the higher sources. Spiritual energies need to be calibrated or modified so that lower energies on Earth can accept and process that higher energy. The inability to calibrate or receive light that is high can result in confusion and even disorientation. In some cases, people could even be overcome and perhaps faint. It is important, then, to look at how your ability to receive energy is doing, and it is important for the masters to calibrate the energy that comes down so that you can process and use it.

Central Sun — The center of a galactic system. All star clusters, nebulae, and galaxies contain a nucleus at their center. The Central Sun of the Milky Way is multidimensional and provides life-giving spiritual energy to the entire galaxy. The center of our galaxy is often referred to in spiritual circles as the Central Sun.

chakras — Energy centers of the human body. These centers provide the integration and transfer of energy between the spiritual, mental, emotional, and biological systems of the human body.

channeling — The process of entering a meditative trance to call forth other entities to speak through you.

Chief White Eagle — An Ascended fifth-dimensional Native American guide who is very connected to Jesus and other higher fifth-dimensional beings.

Chi-Lel — A Chi Gong healing energy work based on a multicosmic thought field. The practitioner of Chi-Lel does Taoist postures while connecting with cosmic group energy to create and maintain a healing group thought field.

codes of ascension — There are certain words in the sacred texts that can be said as mantras to open up the parts of our minds to accelerate and activate our ascension energies. One such sacred phrase is "holy, holy, holy is the lord of hosts" (*Kadosh, Kadosh, Kadosh, Adonai Tzevaoth*).

corridor — A pathway or etheric tunnel on Earth that leads to a higher dimension. Corridors can be found in high-energy places, such as sacred sites on Earth. The Arcturians believe that we can establish corridors within our meditation areas.

cosmic egg — The optimal shape of your aura for health benefits. When the aura is in the shape of an egg, you can express maximum energetic possibilities. The egg is a universal shape of wholeness.

cosmic karma — The idea that karma is played out not only with reincarnation on Earth but on other planets in the galaxy or even on other parts of the universe (cosmos).

crystal temple/crystal lake — An etheric temple in the fifth dimension that has been made available for our use. The crystal temple contains a lake more than one mile in diameter that houses a huge crystal that is half the size of the lake itself. A huge glass dome encompasses the lake and the surrounding area, allowing visitors to view the stars.

dead zone — an area of water in which all oxygen has been depleted and no life can exist. Fertilizers and other chemicals are common culprits that contribute to dead zones.

Earth paradigm — Our current Earth paradigm is based on dualism and polarization. Even spiritual models include male and female dualities. Dualism is part of the group model, group paradigm, and planetary paradigm. When you are using the planetary paradigm of the current era, you run into many contradictions, such as thinking you are deeply separated from the cosmos even though everything is part of the same universal system. You run into the contradiction that you are a spiritual being with eternal life living on a planet as a finite being in linear time. The Arcturians have developed a new paradigm for planetary healing that, if accepted and used, would be transformative.

Eh'yeh — In Hebrew, the supreme name of God. This is the name for God given to Moses in Genesis 3:14.

Ehyeh, Asher, Ehyeh — "I Am That I Am," expanded to include "I Will Be That I Will Be," and "I Have Been What I Have Been."

El na refa na la — A special healing Kabbalistic chant and prayer. It means, "Please, God, heal her now!" Its rhythm creates a healing vibration.

Elohim — The Hebrew name that describes the Creator in Genesis 1.

etheric — A term used to designate the higher bodies in the human system. In India, "etheric" is used to describe the unseen energy and thoughts of humans.

etheric crystals — Invisible crystals containing fifth-dimensional energy that the Arcturians sent to Earth. The purpose of these etheric crystals is to provide healing energies to Earth's meridians. See "twelve etheric crystals."

fifth dimension — A higher dimension of existence that is above the first and third dimensions. We currently live on the third dimension and are bound by the laws of cause and effect and reincarnation. The fourth dimension is the astral realm and the realm of dreams. The fifth dimension transcends this and is the realm of infinite energy and love that can be compared to the Garden of Eden. The ascension focuses on going to the fifth dimension.

first contact — Refers to extraterrestrial beings contacting Earth. The Arcturians refer to first contact as happening on a global level. In ancient history, extraterrestrials contacted groups; however, the first contact we refer to would result in a major reset of Earth's functioning because it would occur globally.

galactic anthropologists — Starseeds who have been on other planetary systems in other incarnations. These starseeds have studied other galactic civilizations and planets and have participated in other societies such as in the Pleiades.

Galactic Kachina — In Native American Hopi and Navajo folklore, a kachina is an intermediary between the higher spirit world and this world. The Galactic Kachina is the intermediary between the Central Sun and this planet. The existence of this new Kachina was announced by Juliano, and as far as the author knows, it has not yet been accepted by the Navajo or Hopi.

galactic spirituality — A spiritual philosophy or theory that accepts the existence of other higher beings throughout our galaxy and takes a galactic view in understanding our planetary evolution.

grid lines — Another name for energy lines that run through the planet. In Chinese medicine, energy lines that run through the body are called "meridians."

Group of Forty — A concept of group consciousness suggested by the Arcturians for use in the group ascension process. According to the Arcturians, forty is a spiritually powerful number. The Arcturians emphasize the value and power of joining together in groups.

A Group of Forty consists of forty members located throughout the world who focus on meditating together at a given time each month. Group interactions and yearly physical meetings are recommended. Members agree to assist each other in spiritual development. The Arcturians have asked that forty Groups of Forty be organized. These groups will assist in the healing of Earth and provide a foundation for each member's ascension.

Helio-ah — A female Arcturian ascended master and Juliano's twin flame.

holes in the aura — The healthy aura is shaped as an egg and is smooth. Holes in the aura are small openings from which a person's vital energy can leak. There are several healing methods that can be used to close such holes.

hundredth monkey effect — A phenomenon based on a Japanese snow monkey study in which a new behavior or idea can spread rapidly by unexplained means from one group to all related groups once a critical number of beings exhibit the new behavior or acknowledge the new idea. In this study, scientists concluded that a small number of monkeys who had a new perception and learned new tools and techniques could dramatically and almost mystically change the behavior of all other monkeys in their cultural group.

harmonic light — Fifth-dimensional light often appearing as gold balls of etheric energy. This light can be transmitted through the noosphere and can spread the energy of balance and harmony wherever it is directed. Starseeds can direct it around the planet through their thoughts and prayers.

Kadosh, Kadosh, Kadosh, Adonai Tzevaoth — "Holy, holy, holy is the lord of hosts." A well-known phrase from a Jewish prayer that starseeds currently use to unlock the codes of ascension.

ladders of ascension — An etheric ladder downloaded by the

Arcturians in various locations around the planet. These ladders can be compared to Jacob's ladder in the Hebrew Bible, in which Jacob, while dreaming, saw angles on a ladder. This ladder was a gateway to the other dimensions. The ladder of ascension is also a gateway for your ascension. It also goes to Juliano's starship. Seven ladders of ascension have been downloaded on Earth.

lightbody — The higher etheric spirit body that is directly connected to one's soul.

Merkabah — A visionary Egyptian word meaning chariot or traveling etheric vehicle.

meridians (Earth) — Energy channels through the earth that are similar in purpose and function to the meridians in a human body as explained in Chinese medicine. The theory is that if the meridians are blocked, illness or planetary imbalance will follow.

Metatron — Tradition associates Metatron with Enoch, who "walked with God" (Genesis 5:22) and who ascended to heaven and was changed from a human being into an angel. His name has been defined as the Angel of Presence, or the one who occupies the throne next to the Divine throne. Another interpretation is that his name is based on the Latin word *metator*, which means "guide" or "measurer." In the world of the Jewish mystic, Metatron holds the rank of the highest of angels, that of archangel. According to the Arcturians, Metatron is associated with the Arcturian stargate and assists souls in their ascension to higher worlds.

Michael — His name is actually a question: "Who is like God?" He is perhaps the best known of the archangels and is acknowledged by all three Western sacred traditions. He has been called the Prince of Light, fighting a war against the sons of darkness. In this role, he is depicted most often as winged and with an unsheathed sword, the warrior of God and slayer of the dragon. His role in the ascension is focused on helping us cut the cords of attachment to the Earth plane, which will allow us to move to higher consciousness.

multidimensional presence — We exist on several different dimensions simultaneously.

multiverse — This is a term used to describe the existence of many universes.

neutralization — The process whereby you can stop negative energy from attacking your energy field or aura. Those who are doing negative actions toward you usually want to take energy away and create an energy deficit. Neutralization means that their actions can no longer take away energy from you or the planet.

noorelativity — The ability to interact with and change in a positive direction the noosphere. It is based on principles similar to biorelativity. The difference is that in noorelativity, you use your powers of thought energy to create and enhance the evolution of both planet Earth and humanity. Thought fields exist and influence the noosphere. Thought forms downloaded into the noosphere create and shape this reality.

noosphere (planetary) — The thought energy field contained in Earth's aura. It can be compared to the planetary subconscious, but it is more than that. The noosphere contains the accumulated collective thought energy of all beings on Earth, past and present. The noosphere is composed of an energy field of subatomic thought particles, or thought waves. These subatomic thought particles exist around planetary bodies in the universe, and they allow the thought energy around a planet to be stored and transmitted instantaneously across the universe at speeds faster than the speed of light (186,000 miles per second). The noosphere affects the overall planetary energy field.

null zone — A zone outside the third dimension and not necessarily in any other dimension. It is an area outside our space-time universe structure, and it's where time is nonexistent. Some have speculated that the photon belt contains null zone regions and that Earth was temporarily in this null zone until the year 2011.

omega light — This is a fifth-dimensional light that has high healing properties. The light can help transcend the world of cause and effect and can help produce miraculous healings. You can increase the effects of this healing light by saying, "Omega light."

omega man or woman — The beautiful image of the omega man represents the perfected evolutionary point of humanity.

Or HaKadosh Baruch Hu — Hebrew phrase for "Holy light, blessed is he."

Orion — A superb constellation that dominates the southern winter sky. The most striking part of the constellation is the belt, which consists of three bright stars. No other constellation contains so many bright stars. Rigel, which is outside the belt, for example, is a giant star more than 500 light-years away. Betelgeuse, another star outside the belt in Orion, is about 300 light-years away.

Orions — An extraterrestrial culture that descended from another ancient civilization near the constellation Orion.

parasitic attachment — Refers to the physical method with which a parasite (a being wanting energy) sends out attachment structures, or hooks, to its host in order to suck energy from the aura.

path work in the Arcturian Tree of Life — There are twelve spheres on the Arcturian Planetary Tree of Life and more than twenty-two lines, or paths, that connect these spheres. The paths help us connect energetically to the spheres, which are often separated into pairs of opposites. The path work then provides the lessons needed to integrate the opposite spheres.

photon belt/energy — An energy emanating from the center of the galaxy that is about to intersect with our solar system and Earth. Some have predicted that the photon belt contains energy particles that could affect Earth's magnetic field, causing all electronic equipment to stop working.

planetary cities of light — Cities of light designated by the Group of Forty project codirector David K. Miller. To obtain this designation, four Group of Forty members must work or live in a city and agree to meditate and work with the energy of the city to help make it more fifth dimensional. A special activation ceremony that includes placing crystals around the city is performed along with a special global meditation ceremony. There are currently forty-five planetary cities of light now activated around the world.

planetary ocean reserves of light — Similar to the planetary cities of light but based on special ocean reserves. The idea is to preserve ocean areas as if they are national parks. The Group of Forty has helped to develop almost ten ocean reserves of light around the globe.

Pleiades — A small cluster of stars known as the Seven Sisters in some mythologies. Some Native Americans believe they are descended from the Pleiades. The system is near the constellation Taurus, about 450 light-years from Earth, and it is the home of the Pleiadians, who have frequently interacted with Earth and her cultures. It is said that the Pleiadians have a common ancestry with us.

portal — An opening at the end of a corridor that allows you to go into an interdimensional space.

pulsing — Describes the speed or vibration of the aura.

pung — A term that originated in the Chinese Tai Chi martial arts world. It describes the elasticity, resiliency, and reflected bounce of someone's energy field. When someone has good pung, then negative energy easily bounces off his or her aura, protecting his or her energy field.

quantum healing — Involves transcending the laws of cause and effect and the normal logical thought processes on Earth. It can include shamanistic healing, sound or vibrational healing, and any technique that uses fifth-dimensional energy.

Quan Yin — A female ascended master of the spiritual hierarchy. In her previous incarnation, she performed many acts of kindness and compassion, and she is known as the Goddess of Mercy.

reset concept — A reset of Earth involves temporarily shutting off the old paradigms so that a new wave of energy and paradigms could be used to move Earth in a new direction. See "first contact."

ritual purification — The Arcturian process for purification now involves detaching from third-dimensional energies, concerns, and Earth attachments in general. Purification is a process in which binding energy is removed from earthly concerns. Some of these concerns are part of everyday life, worries that everyone has. Becoming purified for the ascension means you would not be focused on or have the energy for the mundane or the daily business on Earth. You would not have any energies or attachments to negative interactions with other people. The technique for ritual purification involves doing the shimmering exercise.

Sacred Triangle — A term used by the Arcturians to denote the unification of three powerful spiritual forces on Earth: the White Brotherhood-Sisterhood ascended masters, including Sananda/Jesus; the extraterrestrial higher-dimensional masters, such as the Arcturians and the Pleiadians; and the Native American ascended masters, such as Chiefs White Eagle and Buffalo Heart. The unification of these spiritual forces will create the Sacred Triangle that will aid in the healing and ascension of Earth.

Sananda — the galactic name of Master Jesus, an evolved being who is known and does work throughout the galaxy.

sixth mass extinction — Recently, more than 15,000 scientists from 184 countries concluded that Earth is experiencing its sixth mass-extinction event. The asteroid that hit Earth 66 million years ago was one, killing off the dinosaurs and many other plant and animal species. The current mass extinction is mainly the result of human activities, such as meat consumption, overfishing, ocean acidification, and human overpopulation.

shimmering — A methodology taught by the Arcturians in which third-dimensional starseeds are upgraded into a fifth-dimensional modality. On a personal level, shimmering allows your auric field to vibrate at a frequency that enables the aura to shift the electrons. The atomic structure of your cells transmutes into a vibratory energy field that shifts the cellular structures into the fifth dimension, causing a back-and-forth, or "shimmering," modality. This modality actually affects the atomic and quantum levels of your cellular structures. It is also possible to do a shimmering exercise for Earth, which will help in its ascension. Shimmering is the precursor to the ascension.

stargate — A multidimensional portal into higher realms. The Arcturian stargate is very close to the Arcturus star system, and it is overseen by the Arcturians. This powerful passage point requires that earthlings who wish to pass through it complete all lessons and Earth incarnations associated with the third-dimensional experience. It serves as a gateway to the fifth dimension. New soul assignments are given there, and souls can then be sent to many different higher realms throughout the galaxy and the universe. Archangel Metatron and many other higher beings are present at the stargate. Many people use the term "stargate" to refer to openings on Earth to higher dimensions, but they are describing corridors. The stargate is a magnificent, temple-like, etheric structure that can process and transform many souls.

starseeds — People who have or are born with the awareness of galactic consciousness. Starseeds may also have memories of past lifetimes on and feel connected to civilizations from other planets, such as the Pleiades or Arcturus. Some starseeds have come to Earth at this time to assist her in this evolutionary transformation.

stages of planetary development — The Arcturians report that there are five stages of planetary development. Earth is at the end of stage one, a crisis of survival versus self-destruction. Stage one also exhibits conflict between spiritual wisdom and technology. The other stages of development involve the planet's adoption of spiritual values that allow it to overcome the crisis of stage one.

Teilhard de Chardin — A twentieth-century French philosopher who wrote that people are evolving toward a higher point in species development. He referred to this higher stage of evolution as moving toward the omega point.

thought constructs and thought fields — Similar thoughts join to create a thought field or an energy field. Thought constructs are composed of multiple thoughts that form a series of mental energy that helps to create realities on Earth

thought projection — A technique described by the Arcturians involving projecting thoughts through a corridor to reach the fifth dimension and beyond.

Tikkun — In the Kabbalah, the Hebrew word for "repair of the world." The Arcturians have expanded this concept to include planetary healing, or repairing Mother Earth. In Hebrew, this term also means "restoration," or "the divine restoration of the cosmos."

Tomar — An Arcturian ascended master whose specialty is using and describing the Arcturian temple energy.

tones and sacred sounds — Sounds producing a vibratory resonance that helps activate and align the chakras.

tools of ascension — Spiritual tools offered by the Arcturians and other spiritual masters to assist starseeds in learning the techniques to accelerate ascension work. Some of the spiritual tools include receiving past-life therapy, shimmering, and releasing attachments to third-dimensional reality.

Tree of Life — The Tree of Life was first downloaded by the ancient Kabbalistic rabbis and contains a galactic blueprint for the creation of this reality. It includes ten energy codes placed in spheres in the shape of a tree. The Tree of Life is always multidimensional and holographic. The Tree of Life has pathways for manifestation found in its twenty-two lines. The Tree of Life connects to the energies of the cosmos.

twelve etheric crystals — Part of the Arcturian Planetary Tree of Life. They represent the twelve spheres in the tree of life and have been downloaded by the Arcturians with the help of Group of Forty members in Lago Puelo, Argentina; Volcan Poás, Costa Rica; Copper Canyon, Mexico; Mount Shasta, California; Mount Fuji, Japan; Bodensee, Central Europe; Istanbul, Turkey; Lake Taupo, New Zealand; Grose Valley, Australia; Lake Moraine, Alberta, Canada; Serra da Bocaina, Brazil; and Montserrat, Spain.

unity thinking — The ability to create a thought form that unites the higher dimensions with the lower dimensions. Unity of thoughts repairs or heals the third-dimensional reality.

vibrational speed of the aura — Describes the pulsing speed of the aura. The faster it pulses, the higher the consciousness you can experience.

Vywamus — An ascended master who is considered an expert on soul psychology.

walk-ins — Humans who have received other spiritual entities in their bodies. The term is also used to refer to a new spirit that has entered the body. In some cases, the original spirit of the person may have left (for example, after an auto accident or some other form of severe trauma) and a new spirit "walks in" to the old body. This is always by agreement of the person vacating the body, before incarnating, to allow the body to continue in service after a particular incarnation is complete. It also allows the walk-in spirit to skip the process of childhood and adolescence to get straight to their mission on Earth. The walk-in agrees to honor the commitments of the previous occupant's life.

White Brotherhood-Sisterhood — A spiritual hierarchy of ascended masters residing in the fifth dimension. “White” is not used here as a racial term. It refers to the white light, or higher frequency, that these masters have attained. The masters include Sananda, Kuthumi, Mother Mary, Quan Yin, Sanat Kumara, Archangel Michael, Saint Germain, and many other ascended beings.

White Buffalo Calf Woman — In Lakota Native American folklore, she is the fifth-dimensional spirit being who appeared to them, bringing forth special information about holy ceremonies and accessing higher spirit. She taught the necessity of being in harmony with Earth. Her focus is on the unity of all beings. She is representative of the dawning of a New Age.

About the Author

David K. Miller is the director and founder of an international meditation group focused on personal and planetary healing. He has been the director of this global healing group, called the Group of Forty, for more than fifteen years. David has been developing groundbreaking global healing techniques using group consciousness to help heal areas of Earth that need balance, restoration, and harmony. The technique he uses with his group work is called Biorelativity, which uses group consciousness work to restore Earth's feedback loop system, a complex planetary system that maintains the correct balance of our planet's atmosphere, ocean currents, and weather patterns.

David's meditation group has more than 1,200 members worldwide. In addition to his lectures and workshops, David is also a prolific author, having written fifteen books and numerous articles on Earth healing techniques. Several of his books also have been published in German and Spanish.

David works with his wife, Gudrun Miller, who is a psychotherapist and visionary artist. Together they have conducted workshops in Brazil, Germany, Australia, Mexico, Argentina, Costa Rica, Spain, New Zealand, Belgium, and Turkey. David's foundation for this work lies in his study of and connection to Native American teachings and his intense research in mysticism, including the Kabbalah. He also has an avid interest in astronomy and Earth's relationship to the galaxy. To learn more, go to GroupofForty.com.

Light Technology PUBLISHING Presents

TO ORDER PRINT BOOKS

Visit LightTechnology.com, Call 928-526-1345 or 1-800-450-0985,
or Check Amazon.com or Your Favorite Bookstore

BOOKS THROUGH DAVID K. MILLER

New Spiritual Technology for the Fifth-Dimensional Earth

Information is featured about native ceremonies to connect to Earth healing energies, thought projections, and thought communication.

$19.95 • Softcover • 240 PP.
978-1-891824-79-1

Teachings from the Sacred Triangle, Volume 3

Learn how to use holographic technology to project energies in the most direct and transformative way throughout Earth.

$16.95 • Softcover • 288 PP.
978-1-891824-23-4

Raising the Spiritual Light Quotient

The spiritual light quotient, one's ability to understand spiritual concepts, is similar to the intelligence quotient (IQ) test. Learn how to raise your SLQ.

$16.95 • Softcover • 384 PP.
978-1-891824-89-0

A New Tree of Life for Planetary Ascension

WITH MORDECHAI YASHIN

David Miller has teamed up with Torah expert Mordechai Yashin to provide a unique, expanded perspective on the Tree of Life.

$16.95 • Softcover • 336 PP.
978-1-62233-012-6

Teachings from the Sacred Triangle, Volume 1

This book offers an understanding of the soul, soul evolution, and how the human species is advancing toward the next evolutionary step.

$16.95 • Softcover • 272 PP.
978-1-62233-007-2

Enseñanzas del Sagrado Triángulo Arcturiano

Los capitulos incluyen:

- Los Principios de la Biorelatividad
- La Conciencia y Conexiones de Grupo
- La Estructura Etérea de la Tierra

$19.95 • 416 páginas
978-1-62233-264-9

Teachings from the Sacred Triangle, Volume 2

The teachings continue in this second volume of the *Sacred Triangle* series, focusing on the importance of energy bridges.

$16.95 • Softcover • 288 PP.
978-1-891824-19-7

David K. Miller has an extensive background in psychology and psychotherapy. After thirty-five years of conventional practice, David now focuses exclusively on soul psychology. He has developed several therapy techniques, penned many articles, and authored several books. David is also the founder of the international meditation group known as the Group of Forty. To learn more, go to GroupofForty.com.

All Our Books Are Also Available as eBooks from Amazon, Apple iTunes, Google Play, Barnes & Noble, and Kobo.

Light Technology PUBLISHING *Presents*

TO ORDER PRINT BOOKS

Visit LightTechnology.com, Call 928-526-1345 or 1-800-450-0985,
or Check Amazon.com or Your Favorite Bookstore

BY TOM T. MOORE

THE GENTLE WAY I, II & III

ASK FOR AND RECEIVE BENEVOLENT OUTCOMES

You will be amazed at how much assistance you can receive simply by asking. These inspirational self-help books, written for all faiths, explain how to access and achieve a more benevolent world.

CHAPTERS INCLUDE

- Angels
- How I Began
- Easy Steps
- Home Life
- Politics
- Travel
- The Radiant Effect
- Living Prayers
- "I Hope" Requests

The Gentle Way: 160 PP. • Softcover • ISBN 978-1-891824-60-9 • $14.95

The Gentle Way II: 320 PP. • Softcover • ISBN 978-1-891824-80-7 • $16.95

The Gentle Way III: 352 PP. • Softcover • ISBN 978-1-62233-005-8 • $16.95

All Our Books Are Also Available as eBooks from Amazon, Apple iTunes, Google Play, Barnes & Noble, and Kobo.

Light Technology PUBLISHING Presents

TO ORDER PRINT BOOKS
Visit LightTechnology.com, Call 928-526-1345 or 1-800-450-0985,
or Check Amazon.com or Your Favorite Bookstore

Shamanic Secrets Series Through Robert Shapiro

Shamanic Secrets: Lost Wisdom Regained

Due to wars, natural disasters, a shaman not being able to train a successor, and many other reasons, Isis (through Robert) says that 95 percent of the accumulated shamanic wisdom has been lost. Now it is important to regain this wisdom as young people who are able to learn and use these processes are being born now.

Beings who lived as shamans and healers on Earth at various times now speak through Robert Shapiro and bring these lost teachings and techniques to a humanity waking up and discovering it has the talents and abilities to use this wisdom for the benefit of all.

$16.95 • Softcover • 352 PP. • ISBN 978-1-62233-049-2

Shamanic Secrets for Material Mastery

Explore the heart and soul connection between humans and Mother Earth. Through that intimacy, miracles of healing and expanded awareness can flourish.

$19.95 • Softcover • 528 PP.
978-1-891824-12-8

Shamanic Secrets for Physical Mastery

The purpose of this book is to explain the sacred nature of the physical body and some of the magnificent gifts it offers.

$25.00 • Softcover • 608 PP.
978-1-891824-29-6

Shamanic Secrets for Spiritual Mastery

Spiritual mastery is the underpinnings of multiple ways of being, understanding, appreciating, and interacting in harmony with your world.

$29.95 • Softcover • 768 PP.
978-1-891824-58-6

All Our Books Are Also Available as eBooks from Amazon, Apple iTunes, Google Play, Barnes & Noble, and Kobo.

Light Technology PUBLISHING Presents

TO ORDER PRINT BOOKS

Visit LightTechnology.com, Call 928-526-1345 or 1-800-450-0985,
or Check Amazon.com or Your Favorite Bookstore

BOOKS THROUGH TINA LOUISE SPALDING

You Can Free Yourself from the Karma of Chaos

"We have come here as a group to help you because it is a pivotal time in your planet's evolution. You are seeing monumental changes in your society now. To achieve the shifts that these transfigurations will bring about, you must understand your minds, histories, and human nature as you experience it on the ground, in your hearts, and in your consciousnesses.

"Your baggage, judgments, and fears must be released for you to enter this new world, this new time on your planet, with clear and uncontaminated minds. It is our purpose to bring you through this journey so that you will understand, forgive, and walk unencumbered into your new future."

— Ananda

$16.95 • Softcover • 224 PP. • 978-1-62233-057-7

Jesus: My Autobiography
$16.95 • Softcover • 304 PP.
978-1-62233-030-0

Love and a Map to the Unaltered Soul
$16.95 • Softcover • 240 PP.
ISBN 978-1-62233-047-8

Making Love to God: The Path to Divine Sex
$19.95 • Softcover • 416 PP.
978-1-62233-009-6

Spirit of the Western Way: Wake Up to Your Power — Heal the Collective Consciousness of the Western Mind
$16.95 • Softcover • 176 PP.
978-1-62233-051-5

Great Minds Speak to You
$19.95 • Softcover • 192 PP.
Includes CD
978-1-62233-010-2

CD included!

All Our Books Are Also Available as eBooks from Amazon, Apple iTunes, Google Play, Barnes & Noble, and Kobo.

Light Technology PUBLISHING Presents

TO ORDER PRINT BOOKS

Visit LightTechnology.com, Call 928-526-1345 or 1-800-450-0985,
or Check Amazon.com or Your Favorite Bookstore

SPIRITUAL BOOKS FOR CHILDREN BY LEIA STINNETT

The Little Angel Book series

All My Angel Friends **(Coloring Book)**
$10.95 • Softcover • 64 PP. • 978-0-929385-80-8

The Angel Told Me to Tell You Good-Bye
$6.95 • Softcover • 64 PP. • 978-0-929385-84-6

Animal Tales: Spiritual Lessons from Our Animal Friends
$7.95 • Softcover • 96 PP. • 978-0-929385-96-9

The Bridge between Two Worlds
$6.95 • Softcover • 64 PP. • 978-0-929385-85-3

A Circle of Angels **(Workbook)**
$18.95 • Softcover • 112 PP. • 978-0-929385-87-7

Color Me One
$6.95 • Softcover • 64 PP. • 978-0-929385-82-2

Crystals R for Kids
$6.95 • Softcover • 64 PP. • 978-0-929385-92-1

Exploring the Chakras
$6.95 • Softcover • 64 PP. • 978-0-929385-86-0

Happy Feet
$6.95 • Softcover • 64 PP. • 978-0-929385-88-4

Just Lighten Up! **(Coloring Book)**
$9.95 • Softcover • 48 PP. • 978-0-929385-64-8

The Little Angel Who Could Not Fly
$9.95 • Softcover • 64 PP. • 978-1-62233-025-6

One Red Rose
$6.95 • Softcover • 64 PP. • 978-0-929385-83-9

Principles and Applications of the Twelve Universal Laws
$18.95 • Softcover • 128 PP. • 978-0-929385-81-5

When the Earth Was New
$6.95 • Softcover • 64 PP. • 978-0-929385-91-4

Where Is God?
$6.95 • Softcover • 64 PP. • 978-0-929385-90-7

Who's Afraid of the Dark?
$6.95 • Softcover • 64 PP. • 978-0-929385-89-1

The Adventures of Tee-la and De-Nar in the Land Called One series

The Master Speaks (Book 1)
$9.95 • Softcover • 64 PP. • 978-1-62233-022-5

The Seven Sacred Pools (Book 2)
$9.95 • Softcover • 64 PP. • 978-1-62233-026-3

The Cave of the Ancients (Book 3)
$9.95 • Softcover • 64 PP. • 978-1-62233-024-9

All Our Books Are Also Available as eBooks from Amazon, Apple iTunes, Google Play, Barnes & Noble, and Kobo.

Light Technology PUBLISHING Presents

SEDONA JOURNAL OF Emergence

ORDER NOW

to receive SPECTACULAR SAVINGS on your *Sedona Journal* subscription!

All subscriptions include the annual Predictions Issue

YOU ARE EXPERIENCING AN UNPRECEDENTED EXPANSION into a new reality and a dimensional shift into a new state of being. This movement from one dimension to another while in a physical body has never been done before. It feels as if you are building the rocket you're riding while it is blasting off!

THERE ARE NO ANCIENT BOOKS, NO RULEBOOKS, no manuals or procedures, no record of how to do this thing, because it has never been done before. During previous dimensional shifts, embodied beings would die in the old reality and then be reborn in the new one in new bodies with a different vibrational frequency.

SO LIGHTBEINGS, THROUGH THEIR CHANNELS, EXPLAIN THIS PROCESS and offer guidance and spiritual techniques to help you learn to feel and express love and benevolence — and to encourage you to change your behavior to ensure that Earth remains habitable while you expand into your natural self and awaken to your natural talents and abilities. As this happens, you will allow yourself to flow with all humanity into a more benevolent version of Earth — into another dimensional focus, another of the strata of this existence.

PRINT SUBSCRIPTIONS

Mailed U.S. Subscriptions

1st Class	2nd Class
❒ 2 yrs $129	❒ 2 yrs $79
❒ 1 yr $65	❒ 1 yr $43

Canada

❒ 2 yrs .... $159 ❒ 1 yr $83

All prices are in U.S. currency.

All Other Countries

❒ 2 yrs .... $299 ❒ 1 yr $154

All prices are in U.S. currency.

NOTE: The U.S. Postal Service has changed postal rates, eliminating Canadian and global 2nd class surface and increasing all airmail rates.

Subscription includes the annual double-size PREDICTIONS ISSUE at no extra charge.

ELECTRONIC SUBSCRIPTIONS with Bonus Content

Get the entire journal plus additional content online by subscription — and get it 2 weeks before it hits newsstands!

❒ 2 yrs .... $55 ❒ 1 yr $29

All electronic and combo subscriptions *MUST* be purchased online at SedonaJournal.com to obtain username and password.

Get the Best of Both Worlds!

Special Combo Offers!

U.S.A.

Get BOTH Printed AND Electronic Subscriptions

1st Class	2nd Class
❒ 2 yrs $159	❒ 2 yrs $109
❒ 1 yr $81	❒ 1 yr $59

Canada

Get an Airmail Printed Subscription Along with an Electronic Subscription for Only

❒ 2 yrs ...... $189 ❒ 1 yr $99

NOTE: The U.S. Postal Service has changed postal rates, eliminating Canadian and global 2nd class surface and increasing all airmail rates.

All Countries

Get an Airmail Printed Subscription Along with an Electronic Subscription for Only

❒ 2 yrs ...... $329 ❒ 1 yr $170

Order online: SedonaJournal.com

or call 928-526-1345 or 1-800-450-0985

Light Technology PUBLISHING **Presents**

EASY ORDER 24 HOURS A DAY

1

Order ONLINE!
LightTechnology.com

Order by Email
customersrv@lighttechnology.com

2

Order by Mail
Send to
Light Technology Publishing
PO Box 3540
Flagstaff, AZ 86003

3

Order by Phone
800-450-0985
928-526-1345

4

Order by Fax
928-714-1132

Available from your favorite bookstore or
LIGHT Technology PUBLISHING

MasterCard VISA AMERICAN EXPRESS DISCOVER PayPal

LightTechnology.com
We Offer the Best Channeled and Inspired Books of Wisdom.
Use Our Secure Checkout.
In-Depth Information on Books, Including Excerpts and Contents.
Use the Links to Our Other Great Sites. See Below.

SedonaJournal.com
Read Excerpts of Monthly Channeling and Predictions in Advance.
Use Our Email Links to Contact Us or Send a Submission.
Electronic Subscriptions Available — with or without Print Copies.

BenevolentMagic.com
Learn the techniques of benevolence toward self and benevolence toward others to create global peace. Download all the techniques of benevolent magic and living prayer for FREE!

ExplorerRace.com
All humanity constitutes the Explorer Race, volunteers for a grand and glorious experiment. Discover your purpose, your history, and your future. Download the first chapter of each book for FREE!

ShamanicSecrets.com
What we call shamanism is the natural way of life for beings on other planets. Learn to be aware of your natural self and your natural talents and abilities. Download the first chapter of each book for FREE!